Who Owns the Past?

Who Owns the Past?

Papers from the annual symposium of the
Australian Academy of the Humanities

Edited by
Isabel McBryde

Melbourne
OXFORD UNIVERSITY PRESS
Oxford   Auckland   New York

OXFORD UNIVERSITY PRESS
Oxford London New York Toronto
Delhi Bombay Calcutta Madras Karachi
Kuala Lumpur Singapore Hong Kong Tokyo
Nairobi Dar es Salaam Cape Town
Melbourne Auckland
and associates in
Beirut Berlin Ibadan Mexico City Nicosia

National Library of Australia
Cataloguing-in-Publication data:

Australian Academy of the Humanities.
Symposium (14th: 1983: Australian Academy of
Science).
Who owns the past?

Includes bibliographical references and index.
ISBN 0 19 554565 6.

1. Cultural property, Protection of –
Congresses. 2. Historic sites – Congresses.
I. McBryde, Isabel, 1934– . II. Title.

363.6'9

OXFORD is a trademark of Oxford University Press
Typeset by Syarikat Seng Teik Sdn. Bhd.,
47, Jalan SS21/37, Petaling Jaya, Malaysia.
Printed in Hong Kong
Published by Oxford University Press, 7 Bowen Crescent, Melbourne

Contents

Acknowledgements

The papers in this volume are contributions made to the Fourteenth Annual Symposium of the Australian Academy of the Humanities, held at the Academy of Science, Canberra, in May 1983. It was the second Academy Symposium to be held as an open forum and the large gathering, filling both floors of the Academy's Becker Hall, demonstrated the public interest in the Symposium theme and the work of the Academy. In early 1983 'Who owns the past?' was more than a fascinating topic for academic philosophic debate. It had become a dominant public issue in Australia.

The Academy of Science building proved an excellent venue for our Symposium and I am grateful to our sister academy for the use of their facilities. Other functions for the 1983 meeting were held at University House under the excellent care of Professor Elliott. As usual Ansett Airlines of Australia were the official carriers and it is a pleasure to acknowledge their assistance with organization. As convener of the Symposium I should like to express my deep thanks to Professor Hardy, Secretary of the Academy, and to Mrs Waters, the Executive Secretary for their help and support in so many ways during the time leading up to the Symposium and during the meetings. Also I must thank my mother, Roberta McBryde, for support during the Symposium itself, which sadly coincided with a time of serious illness for a member of our family.

The beautiful poster for the Symposium was designed by Stephen Cole of the Australian National University's Graphic Design Section.

The Symposium proved an exciting and stimulating three days. For this I should like to express my appreciation to those who joined us, many from interstate, and to those who contributed to this volume though unable to be present at the meeting (Ms Sullivan and Sir David Wilson, Director of the British Museum). My thanks to those who chaired sessions, Professor Clark, Professor Golson, Professor Inglis, Professor Passmore, Professor Weaver, and particularly to the speakers, who accepted the invitation to share with us their knowledge and experience. As our overseas guest we were glad to welcome Professor Bruce Trigger of McGill

University in Montreal. These speakers made the 1983 Academy Symposium a memorable occasion.

Moving from meeting to publication, it was a great pleasure to learn that Oxford University Press (Australia) would be the publishers of this volume. My thanks to them, and their editors Ms Sweetland and Ms Dawson for guiding the volume through this important stage.

Every effort has been made to trace the original source of material contained in this book. Where the attempt has been unsuccessful the publishers would be pleased to hear from the author/publisher to rectify any omission.

Isabel McBryde
Canberra
February 1984

Cover illustration:

From 1751 to 1753 architect James Stuart and artist Nicholas Revett travelled in Greece to record classical architecture. They left an invaluable record, particularly this view of the Parthenon standing in the midst of the Turkish garrison, surrounded by houses and enclosing a mosque. It gives an impression of the daunting presence of the Hellenic heritage for the Greeks of Athens at that period. (*The Antiquities of Athens*, measured and delineated by James Stuart (FRS) and Nicolas Revett, 4 vols, London, 1762–1816: vol. 2 (ed. W. Newton, 1787), Chapter 1, Plate 1)

Contributors

Les Groube, Senior Lecturer in Prehistory, University of Papua New Guinea

Elizabeth Jeffreys, Lecturer in Greek, Macquarie University

Isabel McBryde, Reader in Prehistory, Australian National University

John Mulvaney, Professor of Prehistory, Australian National University

Bernard Smith, Emeritus Professor, University of Sydney

Sharon Sullivan, Head, Aboriginal and Historic Resources Section, National Parks and Wildlife Service, New South Wales

Alice Erh Soon Tay, Challis Professor of Jurisprudence, University of Sydney

Bruce Trigger, Professor of Anthropology, McGill University, Montreal

Wang Gungwu, Professor of Far Eastern History, Research School of Pacific Studies, Australian National University

Eric Willmot, Principal, Australian Institute of Aboriginal Studies, Canberra

David Wilson, Director, British Museum, London

Introduction

Isabel McBryde

Rarely has the Academy of the Humanities taken for its annual symposium a theme so controversial or so immediate. Over the last decade heritage issues have become central to many decisions in many countries at the local, national and international level. The philosophic issues of who owns, or controls, the present (or the future) by manipulation of perceptions of the past, or versions of the past, have always been vital. They form a continuing strand through historical enquiry. The Academy Symposium was held in May 1983, following a March election in which conservation issues in south-western Tasmania were dominant in debate. In April 1983 Federal Parliament passed its World Heritage Properties Protection Act, and in July the High Court brought down its decision on the Tasmanian Dams case. So our discussions were relevant to the immediate public issues of mid-1983. Indeed two of our Fellows, Professor Mulvaney and Dr Rhys Jones, were deeply involved in these issues. Alice Tay has expanded her chapter on legal issues to include discussion of these developments.

But beyond the intense debate engendered by this one particular conservation issue, and the turbulent, muddied, waters of the Gordon below Franklin, are continuing questions of fundamental significance. In this symposium we had the opportunity to address these, and to set them in wide perspective by crossing cultural, temporal and political boundaries. Such an approach was not only appropriate to our theme, but also to the wide range of disciplines represented in the Academy. So in the symposium we surveyed the issues of 'who owns the past?' from the perspective of the past of the indigenous peoples of former colonial states, considered questions of law, of the restitution of cultural property, and the uses of heritage and tradition in reconstructing or using the past. We ranged from Byzantium to modern China, from the American Indian to Papua New Guinea and Australia.

'Who owns the past?' is a good symposium title. But what are its implications? To me it seems to present several foci, in terms of who 'owns', 'controls', or 'uses' the past. These relate on the one hand to the physical remains from the past, the objects (artefacts, museum collections, works of art) and the places, monuments and archaeological sites. On the other hand are foci relating to perceptions of the past itself, to questions of the information derived from the past, of who may have access to this, who may investigate it, what aspects of it may be made available to whom, what purposes may this information be made to serve and what controls may be exercised over it.

The past, in the sense of the past of human societies, remote in time, may never be revisited nor apprehended as reality (Collingwood 1946 [1980 reprint]: 3–5, 282–83). It is perhaps, as Collingwood said, 'wholly unknowable; it is the past as residually preserved in the present that alone is knowable' (Collingwood 1946 [1980]: 5). We explore the past through our present perceptions of the evidence for its existence in written records, oral tradition, and in the tangible, physical remains of archaeological sites and artefacts. This perceived past may bear little relation to the vanished reality, and that relationship may be barely amenable to the testing processes applied to scientific hypotheses (Collingwood 1946 [1980]: 5).

Eric Willmot in his paper on Aboriginal history begins from this point to discuss Aboriginal and non-Aboriginal concepts of the past. 'The only real world for you and me is the present, and while we may create a reality which we call the past it is only our reality, it is the story we tell . . . We as human beings, live in a flat time world, our total reality is only an instant thick.' Bernard Smith also addresses this problem, showing how tradition and heritage may be used to turn the personal past, this individual instant, into the social past, encapsulating the experiences and past of the group.

If we ask the question 'who owns the past?', accepting that we have but this ephemeral perception of past reality, the answer may be swift and brutal – 'everyone or no one'. The question seems as elusive as the past. Yet in legislative responses to the question, especially as applied to the tangible remains from the past, we find a clear and consistent assumption. This assumption (embedded in legislation pertaining to sites and artefacts), is that these constitute the common heritage of all. In Australia it is found in both federal and state legislation. In presenting the second reading of the World Heritage Properties Protection Bill in parliament on 21 April 1983, the Minister for Home Affairs and the Environment stated that such important cultural and natural resources 'are properties which belong to all Australians' (p. 6). He referred to the preamble of the World Heritage Convention Treaty which states that 'destruction or disappearance of any item of the cultural or natural heritage constitutes a harmful impoverishment of the heritage of all nations of the world'. The analogy drawn was that important cultural or natural resources presented for World Heritage Listing 'are properties which belong to all Australians' (p. 6). In response to such assumptions, of course, one might further ask: Who determines the legislative answers? Under what motivation and to what purpose? Legislation, by definition, reflects a dominant viewpoint. We shall return to this problem later.

Such concepts have been embodied in international law relating to cultural property since the 1860s; they are clearly stated in the 1954 Hague Convention and the 1970 UNESCO Convention. This last also stressed the vital role of national heritage in promoting a sense of cultural identity.

Some of the earliest arguments for national policies of heritage protection were couched in terms of the site as both symbol and patrimony. The site, or the artefact, may be seen as a physical link with the past, as somehow making the past present, giving as Lévi-Strauss said of historical archives 'a physical existence to history, for in them alone is the contradiction of a completed past and a present in which it survives, surmounted' (1972: 242). This comment was made in the context of considering Churinga as 'palpable proofs of mythical times', so analogous to the archival documents.

The site as national symbol emerges in the nineteenth century, as part of the historical self-consciousness of a number of European states. In Scandinavia this sense of the historical importance of objects and sites from the past was articulated earlier than in many other European countries, and early embodied in legislation. From the seventeenth century Sweden protected ancient monuments by enactments. Implicit in these was the concept that landowners have no right to use ancient monuments on their land for personal ends, since they were in a sense the patrimony of all. The Danish archaeologist Jacob Worsaae wrote in 1843: 'A nation which respects itself and its independence cannot possibly rest satisfied with the consideration of its present situation alone. It must of necessity direct its attention to bygone times . . . So as to ascertain by what means it has arrived at its present character and condition' (*Danmarks oldtid*, quoted in Daniel 1967: 98). In his *Essays on Barrows* (quoted ibid: 104) he argued thus for the preservation of these archaeological sites:

They are national memorials, which may be said to cover the ashes of our forefathers; and by this means constitute a national possession which has been handed down for centuries from race to race. Would we then unconcernedly destroy those venerable remains of ancient times, without any regard to our posterity?

So sites become symbols of collective cultural identity. The Tasmanian Aborigines now so regard Kutikina cave on the Franklin River, as do the modern Greeks the monuments of the Acropolis. At the 1981 'Lost Heritage' Conference in London one delegate put it thus:

. . . a cultural artefact is not merely something which is more or less dead, beautiful and scientific, something which is put in a showcase [be it] in a marvellous museum like the Louvre or the British Museum. It is something that, for a particular people, is a living thing which enables a people to achieve confidence in itself and is, thus, able to imagine its future. So when we are told that these artefacts are better recognized, better protected and better studied in major museums I say 'Quite so'. But I would also say that those same artefacts have a far more important mission than that one . . . (Stétié 1981: 8)

The case of the sculptures and reliefs from the Acropolis temples presents all these issues, but must never be considered isolated from its historical contexts. The Greeks, like the Chinese (see Wang Gangwu's chapter) have an intense sense of heritage, of historical continuity from Mycenaean past to present. The Greeks of the classical period lived in the shadow of Mycenaean grandeur, but left daunting, untranscendable achievements to haunt those of Byzantine and modern days – indeed 'a shadow of a magnitude' (Keats, 'On seeing the Elgin Marbles'). The Parthenon even in 438 BC could be seen as a symbol, built on the ruins of the partly built temple destroyed by the Persians in 480. Its history since then has only enhanced that symbolic quality, apart from its value as a consummate architectural achievement. During 1983 Melina Mercouri, Greek Minister for Culture, argued passionately for the restitution of the sculptures removed by Lord Elgin:

For every Greek they represent our identity, our soul, our blood (Miss Mercouri reported in the *Australian* on 16 January 1984) . . . the Parthenon is a unique symbolic monument. . . . We are talking about the unity of a unique monument of the culture and democracy of Greece (*Guardian*, 23 May 1983, p. 13) . . . the Marbles are part of a monument to Greek identity, part of the deepest consciousness of the Greek people: our roots, our continuity, our soul. The Parthenon is like our flag. (*Sunday Times*, 22 May 1983)

We are reminded that one of the first acts of the newly independent Greek state, in the 1830s, was restoration of the Acropolis buildings to free them from the accretions of Turkish and Frankish occupation. The law passed in 1834 to protect antiquities and monuments expressed the view that 'all objects of antiquity in Greece, as the productions of the ancestors of the Hellenic people, are regarded as the common national possession of all Hellenes'. To use the terms 'Hellenic people' and 'Hellenes' was also to make a statement about continuity with a distant past.

The claims are for restitution of the material in the British Museum, purchased by that institution from the collector in 1816. They are not the first claims presented by the Greeks to the British. They rest on the symbolic value of the sculptures as Greek heritage, *and* their importance to the integrity of the structure from which they were removed. They are not portable works of art, but designed elements of a larger composition, however great the individual quality of each piece. Such claims in the past have not met favourable response. The counter-arguments have rested on three bases. First they stress the legality of Lord Elgin's activities – the removal of the sculptures was undertaken under *firman* from the government of the day. However, here one must note that that government was an occupying power. One might also wonder whether Lord Elgin may not have used his diplomatic position to advantage in negotiations with that government. This response also stresses the legality of the purchase in 1816, and the legal difficulties of restitution of any item from the British Museum's holdings.

The second point usually raised to counter arguments for restitution, or criticism of the original removal, is one of conservation. Certainly the monuments of the Acropolis were in poor shape in 1800 – damaged in successive battles for the commanding heights in various wars, altered, dismantled and in danger of being reduced to lime in local kilns. Elgin and his contemporaries used brutal and damaging methods to remove the sculptures and reliefs, especially the metopes, but they never doubted that they were in a sense rescuing ancient art treasures from certain destruction. In 1882 Michaelis concluded: 'only blind passion could doubt that Lord Elgin's act was an act of preservation' (quoted in Chamberlin 1983: 37). Conservationists also point to the risks faced by any fine marble sculpture in the Parthenon today, from the dangerously polluted atmosphere and the state of the fabric of the structure. Housing in a museum would be essential. So why not in London?

The third strand of argument, that put forcibly by David Wilson in his chapter, rests on the universal qualities of the Parthenon sculptures as artistic heritage. Items of such supreme achievement cannot, in this view, be seen as the possessions of any one nation, but of all mankind.

These arguments were also developed in an article in the *Times Higher Education Supplement* (10 June 1983: 36):

The main objection to the Greek claim is that it is based on a sense of 'ownership' that is hardly appropriate in the case of works of art. This has two more detailed aspects. The first concerns continuity. It is not clear that because a particular work of art was produced in a particular geographical area hundreds or even thousands of years ago that the modern state which now occupies that territory has an uncontested claim to 'own' it. In what sense is the modern Greece of Mr Papandreou and Miss Mercouri the legitimate successor to the Athenian republic of Pericles?

The second aspect of 'ownership' is less straightforward. Almost by definition, a work of art, especially one of the quality of the Parthenon frieze belongs not to a particular nation or state but to the whole of humanity. For its status is intimately related to a recognition of qualities that transcend the particular and approach the universal. This, of course, does not imply that the genius of a particular nation be devalued. But it does perhaps mean that no single nation can claim sole proprietorship of such a work of art.

So national interests and arguments for the restitution of cultural property may rest on entirely different premises from those of arguments about scientific and scholarly values, or those of aesthetics. These issues are surveyed in John Mulvaney's paper, as well as in that of Sir David Wilson, who argues the value of the 'universal' museum, custodian of the heritage of all mankind; he would not concede the necessity for the Parthenon sculptures to be housed on the Acropolis.

The unambiguous answer to our question, that which considers the past and its physical remains the common heritage of all mankind, may mask complexities which cannot be ignored. National concerns intrude, and within them those of other collectives. It could be said that both national and international legislation, by its very nature, must embody the predominant viewpoint. The past is the possession of those in power; the past belongs to the victor.

This aspect, the possession of the past or the use of the past, by the dominant, is discussed by Wang Gungwu in surveying attitudes to the past in China at two critical periods of her history. Eric Willmot also touches on it in commenting on the events of early colonial settlement at Sydney Cove and the historical traditions of Bennelong and Pemulwuy. It has not escaped other Aboriginal commentators, for example Charles Perkins in a letter headed 'History as written by the conquerors' (quoted in White and O'Connell 1983: 233):

Australian colonial history, as it has been compiled from early records is proof of nothing more than the fact that history is always written by conquerors.

As such the carefully sifted 'facts' concerning Aborigines by white settlers and officials have been used as a foundation for all of the self-sustaining social myths that tend to justify the white man's dominance of Australia today.

Similar perceptions may be seen in the statements introducing the recommendations made to the Victorian government by the South-Eastern Land Council relating to proposals for an Aboriginal Heritage Act.

Our history tells of the events that have occurred from that time [The Dreaming] till now. A history that must now be forgotten or bastardized by order of the White invaders in order that we may only know his ways, laws, culture, religions, history, languages and etcetera.

Does that sound harsh?

If you think so then contemplate in what language and method we are to convey this message. It is written in the language of the invaders and takes written form to be handed to the Law men of White Law. Not an oral message in one of our languages before Law men of the Law of this country, the Law that has prevailed here since the Dreaming.

The statement is not a harsh one.

Questions of national concern may be raised regarding rights to investigate the past, or study its physical remains. As Lowenthal puts it, the past is 'nationalized' (Lowenthal 1975: 13). The countries of the eastern Mediterranean are jealous in control of their archaeological sites, while Ethiopia recently refused permits to American teams wishing to work on early hominid sites (Lewin 1983). Eighty years ago Flinders Petrie surveyed archaeological ethics in this context. He saw archaeologists of the present as being in a position of powerful, but 'transitory stewardship'. 'We have no right to destroy or suppress what happens just for the present to be in our power' (1904: 176), for past, present and future all have rights in the surviving monuments of human endeavour. His research was in countries whose governments early controlled investigation and the export of antiquities. He saw these measures as 'nibblings on a wide claim which no state has ventured yet to formulate, namely that all objects of past generations are public property . . . the logical outcome of the present laws and present tendency would be this nationalization of all antiquities' (1904: 185). He also saw the very real benefits accruing from such laws in protection of sites from destruction and alteration (1904: 185–8).

Similarly the interests of specific groups within national entities may be relevant. Minority or dispossessed groups such as the

Australian Aborigines and the North American Indians may demand more than a recognition of traditional rights of access to, or use, of sites important for their economic life. Bruce Trigger in his chapter, 'The Past as Power', surveying the history of the anthropology of the North American Indian shows how this has often ignored the realities of Indian life. Many peoples now argue for control or custodianship of what is seen as their particular heritage, as we have seen in the statement from the Southeastern Land Council. The academic researcher may not be welcome, nor may arguments about the common heritage of all mankind (Figs 4 and 5). Ros Langford, of the Tasmanian Aboriginal Centre, put these arguments to a meeting of the Australian Archaeological Association in December 1982 in a paper entitled 'Our Heritage – Your Playground': 'the issue is control . . . we say that it is our past, our culture, and heritage, and forms part of our present life. As such it is ours to control and it is ours to share on our own terms'.

In 1981 the Southeastern Land Council had made recommendations to the Victorian state government concerning an Aboriginal Heritage Act, its provisions and implementation. These embodied the principles of Aboriginal custodianship for sites and artefacts, that the Act must be administered by Aborigines, and 'that all Aboriginal Cultural Heritage is the property of the Aborigines and not the Crown'. Restitution of cultural property (interpreted in its widest sense to include information, myths and stories as well as artefacts) is clearly required: 'everything must be returned'; it is about time we were given our culture back'.

Are the issues relating to the non-tangible testimonies of the past, the information from and about it, any less complex? These issues may not be seen as demanding legislative solution, or are perhaps less amenable to legal answers than issues pertaining to material objects. Alice Tay comments in her paper that these issues have not been addressed fully by the law. But they pose important moral and ethical questions nonetheless. These relate to the uses of the past and traditions about the past, particularly in the educational, social and political arenas. New visions of the past, or new versions of the past. may serve social and political ends, and a people may be alienated from its past in the process (Durutalo 1983). These visions may be necessary in the search for collective self-conscious identity. Ms Jeffreys discusses these issues in her survey of the Byzantine chroniclers. Political or nationalistic goals may determine which elements of the collective past are chosen as the mould for this new entity. What is perpetuated? What is eliminated? What decisions are made by those Dale Spender calls 'the gate-keepers of history'? Why, for example, does Australia now have a well-publicized convict past, yet a century ago found this past too sensitive for popular appeal? The buildings of Port Arthur's penal settlement were demolished in that period of denial of the convict era, but are now in process of investigation and restoration. The convict era of North American history has never received more than scant attention in historical researches or the popular imagination. To the Chinese the past has always been of significance; yet certain elements of its traditions may dominate – Wang Gungwu explores this question for two vital periods of Chinese history. Considering Chinese history we might also ask why is it that the distant past exerts so powerful a force, its traditions outweighing those of more recent times?

Demands for a 'national' identity in the arena of modern international politics may force many new states of the Third World to create a 'national' history from the disparate traditions of once distinct tribal units. These traditions may derive from perceptions of the past quite alien to those of the Western historical traditions to which the 'national' history must conform. Les Groube surveys these problems in the New Guinean context. He points to the existence of other pressures, derived from the imperatives of economic success and development, as well as from the influences of western Christianity that have led to a denial or shunning of the Melanesian past.

The papers in this volume explore complex issues, approached from broad perspectives in both time and space. The issues are diverse, and those of the present have a long history. Whether we own the past or the past owns us, and whether we use the present to understand the past, or the past to control or direct the actions of the present, and so the future, we still stand 'in the shadow of a magnitude'.

References

Collingwood, R.G. (1946, reprinted 1980), *The Idea of History*, Oxford University Press, Oxford.

Chamberlin, R. (1983), *Loot! the Heritage of Plunder*, Thames & Hudson, London.

Daniel, G.E. (1967), *The Origins and Growth of Archaeology*, Pelican, Harmondsworth.

Durutalo, S. (1983), 'The Liberation of the Pacific Island Intellectual', *Review* 4(10), 6–18.

Langford, R. (1982), 'Our heritage – your playground', paper presented to the Australian Archaeological Association, Hobart.

Lévi-Strauss, C. (1972), *The Savage Mind (La Pensée Sauvage)*, Weidenfeld & Nicolson, London.

Lewin, R. (1983), 'Ethiopia halts prehistory research', *Science* 219, 147–49.

Lowenthal, D. (1975), 'Past time, present place: landscape and memory', *The Geographical Review* LXV(1), 1–36.

Petrie, W.M. Flinders (1904), *Methods and Aims in Archaeology*, New York [re-issued Benjamin Blom, New York, 1972].

Stétié, S. (1981), 'The view of UNESCO's inter-governmental committee', in *Lost Heritage*, report of the symposium held on the return of cultural property at the Africa Centre, London, May 1981, The Commonwealth Arts Centre and the Africa Centre, London, 8–10.

White, J.P. and O'Connell, J.F. (1982), *A Prehistory of Australia, New Guinea and Sahul*, Academic Press, Sydney.

1

The Past as Power

Anthropology and the North American Indian

Bruce Trigger

American anthropologists are proud of the objectivity of their discipline, of the central role that it plays in providing a comparative dimension for the other social sciences, and of its efforts to supply a social conscience for their own society's dealings with native peoples. Yet, with a curious inconsistency, they have come to regard cultural relativism – the assertion that any belief or custom must be judged exclusively in terms of the norms of the society in which it is found – not only as providing a framework for understanding individual cultures but also as a morally superior guide for the conduct of human relations. I believe that this view of cultural relativism is naive and self-defeating, though for reasons quite different from those offered by movements such as the Moral Majority, that merely advocate some other brand of absolute morality. It seems to me to be essential for anthropologists to understand their discipline's changing relationship to their own society and how their findings have been subtly influenced by this relationship. Only by taking advantage of social change to learn how particular conditions shape our interpretations of human behaviour, can we hope to understand our social milieu more objectively and hence make anthropology a more effective and responsible guide for social action.

It is widely acknowledged that what we believe to be true about modern peoples influences our understanding of their history, just as what we believe about historical groups helps to shape our opinions of their descendants. Because of this, it is necessary to examine with particular care the relationship between archaeology on the one hand and ethnology or social anthropology on the other. I hope to demonstrate in this paper that this relationship is more complex and has played a far more important role in shaping the development of anthropology than most historians of the discipline have realized. In studying the history of anthropology in the United States, we are considering the mòst elaborate example of this discipline to have developed in any part of the world where in recent centuries European settlers have overwhelmed an indigenous population. Its early beginnings, the flourishing condition of its various sub-disciplines, and its relatively self-contained institutional structure make American anthropology highly instructive for studying not only the relationship between prehistoric archaeology and ethnology but also how these two branches of anthropology have shaped an understanding of native peoples in what was and for them remains a colonial situation.

Civilization and its antithesis

It is commonly noted that the study of native peoples grew out of the curiosity that was aroused in Europe by the age of discovery. Yet even the earliest European descriptions of native people were far from being neutral observations. They were heavily influenced by classical and medieval speculations about what peoples living in the most remote corners of the world might be like (Dickason 1977). From the beginning, interpretations of native peoples were also enmeshed in the political, social, and economic controversies of Europe. Some of the considerations that influenced these interpretations were narrowly related to the exploitation of native peoples; others were broadly philosophical, though linked to differing opinions about how European society should develop. Hence, while facets of native culture were sometimes accurately recorded, views of native peoples were inevitably coloured by European prejudice and self-interest. By laying the groundwork for future interpretations of native peoples, these early speculations were to begin to shape anthropological thought long before the discipline was formally constituted.

The first English writers who described native North Americans were promoters of colonization. It was not in their interest to portray native peoples as hostile or dangerous. Indeed, references to conflicts between native people and European settlers were sometimes deliberately omitted from printed accounts of early English settlement in Virginia (Quinn 1977: 327). Native Americans were portrayed as having primitive technologies but as being skilful individuals who could easily be taught to work and live as Europeans. Physical differences between the two groups were ignored or thought to be of little importance. The principal failing of native people was seen to be their lack of an acceptable form of religion or even of any religion, but it was believed that this too could easily be remedied by means of Christian instruction. On the seal of the Massachusetts Bay Colony (1679–90) an Indian was depicted beseeching Englishmen to 'come over and help us' (Vaughan 1982: 927–29). Yet associated with this seeming benevolence was a firm belief that the moral and cultural superiority of Englishmen gave them the right to exploit native labour and direct native affairs in perpetuity as recompense for teaching them trades and to be 'tractable, civil, and industrious' (John Smith, quoted in Quinn 1979, 5: 335). While some English settlers sought to obtain formal deeds of purchase for land from its native owners, the general view was that failure to improve the soil meant that Indians did not have a legal claim to it. As John Winthrop put it in 1629, 'if we leave them sufficient for their use we may lawfully take the rest, there being more than enough for them and us' (Vaughan 1979: 110–11). Native rights were further diminished by proclaiming that the New World remained a virgin land, 'even as God made it' (John Smith, quoted in Quinn 1979, 5: 335).

As conflicts between English settlers and native groups became commonplace, English writers emphasized the Indians' idleness, improvidence, ignorance and a host of more serious vices. They were increasingly stigmatized as inferior or conquered peoples and their treachery and rebelliousness were seen as constant threats to colonists unless a 'strikt hand' were kept over them (Levett, quoted in Levermore 1962: 627). Their wretched style of life and enslavement to Satanic superstitions were accepted as evidence of God's displeasure with them, and the epidemics of European diseases that were thinning their numbers were interpreted as providential intervention to encourage European settlement (Gorges 1847: 62). As some Spanish theologians had done still earlier, the leaders of the Massachusetts Bay Colony liked to think of their own people as constituting a New Israel and of the Indians as Canaanites whose possessions God was delivering into their hands. Natives who submitted were to be treated kindly but firmly, while those who resisted were to be sold into slavery or exterminated (Porter 1979: 91–115). Ezra Stiles, the President of Yale University, carried this biblical parallel still further by promoting the idea that the Indians of New England were literally descended from Canaanites who had fled from Palestine at the time of Joshua's invasion (Haven 1856: 4). There was also growing doubt that it would be as easy to convert the Indians to Christianity and to have them adopt a European style of life as had originally been thought.

Until polygenists began to argue that native Americans might have been created separately in the New World, the question of their origins, although keenly debated, posed few serious intellectual challenges. Orthodox religious views maintained that all human beings had been created somewhere in Asia; hence Indians must have spread from there to the New World. As early as 1589, Joseph de Acosta, in his *Historia natural y moral de las Indias*, had suggested that they had come, as primitive hunters, by land from Siberia (Fagan 1977: 21–22). Far more serious problems of an historical nature were posed by cultural similarities that were shared by native American societies and those of ancient Europe and the Near East. Proto-evolutionists saw in America evidence of what the childhood of all mankind had been like. As early as 1592, John White used his remarkable drawings of Virginia Indians as models for a series of illustrations of ancient Britons (Orme 1981: 3–4). During the seventeenth century, it became increasingly fashionable to view certain aspects of Old World antiquity as survivals of a primitive age when cultures had resembled those that had lasted into modern times in the New World (Daniel 1975: 25–27). On the other hand, degenerationists, (such as Joseph-François Lafitau [1724]; Fenton and Moore 1974–77) interpreted these resemblances as surviving vestiges of the divinely-revealed patriarchal way of life described in the Book of Genesis. Only Judaism and later Christianity were thought to be able to prevent human behaviour from declining into barbarism. Both the evolutionary and the degenerationist points of view drew a clear distinction between native North American cultures and those of Europe. The evolutionist position implied that for some reason American cultures had failed to develop; the degenerationist view branded them as having become morally and spiritually corrupt.

During the eighteenth century, environmental explanations tended to supplant theological ones in accounting for cultural change. Yet, suggestions that North America was climatically inferior to the Old World and that this caused its plant and animal life to degenerate were more popular with European scholars than they were with European settlers in North America. This was because such explanations implied that these settlers, no less than native peoples, were being adversely influenced by the environment (Haven 1856: 94).

In the course of the eighteenth and early nineteenth centuries, an evolutionary perspective triumphed over a degenerationist one, at least in scholarly circles. There was also a growing tendency to attribute behavioural differences between native Americans and European settlers to largely unalterable biological factors. Increasing attention was paid to the physical characteristics that distinguished the two groups and, with respect to Indians as well as blacks, a dark skin colour was often cited as evidence of intellectual and moral inferiority to whites. It was more comfortable for whites to believe that the failure of all but a few Indians to adopt

Christianity and a European lifestyle resulted from their biological inferiority, than to contemplate the possibility that native people were rational human beings who did not find European civilization attractive. Native resistance to the expansion of settlement and the Indians' role as military allies of the French prior to 1760 led increasing numbers of Europeans to stigmatize them as irremediably bloodthirsty savages. By the time of the American Revolution, the belief that native people could not be civilized and therefore should be swept aside to make room for the spread of civilization led many Americans to advocate policies of genocide (Vaughan 1982: 929–49).

Throughout the nineteenth century, as white settlement expanded across North America, such arguments were used to justify the routine use of military force to subjugate native peoples or compel them to retreat westward. These ideas acquired spurious scientific respectability, first from the works of polygenists such as John Gliddon and Josiah Nott, who viewed Indians as a separate species that was inferior to Europeans and later by suggesting, as an extrapolation from Darwinian evolution, that the struggle between whites and Indians was only one manifestation of a universal natural tendency to ensure the survival of the fittest (Stanton 1960). The anticipated disappearance of the American Indians was proclaimed to be a price that had to be paid for the general advancement of humanity. In 1846, even the celebrated ethnologist Henry Schoolcraft, whose wife was partly Ojibwa, did not hesitate to observe of whites and Indians that 'it has been given to us (whites) to carry out scenes of improvement, and of moral and intellectual progress, which providence in its profound workings, has deemed it best for the prosperity of man, that we, not they, should be entrusted with' (Hinsley 1981: 10). The desperate struggles that native peoples waged to defend their territories against encroachment by white Americans or by tribes that had already been displaced by white expansion were cited as further evidence of their ferocity and inability to become civilized. Racist myths transformed native victims into bloodthirsty monsters, while white aggression was justified in the name of human progress. Such attitudes may be seen reflected in illustrations of the period, the images contrasting markedly with the realities of Indian life (see Figs 6,7 and 8).

Because modern Indians were widely regarded as primitive and incapable of adopting a civilized way of life, it was assumed that their past would exhibit little evidence of change or cultural development. Yet, as European settlement penetrated west of the Appalachians in the late eighteenth century, huge mounds and earthworks containing sophisticated copper and mica ornaments, worked marine shell, stone pipes, and fancy pottery began to be found throughout the Ohio and Mississippi valleys. Amateur archaeologists and the general public attributed these finds to Danes, Hindus, Israelites, or Toltecs, who were believed to have lived in that region in the remote past. It was further imagined that these peaceful and civilized 'Moundbuilders' had been dispersed by savage hordes of North American Indians. Such speculations romantically justified the wars being waged against the native inhabitants of North America as a crusade to avenge the Moundbuilders. When, towards the end of the nineteenth century, the archaeologist Cyrus Thomas demonstrated that the Moundbuilders were among the ancestors of the North American Indians, he sought to make his argument convincing by suggesting that their level of culture had not been essentially different from that of native groups who lived in eastern North America in historic times. To do this, it was necessary to ignore many of the most impressive achievements of the prehistoric Hopewellian and Mississippian cultures (Silverberg 1968).

During the nineteenth century, there was also a tendency for archaeologists to assume that many Indian artefacts of exceptional quality had been produced after European contact. It was argued that iron tools were needed to work stone, bone, and native copper effectively. An example of this type of thinking was the assumption that the elaborate paraphernalia associated with the Southern Cult indicated that this mortuary ritual was a response to the shock of massive epidemics that followed Spanish intrusion into the southeastern United States in the early sixteenth century. It has since been established that this was an entirely prehistoric phenomenon (Martin, Quimby and Collier 1947: 361–66). This was very different from Europe, where prehistoric archaeology was valued because it could demonstrate that even from earliest times to the dawn of history cultural progress had characterized the ancestors of modern Europeans.

Evolutionary anthropology

Anthropology emerged in both Europe and America in the course of the nineteenth century as a discipline concerned with the study of 'primitive peoples'. It developed in an age of worldwide colonialism and at a time when the ideas of cultural evolution formulated by the philosophers of the French Enlightenment were in the ascendant. Yet it was also a period when Enlightenment faith in the psychic unity of mankind was being eroded in Europe by a growing conviction that cultural differences among various groups of people could be accounted for by racial factors. Scholars such as John Lubbock popularized the belief that primitive peoples throughout the world were biologically inferior to Europeans. They were doomed to vanish with the spread of civilization, since no amount of education could compensate for the thousands of years during which natural selection had failed to adapt them biologically to a more complex way of life (Lubbock 1865; 1882). It is also worth noting that Lubbock and other racially oriented thinkers believed that, as a result of natural selection, within Western civilization the criminally-inclined and lower classes were biologically inferior to the middle and upper classes. Thus a single set of reasons was used to justify colonialism and to explain social inequality within Western society.

In England, nineteenth-century European (and in particular Anglo-Saxon) society was esteemed to be the supreme achievement of cultural evolution to date. History was viewed as a chronicle of human progress which moved from the dawn of civilization in the Near East, to ancient Greece and Rome, and finally to Western Europe. The idea that the torch of civilization had been passed from one group to another allowed Western Europeans to appropriate as their own the historical achievements of neighbouring peoples and places. At the same time, anthropology emerged as the study of geographically or temporally more remote peoples who did not have their own history. It was intended partly to elucidate the character of tribal groups whom European settlers and colonial administrators were encountering in many parts of Africa, Asia, and the Pacific, but also to be a source of information about the development of European society prior to recorded history.

During the nineteenth century, European anthropology had four main branches, although they were differently labelled and interrelated at various times and in different countries. Ethnology sought to document the simpler cultures that had existed in different parts of the world prior to European domination. Within an evolutionary perspective, it was assumed that these cultures were less evolved than those of modern Europe and that, by selecting ones at different levels of development, ethnologists could illustrate the nature of European society at successive stages of prehistory. Physical anthropology studied biological differences among human groups to see if these correlated with variations in their behaviour. Linguistic studies sought to document diversity among human languages, but also to reinforce an evolutionary viewpoint by demonstrating that the languages spoken by simpler societies were grammatically and lexically less sophisticated than were those of civilized peoples. Prehistoric archaeology was concerned primarily with Europe. It sought to prove that cultural evolution had characterized that part of the world from the earliest period of human occupation to the dawn of recorded history (Daniel 1975: 29–151). Because of this, even when there was the greatest amount of interest in unilinear evolution (between the 1850s and the 1880s) no antithesis was perceived between an evolutionary and an historical approach to the study of European prehistory. For Europeans, prehistoric archaeology was primarily an extension of the study of their own history into earlier times. As evolutionary interests declined and the European social sciences shifted towards an historical particularist perspective near the end of the nineteenth century, European archaeology gradually moved away from anthropology and became either a branch of history or an independent discipline (Daniel 1975: 228–58).

In nineteenth-century America, history was viewed almost universally as the study of European society before (as well as after) its arrival in the New World (one partial but significant exception is Winsor 1889). It was concerned with commemorating the achievements of a people who had progressed steadily from prehistoric times, and whose leading countries had achieved world hegemony by the nineteenth century. In contrast, the primary task of anthropology was to study the native peoples of North America. Some anthropologists, such as John Wesley Powell, the first director of the Bureau of American Ethnology, saw the purpose of anthropology as being to ameliorate the treatment of native people by the American government by helping white Americans to understand them better (Hinsley 1981: 287). The majority of anthropologists probably agreed with Schoolcraft that their main goal was a more modest one: to preserve for future ages some records of a dying race (Schoolcraft, quoted in Hinsley 1981: 20). As native people ceased to be rivals for the control of a continent, a widespread romanticism developed about them, that was manifested in anthropology no less than in art and literature (Keiser 1933, Monkman 1981).

The same four divisions of anthropology emerged in America as in Europe, although from the beginning they were more unified since they were all concerned with the same people. Ethnologists sought to reconstruct the traditional cultures of native American tribes, relying on the memories of elderly informants who claimed to remember what life had been like prior to disruptions by smallpox epidemics and European occupation. In the east, where European influence had been exerted much earlier, historical records were used to help in this task. It was generally assumed that native cultures had been stable prior to the arrival of the Europeans and so these descriptions were deemed valid for prehistoric times as well.

Archaeologists were expected to confirm this by demonstrating that the patterns recorded by ethnologists were present in prehistoric times. In the southwestern United States, it was possible for them to locate vast numbers of prehistoric sites that closely resembled those of modern Pueblo groups; thus confirming the expected continuity (Willey and Sabloff 1980: 50–51). Yet, in many parts of the east, where archaeologists had been active for a long time, it was already evident that many prehistoric sites did not resemble those associated with groups that had lived in the same area in historic times. In these cases, it was generally assumed that the discrepancy resulted from tribes moving about on a thinly populated continent rather than from cultural changes within particular groups (Parkman 1927: 3; Hunt 1940: 13). For example, New York State archaeologists believed that the Middle Woodland cultures which had preceded prehistoric ones almost identical to those of the historic Iroquois belonged to Algonkian peoples whom the Iroquois had later displaced. The pottery found in these Middle Woodland sites resembled, in a general fashion, pottery that had been produced by Algonkian speakers to the north and east of the Iroquois area in historic times. A still earlier aceramic culture in New York State was thought to have Eskimo affinities (Parker 1922). While archaeologists were capable of noting major alterations in the archaeological record, their conviction that native cultures had been largely static prior to the arrival of the Europeans led them to avoid explanations couched in terms of changes occurring within cultures.

Almost no attention was paid to establishing detailed cultural chronologies during the nineteenth century, although the techniques of stratigraphy and typological seriation that were the backbone of European evolutionary archaeology were known to American archaeologists and used by them (Trigger 1980: 664). Archaeologists were mainly interested in determining what artefacts were used for, how they were made, and what area or people had produced them. These were the same questions that, so far as material culture was concerned, were of interest to American ethnologists (Hinsley 1981: 87–91).

The strongly ethnographic orientation of archaeology may help to explain why only a few archaeologists were interested in searching for the earliest evidence of humanity in the New World. The evidence from any seemingly early cultures could not easily be interpreted by direct analogy with historic ones. It also remained an article of faith among many anthropologists that human beings had arrived but recently in the New World and that their cultures had developed into essentially their modern form soon after Indians had spread across the continent (Willey and Sabloff 1980: 46–50).

North American anthropologists also either belittled the achievements of the native civilizations of Mexico and Peru or regarded them as irrelevant for understanding the North American Indians. Lewis Henry Morgan argued that the Aztecs had been at the same stage of development as the Iroquois (Middle Barbarism) and that historians such as W.H. Prescott, who described them as being civilized, had been misled by Spanish efforts to exaggerate the importance of their conquests (Resek 1960: 133). Morgan's view accorded with the strong prejudices that were expressed against the Mexicans, during and after the Mexican War (1846–48), as a nation whose leadership had been destroyed through interbreeding with a racially inferior Indian population (Horsman 1975). In coming to this conclusion, no attention was paid to the already well-known architectural and artistic accomplishments of the prehistoric Maya and the Aztecs (Stephens 1841). Moreover, even archaeologists who acknowledged the creative accomplishments of the Indians of Mexico and Peru generally regarded the native peoples of North America as being inferior to them and incapable of evolving beyond the tribal level.

Perhaps the most significant feature of nineteenth-century American anthropology was that no provision was made to study the important changes that had occurred in native American societies as a result of European contact. In part this was because ethnologists believed that their most urgent responsibility was to study native cultures before they totally vanished. It may also reflect a lack of confidence among ethnologists that they were well enough trained to engage in archival research. Yet neither of these explanations accounts for their general failure to record systematically what was happening to Indians as they were studying them. The changes that were taking place generally were thought to be a random process of disintegration that would terminate either with native peoples becoming totally extinct or with those who survived being assimilated into the dominant white culture. These changes were mainly deplored as obstacles to studying traditional native cultures which ethnologists had to find ways to circumvent. A striking exception to this view was James Mooney (1896), who portrayed native societies as dynamic entities struggling to survive the shock of acculturation and loss of power in his study of the Ghost Dance, an indigenous religious movement that late in the nineteenth century sought to revive the morale of the Plains Indians. Curtis Hinsley (1981: 207–8) has suggested that Mooney's Irish background may have helped him to understand that native responses to white pressure should not automatically be interpreted as evidence of cultural disintegration.

The manner in which nineteenth-century white Americans regarded native peoples was revealed by their making them an object of anthropological rather than historical study. It was also dramatized by displaying their material culture, alongside collections of rocks and stuffed animals, in museums of natural history rather than in museums of fine arts, where visitors were invited to admire the cultural achievements of Europe and Asia. In this fashion, it was (and continues to be) implied that Indians were more akin to the natural world than to civilized humanity. Moreover, like bisons and virgin forests, they were a part of nature that had to be swept aside if the manifest destiny of white Americans was to be realized. Archaeological and ethnological collections were repositories for the trophies taken from a vanquished and disappearing realm.

Boasian anthropology

Anthropology became established as a discipline in American universities only towards the end of the nineteenth century. Most of the key positions were filled by students of Franz Boas, who had been born and trained in Germany. Boas rejected the evolutionary anthropology of his American predecessors and sought to alter both anthropology and traditional American views of native people. His efforts to demonstrate the absence of any scientific support for racist beliefs and to show that all peoples possessed an equal capacity for development were well received by immigrants from central and eastern Europe who were coming to the United States in large numbers at this time and encountering much racial prejudice from Anglo-Americans (Grant 1916). In accord with current trends in European scholarship, Boas also rejected unilinear evolutionism for its unacceptably deterministic view of cultural change. He and his students sought to document the numerous and unpredictable ways in which economic, social, and intellectual traits combine to produce individual cultural configurations. They rejected the distinction between more and less evolved cultures as being unacceptably ethnocentric and sought to demonstrate that the achievements of tribal societies were no less worthy of respect than were those of technologically more complex ones. They also believed that there was no scientific method for establishing that the values of one society were more evolved or superior than those of another. Boasian cultural relativism routinely stressed, as only a few individual anthropologists had ever done before, the dignity of native peoples and of the many ways of life they had evolved prior to the coming of the European. The interest that Boasian anthropologists had in cultural variation also encouraged them to try to record the total cultural patterns of individual tribes to a greater degree than had been done previously. American ethnologists and British social anthropologists both regarded these descriptions as constituting the basis for a comparative study of cultural diversity independently of any historical considerations (Stocking 1974; Harris 1968: 250–89).

As part of its rejection of cultural evolutionism, Boasian anthropology stressed that diffusion had played a major role in bringing about cultural change. While American anthropologists had invoked diffusion in the nineteenth century, it was now viewed as crucial for shaping cultural patterns (Adams et al. 1978). In combating cultural evolutionism, Boasians tended to minimize the importance of independent development and argued that most of the features associated with any one culture were derived from older or neighbouring ones. Cultural change was conceptualized mainly as a process by which increasing numbers of human groups were able to share existing ideas. Yet, the transmission of ideas from one culture to another was thought to depend to a large degree upon idiosyncratic factors and therefore to be an unpredictable process. This in turn accounted for the cultural diversity observed in the ethnographic record (Harris 1968: 258–59).

The increasing importance that ethnologists assigned to diffusion as a mechanism of cultural change began to influence American archaeology. After 1910, there was growing interest in studying changes that had occurred in prehistoric times. Archaeologists began to use both seriation and stratigraphic techniques in a routine fashion to delineate local sequences of cultural change. In the 1920s, the discovery of Palaeo-Indian cultures extended these sequences substantially further into the past (Willey and Sabloff 1980: 121–23). Archaeologists now believed that important changes had occurred in prehistoric times not only as a result of migrations of people from one part of North America to another but also because diffusion had altered cultures that remained in the same place. Yet, into the early 1950s, massive replacements of population continued to be invoked to account for major and abrupt changes in the archaeological record (e.g. Quimby 1960: 49–50), while important innovations that were believed to have diffused widely among North American cultures often were traced to a presumed point of origin in Central America or eastern Siberia. These included such major items of archaeological interest as pottery, cultigens, and burial mounds (Willey and Sabloff 1980:

118–20). Although archaeologists now regarded native North Americans as being flexible enough to adopt and utilize innovations, their views about diffusion continued to imply that these people were unlikely to invent anything significant. Little attention was paid to understanding the internal dynamics of cultural change, or even to determining why a particular innovation did or did not diffuse from one group to another. While the mechanical employment of concepts of diffusion and migration to account for change in the archaeological record was not very different from contemporary culture-historical explanations of European prehistory, in the American context it reflected a continuing limited faith in the cultural creativity of native North Americans.

Archaeological cultures were now generally defined by lists of surviving material culture and archaeologists sought to relate cultures by comparing the number of traits that they shared or did not share. As a result of this growing preoccupation with typological analysis, many archaeologists began to shun the functional ethnographic interpretation of artefacts as being speculative and unscientific (Taylor 1948: 73–80). Yet some archaeologists attempted to infer from settlement patterns and artefact distributions how native groups had lived in the past and it soon became clear that cultural patterns had existed in prehistoric times that were radically different from any attested in the ethnographic record (Willey and Sabloff 1980: 115–26). Yet even this knowledge did not stimulate significant interest in understanding cultural change in terms of concepts other than those of diffusion and migration. A notable exception to that point of view was A.V. Kidder, whose *An Introduction to the Study of Southwestern Archaeology*, published in 1924, provided the first culture-historical synthesis of archaeological data for a major region of North America. In that book Kidder stressed that the prehistoric southwest owed little more than the 'germs' of its culture to the outside and that its development had been a local and almost wholly independent one that was cut short by the 'devastating blight of the white man's arrival' (Kidder 1962: 344). In this, as in much else, Kidder was ahead of his time (Woodbury 1973).

Ethnohistory

A much later development within the context of Boasian anthropology was the emergence of ethnohistory as a fifth branch of the discipline. Ethnohistorians use historical documentation and oral traditions to study what has happened to native American societies since European contact. There is considerable debate about the origins of ethnohistory as a discipline. A.F.C. Wallace (1982: 533–34) notes that anthropologists have used historical documents in conjunction with archaeological, linguistic and ethnographic evidence to illuminate native cultures since the time of Morgan, while T.H. Charlton (1981: 138) suggests that in the 1930s archaeologists who adopted the direct historical approach began to use ethnohistorical data as a bridge between historic and prehistoric times. Their examples seem, however, to refer more to the use of written documents for purposes of historical ethnography than to ethnohistory as a systematic study of cultural change. James Axtell (1981: vii), on the other hand, sees ethnohistory as beginning with anthropologists' involvement in Indian land claims after 1946.

It seems fairly clear, however, that, while adumbrated by the work of James Mooney and Alfred G. Bailey (1937), ethnohistory developed as a discipline within the context of anthropological studies of acculturation that began in the 1930s. The original aim of these studies was to help government agencies to formulate more humane policies for dealing with native people by examining how native cultures had responded to various forms of European coercion and control. As a result of these studies, some anthropologists became convinced of the need to compare the transformations of native cultures that resulted from European contact in terms of a historical perspective and finally concluded that the history of these processes was itself a subject worthy of study. 'Outline for the Study of Acculturation' by Robert Redfield, Ralph Linton, and M.J. Herskovits (1936), Linton's *Acculturation in Seven American Indian Tribes* (1940), and Edward Spicer's *Perspectives in American Indian Cultural Change* (1961) and *Cycles of Conquest* (1962) were milestones in the development of studies of acculturation into what by the 1950s had come to be called ethnohistory. Along the way, ethnohistorians had to evolve a methodology that would permit them to use documentation largely provided by previous generations of European traders, missionaries or administrators who had varying knowledge of indigenous cultures and different motives for contacting native peoples, to understand the behaviour of past generations of these people (Trigger 1976: 1–26). Ethnohistorians learned much about using archival data from their involvement in land claims research and in recent decades many professional historians have been attracted to the field, making ethnohistory more interdisciplinary in character. There are significant differences in orientation and approaches between American ethnohistorians who have been trained in anthropology and those who have been trained in history (cf. Axtell 1981 and Wallace 1982). This produces creative tensions that in the long run should benefit ethnohistory.

However ethnohistorians perceive their relationship to anthropology and history, their work adds a major dimension to the study of native Americans that was absent from the original constitution of North American anthropology. Investigating what has happened to native peoples since the coming of the Europeans, ethnohistory is the equivalent for them of the study of colonial and modern history for white Americans. European anthropology never required a similar branch since that gap was already filled by the well-established discipline of European history.

More importantly, ethnohistory has begun to document the resilience and dynamism of native peoples and their cultures from earliest European contact to the present. Despite the demographic tragedy that overwhelmed them and despite the unremitting physical and spiritual assault that Europeans (sometimes with good and sometimes with bad intentions) have unleashed against them, post-contact native history is not, as it was once imagined to be, a bleak chronicle of decline and extinction. Rather, as Mooney realized, it is a record of valiant struggle, transformations, and the continual reaffirmation of a will to survive in the face of indifference, hostility and paternalism from a seemingly ever more powerful adversary.

A combination of social factors makes the study of native history comprehensible and of growing interest to a large number of white Americans. Native Americans are increasing rapidly in numbers and hence are posing unanticipated social and economic problems for the dominant white society, which for a long time had expected them to die out or be assimilated. Many native people are also engaging in new and effective forms of political action that are designed to regain control for their people over their own destiny, while the work of native artists is winning unprecedented international acclaim. For the first time in over a century, white Americans have been forced to recognize that native peoples are a living and vital part of a present reality, not merely inert survivals from the past. Simultaneously, unprecedented economic constraints and environmental problems are forcing many white Americans to question the crassly expansionist ethic on the basis of which their society has operated since the seventeenth century.

Yet, if ethnohistory has created a substantial niche for itself within anthropology and history and attracted considerable public interest, it continues to be treated, as studies of native American activities always have been, as peripheral to mainstream American history. The very use of the term ethnohistory to denote a field of scholarship, rather than a set of techniques for studying peoples who did not produce their own written records, suggests that ethnohistorians themselves accept a separate status for their field and one that is marginal to history. Only occasionally is it argued that ethnohistory should be viewed together with prehistoric archaeology as part of a broader and more significant study of American history (Trigger 1982). This contrasts with more specialized studies of European or white American perceptions of native people which are accepted as an integral and important part of intellectual history (e.g. Chiappelli 1976; Vaughan 1965; Kupperman 1980).

Historians generally regard ethnohistory as the extension of historical investigation to an ethnic group that they did not routinely study in the past. There is little realization that this process could have any significance for established areas of historical enquiry. Yet it is obvious that native people played a far from negligible role in the development of white American society over the last five hundred years. For a long time Indians were numerically and militarily superior, and for a still longer period some native groups possessed economic resources that constrained Europeans to depend on their goodwill. In these situations, native values and expectations played a major role in shaping colonial development. The military seizure of the United States from its native inhabitants involved enormously expensive military operations and governed the initial patterns of European settlement over vast areas. In *The Invasion of America* (1975), Francis Jennings demonstrated that only by means of an ethnohistorically based study of the native peoples of New England could the real motives for the behaviour of the early Puritan settlements in New England towards each other be elicited from the contemporary self-serving Puritan versions of these events that American historians had long accepted at face value. Jennings totally demolished the view that while native history must be understood in the broader context of colonial history, the findings of ethnohistorians are irrelevant for understanding white history. Much of colonial history must be studied as part of a larger whole that embraces native history. Moreover, while the relative significance of native peoples has varied through time and space their history is important, and is likely to become even more important in the future, for understanding the whole of American history. So historians such as James Axtell (1981) are working towards a holistic view in which the study of native Americans becomes an integral part of American history.

Archaeology and ethnology

As part of their historical studies, ethnohistorians have been able to document changes in native cultures during the historic period. In many cases they have shown that what previous generations of ethnologists had accepted as traditional native cultures were ones that had been significantly altered as a result of European contact. Fred Eggan (1966: 15–44) presciently demonstrated that much of what were formerly thought to be ordinary cultural variations in Crow kinship terminology among tribes of the southeastern United States had been produced by the differing acculturative experiences of these societies. Such findings have important implications for all cross-cultural generalizations that do not situate ethnographic data in an historical context. Driver and Massey (1957) might have obtained significantly higher functional correlations for trait distributions in native North American cultures had they been able to use data that adequately reflected the state of these cultures prior to European influence. These findings also have significance for the interpretation of archaeological evidence. Martin Wobst (1978) and Carmel Schrire (1980) have cautioned against assuming that the Bushman peoples of southern Africa, who have interacted for long periods with their Hottentot, Bantu and European neighbours, necessarily provide a model of what a Palaeolithic hunter-gatherer society was like. That they do is an assumption based on evolutionist thought, not something that has been proved to be true. It is, moreover, an assumption that only archaeological research can test empirically.

In some cases, ethnohistorians have been able to use written documents to reconstruct the nature of particular cultures for an earlier period than when previous generations of anthropologists believed that they still preserved most of their pre-white characteristics (Hickerson 1970). Invariably, they discern significant differences. In recent years, archaeologists have been discovering that major changes also occurred in native cultures between the time when European goods first appeared in the archaeological record and the earliest written descriptions were recorded that provide ethnologists and ethnohistorians with information about these cultures (Trigger 1982b). The interval between these two events often lasted a century or longer. When the Huron people of southern Ontario were first described in 1615, they were a confederacy of four tribes with a total of about 25 000 people that inhabited some twenty communities located close to each other near the shores of Georgian Bay (Trigger 1969). Archaeological evidence demonstrates that fifty years earlier these same people had lived in many clusters, each composed of one or two villages, scattered over a much larger area that stretched as far south as Lake Ontario and eastward into the Trent valley (Ramsden 1977). Such radical alterations in settlement pattern indicate that major changes in social and political organization must have occurred as the Huron moved north to be closer to the trade routes along which European goods were reaching southern Ontario. Vast problems are also posed for understanding the late prehistoric social organization of southern New England, where epidemics are known to have destroyed much of the population prior to significant European documentation (Salwen 1978). It is clear in both of these cases, and for most tribal groups in North America, that ethnographic and ethnohistorical data do not provide either a baseline for understanding changes brought about by the arrival of Europeans or information that can be used with confidence to generalize about what native cultures were like prior to that time. If we are to establish an 'ethnographic present', in the sense of defining what cultures were like prior to changes brought about by European activities, it will have to be done archaeologically (Wilcox and Masse 1981).

Yet archaeology has already dispelled the idea that native cultures were generally static prior to European intervention. The concept of the ethnographic present derived much of its importance from the belief that native cultures changed only very slowly. Latterly, ethnologists believed that these cultures were static, not because of the inflexibility or mental inferiority of native peoples, but because they were sensitively attuned to a stable environment. Yet the archaeological record reveals not only ubiquitous cultural change in the prehistoric period but change occurring rapidly in many areas at the time of European contact. The same prehistoric archaeological cultures that can be used as a baseline for measuring changes that occurred following the earliest evidence of European intervention are themselves only the latest product of changes that took place in prehistoric times.

Ethnohistory and prehistoric archaeology are transforming American anthropology by making ethnologists aware that, because of cultural change, ethnographic descriptions must be understood within a historical context. If they are not, the resulting conflation of ethnographic data about cultures experiencing different types of change may result in erroneous cross-cultural generalizations. It would also appear that no society can be understood from a structural or functional point of view without first ascertaining its historical antecedents and knowing something about the broader social network of which it is a part. Inasmuch as ethnologists and ethnohistorians can only investigate non-literate cultures after these cultures have been drawn into the European world-system, they cannot study the full spectrum of cultural variation, as they frequently claim to do, but only the range that is represented by cultures that are experiencing varying degrees of acculturation. Ethnologists traditionally have taken great pride in the holistic nature of their data, which they have seen as providing a framework that can be used to understand the more fragmentary information that is available to ethnohistorians and archaeologists. They have also assumed that a comparative study of ethnographic data constituted an adequate basis for generalizing about human behaviour. It is therefore understandably difficult for them to accept this serious limitation on the significance of their data. Yet it appears that whatever we are going to know for certain about the nature and evolution of culture prior to the expansion of the European world-system must come from archaeological and historical sources rather than from ethnographic ones. This in turn must become the basis for defining a new relationship between archaeology and ethnology as anthropological disciplines.

Processual archaeology

The new or processual archaeology marked a major advance in understanding native American prehistory not only because it advocated more aggressive efforts to interpret archaeological data but more particularly because, for the first time, it encouraged archaeologists to study change from the viewpoint of what happens within societies or cultures (Binford 1972). The new archaeology thus united and carried forward separate efforts that had been made in the 1950s to understand prehistoric cultures as adaptive systems (Caldwell 1958) and as changing patterns of social organization (Willey 1953). This emphasis on internal change, although sometimes carried to an extreme, necessarily complements the concepts of diffusion and migration as explanations of the transformations observed in the archaeological record. By making it central to the analysis of its data, the new archaeology has eliminated a major source of bias that has been directed against native peoples by American archaeology since its inception: the notion that they were uncreative or at least less creative than were peoples of European descent. By eliminating the last vestige of this idea from archaeology, the new archaeology has established native peoples on an equal basis with others as objects of historical study.

Unfortunately, the new archaeology has diminished the effect of this extremely positive and important contribution by insisting that the primary aim of archaeology should be, not to understand the past, but to establish general laws of human behaviour that are of practical value, presumably for modern white American society (Watson, Redman and LeBlanc 1971). It has been pointed out that this emphasis on nomothetic goals is a response to the generally low esteem in which American social scientists, and American society generally, hold historical studies (Bronowski 1971: 195). It has also been noted that the desire to produce useful information reflects

the values of a culture in which 'technocratic efficiency is considered as the supreme virtue' (Kolakowski 1976: 229). Yet it is
appalling that native people should be told that the main value of
a study of Arizona prehistory may be a series of generalizations
about human behaviour under stress that will be helpful for assess-
ing the effects of poverty and overcrowding on black and Mexican
Americans in the ghetto areas of modern Arizona cities (Martin
and Plog 1973: 364–68). There is no suggestion in such works that
native prehistory is worthy of study for its own sake. Indeed, in
one of his early pronouncements, L.R. Binford (1967: 235) suggested that the 'reconstruction and characterization of the past' is
of value mainly for 'the general education of the public'. In his
popular history of American archaeology, Brian Fagan (1977: 349),
a British-trained archaeologist, noted with some surprise the degree to which American Indian prehistory is regarded as irrelevant
to American history. In particular, he pointed to the lack of attention that was paid to it during the American bicentennial cel-
ebrations of 1976. This situation persists, despite some recent
evidence of growing public interest in the findings of prehistoric
archaeology.

Another result of the current nomothetic orientation of
American archaeology is the strong emphasis that is placed on
studying problems related to ecology, social hierarchies, and other
aspects of social behaviour that can be analysed in terms of general
postulates, at the expense of no less important problems that must
be investigated by understanding what is cognitively specific to native North American cultures. The value of the latter type of studies is demonstrated by the use that Robert Hall (1976) has made
of a comparative understanding of native American symbolism to
suggest the possible meaning of certain aspects of prehistoric
Adena burial rituals, including the manner in which they constructed their mounds and enclosures. It is also demonstrated by
George Hamell's (1980) studies of the supernatural significance of
natural substances such as crystals, native copper, and marine
shells, which among the native peoples of eastern North America
in historic times were valued for their life-giving powers, especially
in connection with the survival of souls after death. The continuous
association of these substances with burial rituals for over six millennia in eastern North America suggests persistence in their ritual
significance. Despite the problems that are involved in equating
specific myths and rituals over long periods, this in turn provides
insights into the meaning of grave offerings in specific prehistoric
cultures. Similar treatment of crystal and European glass beads and
of native copper and fragments of European copper and brass also
suggests how the Indians of eastern North America first perceived

these European goods and why the heaviest concentrations of them are found in funerary contexts (Fitzgerald 1982). There is some evidence of growing interest in studying symbolism and scientific knowledge in prehistory, especially in the field of archaeoastronomy (Aveni 1981). Yet the relative infrequency of such studies and the strong commitment of American archaeologists to nomothetic research provide evidence of the continuing alienation of many archaeologists from their subject matter.

This estrangement is exacerbated by acrimonious confrontations between archaeologists and native people over who controls the cultural resources of the past, which archaeologists traditionally assumed belonged to landowners or to themselves. These disputes often take the form of legal efforts by native people to halt the excavation of cemeteries, or of any kind of archaeological site, on the grounds that these activities violate the sanctity that native peoples ascribe to such places. The claims often seem to archaeologists to be unreasonable because they are formulated in terms of a pan-Indian perspective that makes Indians of today responsible for sites of any age or tribal affiliation, rather than merely for those associated with their own recent past (Rosen 1980). Yet this is an emotional issue about which native people can arouse sympathy and support among a substantial number of non-Indian citizens and government officials who are normally not inclined to pay attention to their claims for political and economic justice. It is equally significant, however, that a growing number of archaeologists are learning to work with and for native groups and are finding that their research benefits from such cooperation. There is hope that in the future more native people may find that the study of North American prehistory has positive meaning for them.

In the long run, however, such a change in attitude will be encouraged, not by direct confrontation or by clever public relations, but by archaeologists identifying, and where possible eliminating, the causes of their discipline's alienation from the people whose history they study. They must be prepared to acknowledge, both publicly and among themselves, that in the past archaeology unwittingly helped to sustain the view that native people were incapable of progress and therefore had no future in North American society. They must also be ready to admit that, while archaeologists long ago produced evidence which demonstrated that view to be false, they were extremely slow to appreciate the dynamic qualities of native cultures in prehistoric times. It follows that Indians who have rejected the work of most archaeologists as inimical to their own interests and aspirations have evaluated the history and current state of archaeology more accurately than archaeologists themselves have done, and that their acceptance of the discipline requires many archaeologists to overcome their own continuing indifference and bad attitudes with respect to native peoples.

A successful reorientation of American archaeology must be based on recognizing that the current nomothetic orientation of the discipline expresses, albeit in a more intellectualized fashion than before, its continuing alienation from native peoples. If archaeology is to have meaning for native peoples, understanding their past must become a major objective of research. Such a goal would not threaten the positive accomplishments of the new archaeology, which has already done much to enhance the image of the American Indian. On the contrary, it would accord new value to nomothetic research as an instrument for understanding prehistory, while at the same time enriching archaeology by placing new emphasis on studying cognitive and symbolic aspects of the past (Hodder 1982).

Prehistoric archaeology and ethnohistory could then become the basis for the study of native American history from earliest times to the present day. This would parallel the role that archaeology and history play in studying Europe and other parts of the world. By overcoming its alienation from native peoples, American archaeology not only can hope to eliminate a political threat to its continued collection of data but also stands to advance scientifically and to enhance its social significance. Yet to accomplish this, disciplinary inertia and a heavy legacy from America's colonialist past must be overcome.

Anthropology as history

The need for a historical orientation is not restricted to the ethnohistorical and archaeological branches of anthropology. We have already argued that an historical perspective is required to understand ethnographic data. Moreover, American ethnology finds itself caught on the horns of a dilemma. It is becoming increasingly evident that neo-evolutionary approaches have been unduly simplistic. They have underestimated the diversity of cultural patterns and, by treating individual cultures as if they were isolates, have also ignored patterns of interaction that play a major role in bringing about cultural change. As a result, neo-evolutionary anthropologists have failed to recognize many of the regularities that characterize societies at similar levels of complexity or in similar environmental settings and at the same time have been guilty of treating specific phenomena as if they were universal ones. For example, generalizations about tribal cultures generally have been based on New Guinea 'big man' societies (Sahlins 1968; Service 1962), although very different forms of political organization are found in North American societies that share a similar mode of production (Whallon 1982: 156). Like nineteenth-century evolutionism, neo-evolutionary anthropology encourages the view that any society different from technologically-advanced ones is in all respects less advanced than they are. There is a danger that this sort of cultural evolutionism will provide a pseudoscientific justification for bigotry and exploitation. On the other hand, extreme cultural relativism can become a licence for romantic self-indulgence and a historical particularism that fails to explain important structural regularities that are found in historically-unrelated societies that are of similar levels of complexity (Trigger 1982*a*).

What is required is a theoretical framework that allows every society to be studied as a structural transformation of its own past, the elements of which have been altered as a result of ecological and social strategies operating within a field of interaction that includes neighbouring societies. By analysing societies as systems that interact not only with their natural environment but also with neighbouring peoples, it is possible to take account of the full range of processes that bring about cultural change. These include diffusionary ones as well as innovation and adaptation (Trigger 1978: 216–28). By analysing change in terms of units that are characterized by at least enough integration to supply the basic prerequisites necessary for their survival (Aberle et al. 1950), the excesses of historical particularism can be avoided. Studies of cultural evolution should seek to account not merely for changes that take place in closed systems, as neo-evolutionists following the advice of Julian Steward (1955: 82) have done, but also for the kind of changes that are studied within the context of the anthropology of development. It must be realized that a significant amount of social change is constrained and influenced by the ties that link together neighbouring societies, whether they are at different levels of development or vary only in seemingly minor respects. There is reason to believe that a considerable degree of regularity governs these relations. This is witnessed by a growing interest in applying the concepts of world-system theory (Renfrew and Shennan 1982) and similar approaches (Wolf 1982) to anthropology. There is also in Britain a growing convergence between social history and social anthropology (Macfarlane 1970). The result could be a body of cultural evolutionary theory that is infinitely more complex than that associated with neo-evolutionary anthropology but which would be better able to explain the social changes that are observed in the archaeological, historical, and ethnographic records. This kind of theory eliminates the distinction between history and evolution since it aims to explain specific as well as general changes that have occurred in the course of human history. Moreover, inasmuch as human consciousness and behavioural patterns change in relationship to the material basis of their existence, history becomes the matrix in terms of which the various nomothetic generalizations of the social sciences acquire their significance (Childe 1947; Friedman and Rowlands 1978). All of this raises the question of whether the distinction between history and anthropology is any longer justified.

The original differentiation between history and anthropology was a product of colonialism and ethnocentrism. Anthropology was initiated as the study of peoples who were alleged to lack history. The view that native people are not proper subjects for historical research was reiterated as recently as 1965 by the Regius Professor of Modern History at Oxford University, Hugh Trevor-Roper, when he proclaimed that 'there is only the history of Europeans in Africa. The rest is darkness . . . and darkness is not a subject of history' (1965: 9). The emerging discipline of native American history challenges the dichotomy between history and anthropology by drawing upon data studied by archaeologists, ethnohistorians, ethnologists, physical anthropologists, historical geographers and professional historians to produce a synthesis of what is known about native peoples from earliest times to the present. The growing realization that structural-functional interpretations have significance only when the societies being studied are located in their specific historical setting challenges it on an even more fundamental basis.

Yet it is clear that the specialized disciplines that have developed over the past two centuries cannot disappear. Each has developed techniques for collecting and analysing data that require a high degree of specialization to master satisfactorily. Physical anthropology, historical linguistics, ethnohistory, and ethnology are essential sources of information about human behaviour. They cannot be abandoned as techniques for analysing specific kinds of data without seriously weakening our overall ability to understand the past.

Temperamental barriers reinforce disciplinary ones. Anthropologists generally view historians as being too data-bound and particularistic in their style of explanation, while historians mistrust what they see as a tendency for anthropologists to overgeneralize on the basis of limited data. Yet it is to be hoped that in the future researchers from all of the social-science disciplines will learn to work together more closely to produce a unified understanding of human behaviour. A model for this is provided by the interdisciplinary links that have created the fields of social and economic history. These have transformed history from being a discipline that was narrowly concerned with political events into a more holistic investigation of the development of Western society. This change provides a foretaste of what anthropologists, archaeologists, ethnohistorians, and other social scientists, by cooperating, can accomplish on an even broader scale.

In particular, closer ties between history and anthropology would help to decolonize both disciplines by transforming the study of indigenous peoples by colonizing ones into studies that have greater significance for both. In post-colonial Africa, what Americans would call anthropology has come to be restructured as history and sociology. Perhaps the same should happen in North America. More emphasis on native history would acknowledge that native Americans are not static entities but possess a past that is worthy of study in its own right. It would also recognize that they are not living representatives of their colonizer's prehistory but exist and hence have rights in the present as concretely as white people do.

The social sciences must also decolonize themselves by recruiting native people as agents of research. Native scholars must be provided with the training and resources that will permit them to study white people's history and culture as well as their own. The results of such mutual study do not always produce what the other side expects or wishes but in the long run they should lead to a more detailed and objective understanding of human behaviour. That understanding in turn may make the social sciences a more reliable guide than they have been for predicting the consequences of proposed public policy. Yet recruiting substantial numbers of native people into the social sciences will require vast changes in both the academic community and the broader social realm of which the academic community is a small part. How North American anthropologists and historians respond to this challenge in future years will be a touchstone of their professional and social integrity.

* This paper was written while the author was recipient of a Leave Fellowship of the Social Sciences and Humanities Research Council of Canada and sabbatical leave from McGill University.

References

Aberle, D.F. *et. al.* (1950), 'The functional prerequisites of a society', *Ethics* 60, 100–11.

Adams, W.Y., Van Gerven, D.P. and Levy, R.S. (1978), 'The retreat from migrationism, *Annual Review of Anthropology* 7, 483–532.

Aveni, A.F. (1981), 'Archaeoastronomy' in Schiffer, M.B. (ed.), *Advances in Archaeological Method and Theory*, volume 4, Academic Press, New York, 1–77.

Axtell, James (1981) *The European and the Indian: Essays in the Ethnohistory of Colonial North America*, Oxford University Press, Oxford.

Bailey, A.G. (1937), *The Conflict of European and Eastern Algonkian Cultures, 1540–1700: A Study in Canadian Civilization*, New Brunswick Museum, St John.

Binford, L.R. (1967), 'Comment', *Current Anthropology* 8, 234–35.

——, (1972) *An Archaeological Perspective*, Seminar Press, New York.

Bronowski, Jacob (1971), 'Technology and culture in evolution', introduction to Symposium on Technology and Social Criticism: *Philosophy of the Social Sciences* 1, 195–206.

Caldwell, J.R. (1958), *Trend and Tradition in the Prehistory of the Eastern United States*, American Anthropological Association, Memoir 88, Menasha.

Charlton, T.H. (1981), 'Archaeology, ethnohistory, and ethnology: Interpretive interfaces,' in Schiffer, M.B. (ed.), *Advances in Archaeological Method and Theory*, volume 4, Academic Press, New York, 129–76.

Chiappelli, Fredi (1976), *First Images of America: The Impact of the New World on the Old*, University of California Press, Berkeley and Los Angeles.

Childe, V.G. (1947), *History*, Cobbett, London.

Daniel, Glyn (1975), *A Hundred and Fifty Years of Archaeology*, Duckworth, London.

Dickason, O.P. (1977), 'The concept of *L'homme sauvage* and early French colonialism in the Americas', *Revue française d'Outre-Mer* 64, 5–32.

Driver, H.E. and Massey, W.C. (1957), 'Comparative studies of North American Indians', *Transactions of the American Philosophical Society* 47, 165–456.

Eggan, F.R. (1966), *The American Indian*, Weidenfeld & Nicolson, London.

Fagan, Brian (1977), *Elusive Treasure: The Story of Early Archaeologists in the Americas*, Charles Scribner's, New York.

Fenton, W.N. and Moore, E.L. (eds) (1974–77), *Customs of the American Indians Compared with the Customs of Primitive Times, by Father Joseph Francois Lafitau*, 2 vols, Champlain Society, Toronto.

Fitzgerald, W.R. (1982), 'A refinement of historical Neutral chronologies: evidence from Shaver Hill, Christianson and Dwyer', *Ontario Archaeology* 38, 31–46.

Friedman, J. and Rowlands, M.J. (eds) (1978), *The Evolution of Social Systems*, Duckworth, London.

Gorges, Sir Ferdinando (1847), *A brief Narration of the Original Undertakings for the Advancement of Plantations in America*, Maine Historical Society, Collections, Series I, 2.

Grant, Madison (1916), *The Passing of the Great Race*, Charles Scribner's, Boston.

Hall, R.L. (1976), 'Ghosts, water barriers, corn, and sacred enclosures in the Eastern Woodlands', *American Antiquity* 41, 360–64.

Hamell, George (1980), *Sun Serpents, Tawiskaron and Quartz Crystals*, Rochester Museum and Science Centre, Rochester, (mimeographed).

Harris, Marvin (1968), *The Rise of Anthropological Theory*, Crowell, New York.

Haven, Samuel (1856), Archaeology of the United States. *Smithsonian Contributions to Knowledge* 8(2), Washington.

Hickerson, Harold (1970), *The Chippewa and their Neighbors: A Study in Ethnohistory*, Holt, Rinehart & Winston, New York.

Hinsley, C.M. Jr. (1981), *Savages and Scientists: The Smithsonian Institution and the Development of American Anthropology, 1846–1910*, Smithsonian Institution Press, Washington.

Hodder, Ian (ed.) (1982), *Symbolic and Structural Archaeology*, Cambridge University Press, Cambridge.

Horsman, Reginald (1975), 'Scientific racism and the American Indian in the mid-nineteenth century', *American Quarterly* 27, 152–68.

Hunt, G.T. (1940), *The Wars of the Iroquois: A Study in Intertribal Trade Relations*, University of Wisconsin Press, Madison.

Jennings, Francis (1975), *The Invasion of America: Indians, Colonialism, and the Cant of Conquest*, University of North Carolina Press, Chapel Hill.

Keiser, Albert (1933), *The Indian in American Literature*, Oxford University Press, New York.

Kidder, A.V. (1962), *An Introduction to the Study of Southwestern Archaeology, with an Introduction on Southwestern Archaeology Today*, edited by Irving Rouse, Yale University Press, New Haven [original work published 1924].

Kolakowski, L. (1976), *La philosophie positiviste*, Denoel, Paris.

Kupperman, K.O. (1980), *Settling with the Indians: the Meeting of English and Indian Cultures in America, 1580–1640*, Rowman and Littlefield, Totawa.

Levermore, C.H. (ed.) (1912), *Forerunners and Competitors of the Pilgrims and Puritans*, New England Society of Brooklyn, Brooklyn.

Linton, Ralph (1940), *Acculturation in Seven American Indian Tribes*, Appleton-Century, New York.

Lubbock, John (1865), *Pre-historic Times, as Illustrated by Ancient Remains and the Manners and Customs of Modern Savages*, Williams and Norgate, London.

—— (1882), *The Origin of Civilization and the Primitive Condition of Man*, Fourth edition, Longmans, Green, London.

Macfarlane, Alan (1970), *Witchcraft in Tudor and Stuart England*, Routledge & Kegan Paul, London.

Martin, Paul, and Plog, Fred (1973), *The Archaeology of Arizona: A Study of the Southwest Region*, Natural History Press, Garden City.

Martin, Paul, Quimby, George and Collier, Donald (1947), *Indians Before Columbus: Twenty Thousand Years of North American History Revealed by Archaeology*, University of Chicago Press, Chicago.

Monkman, Leslie (1981), *A Native Heritage: Images of the Indian in English-Canadian Literature*, University of Toronto Press, Toronto.

Mooney, James (1896), The Ghost-Dance Religion and the Sioux Outbreak of 1890, *Fourteenth Annual Report, Part 2, Bureau of American Ethnology*, Washington.

Orme, Bryony (1981), *Anthropology for Archaeologists: An Introduction*, Duckworth, London.

Parker, A.C. (1922), The Archaeological History of New York State, *New York State Museum Bulletin*, 235–38, Albany.

Parkman, Francis (1927), *The Jesuits in North America in the Seventeenth Century*, Little Brown and Company, Boston [orginally published 1867]

Porter, H.C. (1979), *The Inconstant Savage: England and the North American Indian, 1500–1660*, Duckworth, London.

Quimby, G.I. (1960), *Indian Life in the Upper Great Lakes, 11,000 B.C. to A.D. 1800*, University of Chicago Press, Chicago.

Quinn, D.B. (1977), *North America From Earliest Discovery to First Settlements: The Norse Voyages to 1612*, Harper & Row, New York.

—— (1979), *New American World: A Documentary History of North America to 1612*, 5 vols, Arne, New York.

Ramsden, P.G. (1977), *A Refinement of Some Aspects of Huron Ceramic Analysis*, Archaeological Survey of Canada, Mercury Series, 63, Ottawa.

Redfield, Robert, Linton, R. and Herskovits, M.J. (1936), 'Outline for the Study of Acculturation', *American Anthropologist*, 39, 149–52.

Renfrew, Colin and Shennan, Stephen (eds), (1982), *Ranking, Resources and Exchange: Aspects of the Archaeology of Early European Society*, Cambridge University Press, Cambridge.

Resek, Carl (1960), *Lewis Henry Morgan: American Scholar*, University of Chicago Press, Chicago.

Rosen, Lawrence (1980), 'The excavation of American Indian burial sites: a problem of law and professional responsibility', *American Anthropologist* 82, 5–27.

Sahlins, Marshall (1968), *Tribesmen*, Prentice-Hall, Englewood Cliffs.

Salwen, Bert (1978), 'Indians of Southern New England and Long Island: Early Period' in *Handbook of North American Indians*, vol. 15, *Northeast*, Trigger, B.G. (ed.), Smithsonian Institution, Washington, 160–76.

Schrire, Carmel (1980), 'An inquiry into the evolutionary status and apparent identity of San hunter-gatherers', *Human Ecology* 8, 9–32.

Service, E.R. (1962), *Primitive Social Organization*, Random House, New York.

Silverberg, Robert (1968), *Mound Builders of Ancient America: the Archaeology of a Myth*, New York Graphic Society, Greenwich.

Spicer, E.H. (ed.) (1961), *Perspectives in American Indian Cultural Change*, University of Chicago Press, Chicago.

—— (1962), *Cycles of Conquest*, University of Arizona Press, Tucson.

Stanton, William (1960), *The Leopard's Spots: Scientific Attitudes toward Race in America, 1815–59*, University of Chicago Press, Chicago.

Stephens, J.L. (1841), *Incidents of Travel in Central America, Chiapas and Yucatan*, Harper, New York.

Steward, J.H. (1955), *Theory of Culture Change*, University of Illinois Press, Urbana.

Stocking, G.W. (1974), *A Franz Boas Reader: The Shaping of American Anthropology, 1883–1911*, University of Chicago Press, Chicago.

Taylor, W.W. (1948), *A Study of Archeology*, American Anthropological Association, Memoir 69, Menasha.

Trevor-Roper, Hugh (1965), *The Rise of Christian Europe*, Harcourt, Brace & World, New York.

Trigger, B.G. (1969), *The Huron: Farmers of the North*, Holt, Rinehart & Winston, New York.

—— (1976), *The Children of Aataentsic: A History of the Huron People to 1660*, 2 vols, McGill-Queen's University Press, Montreal.

—— (1978), *Time and Traditions: Essays in Archaeological Interpretation*, Edinburgh University Press, Edinburgh.

—— (1980), 'Archaeology and the image of the American Indian', *American Antiquity*, 45, 662–76.

—— (1982), 'Ethnohistory: problems and prospects', *Ethnohistory*, 29(1), 1–19.

—— (1982a), 'Archaeological analysis and concepts of causality', *Culture* 2(2), 31–42.

—— (1982b), 'Response of native peoples to European contact', in Story, G.M. (ed.), *Early European Settlement and Exploitation in Atlantic Canada*, Memorial University of Newfoundland, St John's, 139–155.

Vaughan, A.T. (1979), *New England Frontier: Puritans and Indians, 1620–1675*, Little, Brown, Boston [revised ed. Norton, New York].

—— (1982), 'From white man to red skin: changing Anglo-American perceptions of the American Indian', *American Historical Review* 87, 917–35.

Wallace, A.F.C. (1982), Review of Axtell, J. *The European and the Indian, The William and Mary Quarterly* 39, 532–34.

Watson, P.J., Redman, C. and LeBlanc, S. (1971), *Explanation in Archaeology: An Explicitly Scientific Approach*, Columbia University Press, New York.

Whallon, Robert (1982), 'Comments on explanation', in *Ranking, Resource and Exchange*, Renfrew, C. and Shennan, S. (eds), Cambridge University Press, Cambridge, 155–58.

Wilcox, D.R. and Masse, W.B. (1981), *The Protohistoric Period in the North American Southwest, A.D. 1450–1700*, Arizona State University, Anthropological Research Papers, 24, Tempe.

Willey, G.R. (1953), *Prehistoric Settlement Patterns in the Viru Valley, Peru*, Bureau of American Ethnology, Bulletin 135, Washington.

—— and Sabloff, J.A. (1980), *A History of American Archaeology*, Second edition, Freeman, San Francisco.

Winsor, Justin (1889), *Narrative and Critical History of America*, vol. 1. Houghton, Mifflin, Boston.

Wobst, H.M. (1978), 'The archaeo-ethnology of hunter-gatherers or the tyranny of the ethnographic record', *American Antiquity* 43, 303–09.

Wolf, Eric (1982), *Europe and the People Without History*, University of California Press, Berkeley.

Woodbury, R.B. (1973), *Alfred V. Kidder*, Columbia University Press, New York.

2
The Dragon Principle

Eric Willmot

Professor Eugene Kamenka recently said that 'Australia has been insulated from the real problems of the real world' (Humanities Profile, ABC telecast, 1983) It could be said that the theme of this conference 'Who owns the past?' begs a question of reality. Obviously no one owns the past, for the past does not exist. The things we call objects from the past are in fact objects of the present. Albeit they may have been constructed, or come into being at some past time. They represent evidence that a past has existed but we can never know such things as they were in the past. We can only know that part of the past in which we once existed. The only real world for you and me is the present, and while we may create a reality which we call the past it is only our reality, it is the story we tell; or the story that someone who did exist in the past has told and managed to record.

We, as human beings, live in a flat time world, our total reality is only an instant thick. Nevertheless, it is the nature of human beings to want to build around us a round world, to push our reality forward and backwards through dimensions which ceased to exist or which do not yet exist, to create an intellectually, and emotionally satisfying living space. The forward dimension is relatively easy to construct, for it is made of the stuff of dreams. At the time we create it, it cannot be demonstrated by any means to be necessarily untrue. When we try to fill our living space out in the other direction however, we run into a world which did once exist and about which we can know some things. It is a world written in stone, on magnetic tape, in paper and ink, in memories and in myths and legends. Unlike the forward, this reverse dimension has built-in problems. Since we choose to broaden our reality backwards from the present we must find a way of dealing with known facts and worse still with truths which may not be compatible with our desirable, round, present. Furthermore, others know of these facts and perhaps some of the truths. The past then may be more an area of conflict than a piece of valuable equity.

Throughout the ages this problem has been tackled in many different ways. However, it seems that no matter what particular strategy is adopted, there exist two fundamental elements that are necessary for success. These two elements consist firstly of constructing some kind of a story to describe and explain the past, and secondly to erect a custodian or a holder of this postulated truth. For want of a better term we may call the story 'history'. History differs from almost any other kind of story that human beings construct for themselves or for each other. Stories may be complete reports of fact or they may be constructions that have no basis in fact whatsoever. History contains something of both of these things. There is always some kind of fact, if only the evidence of the activity of nature. Human history has also to be the story of human beings and therefore it must describe people who no longer exist. The historian therefore, must construct his characters, using much the same skills as the writer of stories that are based on imagination alone, and yet he or she must accommodate a constellation of known facts.

In the distant human past the problem of facts was not so great, since much less was known of the workings of nature and hence one only had to construct a convincing explanation. Into this constructed world of reasonable explanations could then be woven the tales of the human actors. The story-teller then had only the problem of establishing his or her role as the custodian, the guardian of this constructed truth.

The society of human beings that dwelled in this continent for many thousands of years, had taken this approach to some lengths. Further they introduced an interesting principle. The Australian Aborigines first of all joined the temporal world of present with a constructed spiritual world of present and past. This 'history' was then, over many thousands of years, applied to the nature of this continent. The continent in turn responded by moulding and modifying the mind and spirituality of the humans that dwelt here. This peculiar approach produced a landscape that was moulded to minds and ways of human beings, and human beings who were moulded to the nature of this land.

Problems must have arisen from time to time. These would often be the result simply of the diverse nature of human beings, and at times they must have confronted the truth of 'dreaming'. One solution to this was to define truth in such a way that it could be partitioned. This division provided a strategy for dealing with human situations outside of the 'dreaming'. Truth was divided into three parts. One part provided for the evidence of nature, and two for human interpretation.

Stephen Albert (1978), the first chairman of the National Aboriginal Education Committee, in a paper to the Law Society in Sydney explained this concept with a small anecdote from his home town. He said that an old man of his own people had become highly skilled in the art of being an honest broker. This man was polylingual and his repertoire included English. He was able to represent his own people before the courts of the Europeans. One day we are told he went mad, the police came, handed him to men in white coats and he was locked away in some institution. This ended the service which he so ably provided in the area. This Stephen told us was the first part of truth. It was the actuality. It is what could be observed. Stephen explained that the old man had come under great stress because of his ability to make understandable to all parties the laws of the white and black worlds. As a result he was making both his own people unhappy and in many cases the people responsible for administering the white law. This stress situation appeared to become too much for him to bear, for he broke down under the strain and went mad. This is the second part of truth; it is an understandable and observable circumstance which gave rise to the first part. Stephen went on to tell us that the old man thought a great deal about the situation. He realized he was bringing conflict not only to the white and black people of this place, but also to himself. Furthermore, he could see that by bringing understanding into this situation he was in fact making the situation more difficult than when there was no understanding. He thought about this situation for a long time and decided that he must end it; the simple way to do this was to remove himself in some way from the situation. The way he chose was to conduct himself into madness. This is the third part of truth; the human reason.

With such an understanding of truth the 'dreaming' becomes workable, so workable in fact that Australia is the only world we know of in which violence between nations, in terms of wars of land aggrandizement, was eradicated. This remains the problem which confronts all of humanity. If we fail to solve it over the next century, the question of who owns the past will be irrelevant. There will be no one here to own anything.

There is little doubt that Europeans constructed histories something along these lines in the distant past; there is ample evidence in the recorded mythology of Europe, that some steps in this direction were taken. The Europeans, however, applied a different principle to their mythology; rather than allow the continent of Europe to mould their mythology and historical conceptions, the

Europeans began to adopt a process which allowed them to formulate and understand more critically the laws which govern
nature. This caused a difficulty for custodians. These early beginnings of science produced facts and truths which could be known
by anyone, not just the tellers of the stories. The problems of custodianship began to mount. The strategy adopted by the Europeans to deal with this new difficulty was to redefine, not truth,
but custodianship. These guardians of the new records, became
guardian-keepers.

The Australian custodians, were *guardian-teachers.* Along with
the privileges of guardianship went the responsibility of teaching
all of the society. The people of ancient Australia had a right to
this knowledge as a consequence of a compulsory education system, and the achievement of adulthood. Education for Australians
was a right which belonged to all human beings; but for the
Europeans this key to custodianship and the records became very
quickly a property of the few. These European custodians became
like Tolkien's dragons. They looked after the treasures, very carefully guarded them with their lives, but they kept them to themselves. The people to whose world the treasures belonged
remained mendicant and without access to these truths of their
existence. The dragons became priests, the priests became the literate and the literate became the scholars, and the scholars became
the academics.

There was, however, a saving grace in all this. The Europeans
continued to pursue truth in the form of science and while some
of its adherents, like Galileo, didn't fare too well, the progress of
science slowly brought an enlightenment to the European world.
The descendants of the dragons began to change, slowly but ben-
evolently, and within their own societies slaves began to be freed
and the small flame' of democracy kindled. By the eighteenth century the dragons were a mixed bag; Australia, unfortunately inherited some of the worst. It seemed that while the dragons had
changed for the better in Europe, European expansion into Africa,
the Americas and the Pacific, was accompanied by a considerable
regression and re-recreation of the old dragons' lairs. In fact,
rather than bring European enlightenment to the new polygeneric
nations to which they gave birth, the Europeans brought a darkness from their own past. Even after the initial darkness had
drained away, the Europeans still continued to apply this Dragon
Principle. With all good intentions they gathered the treasures of
Australia's past to themselves, bestowed it on their own, but excluded the people whose birthright they had collected.

Earlier I spoke of polygeneric nations. I have defined
polygenesis (Willmot, 1982) as the process whereby a new society is

born from people of different origins: such nations as Canada, the United States, the South American countries, New Zealand, Australia and South Africa. Others such as Rhodesia were experiments in polygenesis that failed. I've also defined an indigenous nation as one whose population is indigenous to the nation of origin, Japan or Greece for instance. By indigenous I mean a people who are not migrants, that is, people who have no other race history except from the place where they live. This is a definition proposed by (the then Senator) Neville Bonner, at a lecture at Macquarie University in 1982.

Polygenesis is a process which has no doubt occurred many times before in human history. Curiously while this process has in the past lead to the formation of an indigenous population, it is unlikely to ever do so again in the future. Modern methods of recording and archiving almost ensure that people like 'white' Australians are condemned to be migrants forever.

The Dragon Principle, the gathering and keeping of the information which is bestowed only on to an elite, may not necessarily be socially undesirable in an indigenous nation. This is particularly true if the processes are applied in some generally acceptable way. It is however disastrous in a polygeneric nation. Let me explain this.

Human identity in an indigenous nation is, I believe, more or less a direct consequence of the race history of the people of that nation. This is a race history shared commonly by all who inhabit the nation. In a polygeneric nation human identity is not simply the product of one's own particular social group. In a country for instance like America, there would certainly be a great variety of powerful primary identities. These are similar to those in an indigenous nation. These would include for instance the identity of a black American, a native American, various European Americans. These communities however, do not live in isolation, and as a result there is an embedding (Willmot 1981: 8), which incorporates a projected component from the primary identity of others who co-inhabit this society. This projected identity is the identity cast onto one group by another.

In the early days of modern Australian polygenesis, the projected identity of Aborigines that Europeans bestowed, had little effect on Aborigines' own primary identity. This was because there was very little embedding of the two societies at that stage. As the embedding grew, however, this projected identity became devastating. Recovery from that situation has been very slow, and this is at least partly due to the application of the Dragon Principle.

Over the last hundred years Europeans have become the custodians of the knowledge of Australian languages, Australian anthropology, Australian archaeology. This appeared to lead Aborigines in the 1930s and 1940s towards outright rejection of their primary identity. In 1938 William Ferguson published a document called the 'Aboriginal Manifesto' which made three essential demands (Willmot 1978):

1. Make miscegenation legal.
2. Educate our children in the same way as yours.
3. Allow us to assimilate into your population.

This could be seen as a plea by mixed-race Aborigines to be recognized as Europeans. I might add that one would be hard pressed to find a *Koori* in the country today who would have a bar of such a proposition. This precise application of the Dragon Principle in Australia has reduced Aborigines not so much to a mendicant race, but to something less than human, the subject of a study. Kevin Gilbert (1976) says:

It is not so much my black Aboriginality that you deny me as my right to human growth and human potential. While you deny me this, you can build me all the houses and all the mansions in the world and my spirit will not inhabit any of them.

This Dragon Principle however, is a little like genocide: if it is not a complete success it will haunt the perpetrators all the days of their lives. In the case of genocide we have seen the fate of Nazi Germany and colonial Tasmania. The Dragon Principle too has become a kind of uncomfortable albatross about the necks of many white Australian scholars. This principle has been so applied, and has become so much a part of Australian academic life, that it will take Aborigines at least another generation to begin to approach custodianship in most fields of Aboriginal studies.

The historians also applied this principle, but somehow got it wrong. They told a one-sided story which not only failed to convince the Aborigines, but has also failed to convince the rest of the world. It is into this breach that young Aboriginal scholars are moving quickly and easily. The European historians caught up in a vision of an arcadian myth (Smith 1960: 199) presented Australia as an 'antipodal brigadoon'. This was both destructive and sad: destructive in that their story almost destroyed the identity of the entire society of the first Australians; sad in that it missed the important birth of polygenesis in this country.

When the British landed in what is now Sydney, in the land of the Eroa people, it must have been a time of great concern, and for that matter of great excitement. There would have obviously been many schools of thought among the Eroa as to the consequences of this new event on the east coast of their hidden world. We know there were at least two such schools of thought. One is represented by a man called Bennelong (see Fig. 9) whose interest and optimism at the British arrival is well recorded by British historians. An opposing view held by a man called Pemulwuy was never recorded by the same historians. This extraordinary man carried on a twelve-year campaign of opposition against the British. It must represent one of the most important events associated with the early British settlement, and yet remains uncelebrated in the books of white historians. There is however a bright side to this coin. While Bennelong's story is strained through the Dragon Principle, the story of Pemulwuy will be told by Aboriginal historians. It will be their telling, their construction, their Pemulwuy.

It is the mistake of the white historians which has, in my view, contributed substantially to the sudden puzzling rise of Aboriginal political power in the last two decades. Bernard Smith (Humanities Profile, ABC, 1983) said recently that if Australia has not made some gesture towards covenant or treaty by 1988, then, as a nation, Australia is in trouble. The brigadoon retreat is no longer available, and Australia must face a community of nations that is rapidly being surprised by a different kind of Australian history.

Australian Aborigines had been singularly unsuccessful as a group in employment, schooling, technical education, and yet, in recent times startlingly successful in tertiary education. In 1970 there were approximately twenty Aborigines in Australian tertiary institutions as students; in 1980 there were 881 (Department of Education: 1981). Aborigines are fast learning the strength and the weaknesses of the dragons. It is highly significant that the first Aboriginal to gain an academic appointment at a university was in history, at Macquarie University, Sydney.

In the study carried out by the National Aboriginal Education Committee as part of the NITE Enquiry in 1979 (NAEC, 1979), it was found that the most significant common subject interest among Aboriginal teacher trainees was history. More than 70 per cent of the funds approved for Aboriginal-requested research from the Australian Institute of Aboriginal Studies is for the field of history. It is reasonable to expect that the initial modern thrust of Aboriginal scholarship will be in history. Aborigines it seems are determined, if not to own the past, then to have a major part in the telling of the story.

This is, however, far from the end of the story. The Aboriginal population as a community forms a very small minority within the general Australian population. As such, it is faced by the spectre of social marginality. For academic survival Aborigines themselves may be tempted to apply something like a dragon principle. Aborigines are very concerned about custodianship, about who shall be the guardian of the knowledge of the past and how shall such a small society manage the task. Traditionally, Aborigines have had a different view of custodianship: the custodian has been a guardian-teacher, rather than the guardian-keeper of the European model. Twentieth and twenty-first century Aboriginal custodians will be, however, in a very different situation to their forebears. Australian Aborigines no longer constitute an indigenous nation, but rather they are the children of polygenesis like all other Australians. As such they own the future, and the past belongs to the past and the story-tellers. Aborigines are determined, in the future, to be among the story-tellers.

References

Albert, Stephen (1978), address to Law Society (NAEC Files), Sydney.

Bonner, Neville (1982), opening address in the Australian Aboriginal History Unit, Macquarie University, Sydney.

Gilbert, Kevin (1976), Report on the Perfleet Project, unpublished paper.

Kamenka, Eugene (1983), Humanities Profile, ABC Telecast.

National Aboriginal Education Committee (1979), *The Education and Training of Indigenous Teachers in Australia*, Submission to NITE.

Smith, Bernard (1960), *European Vision and the South Pacific, 1768–1850: A Study in the History of Art and Ideas*, Clarendon Press, Oxford.

—— (1983), Humanities Profile, ABC Telecast.

Tolkien, J.R.R. (1969), *Lord of the Rings*, Allen & Unwin, London.

Willmot, Eric (1982), Barry Scott Memorial Lecture, Macquarie University, Sydney.

—— (1978), 'Recent trends in Aborignal education: an experiment in accommodation', *Survival International Review*, 3(4), 18–19.

—— (1981), *Social Development in Northern Australia and the Effect of Social Institutions*, University of Northern Territory, Planning Authority, 10 August 1981.

3
The Ownership of Diversity
The Problem of Establishing a National History in a Land of Nine Hundred Ethnic Groups

Les Groube

Greater New Guinea is a large and complex region. Incorporating Irian Jaya, Papua New Guinea and Island Melanesia, this small fraction of the land surface of the earth contains over one-quarter of the world's languages, and if we could measure it properly, probably a third or more of the total cultural diversity in the world.

Such facts have serious historical implications, stretching to the limit the standard 'models' of the past derived from other less complex and more homogeneous regions. The explanation for, and the documentation of, the development of this extraordinary diversity is one of the most challenging tasks of modern archaeology. Yet this problem, despite its importance for an understanding of the process of physical and cultural change, is the charge of a mere handful of archaeologists and historians. One-half of the main island of New Guinea, Irian Jaya, is yielding little information while in Papua New Guinea, after a burst of activity in the late 1960s and early 1970s, the facts of Melanesian prehistory remain stubbornly embedded in the ground, subject to the powerful forces of tropical decay and human indifference.

Sadly, but not surprisingly, there is little national or individual interest in the past of Papua New Guinea. An obvious and important reason for this is the very youth of this newly independent nation; the requirements of survival in an increasingly competitive world, the pressures on development and the excitement of 'nation-building' leave little time for the tranquillity of examining the past. Papua New Guinea is an emerging nation in the Pacific and Asia, and to most Papua New Guineans, including politicians, the past is now largely irrelevant. Many aspects of it, particularly traditional attitudes to land tenure, health and law, are indeed being deliberately modified for the national 'good'.

It is a land of over three million people with a population growth of approximately 2.3 percent per annum. It is undergoing rapid physical and cultural change masquerading under the economic banner of 'development'. Ancient forests are tumbling down under the chain saws of Australian, Filipino, Korean and Japanese contractors; cattle, sometimes sheep and, ominously, goats are occupying the kunai grasslands where once the wallaby was supreme; cash-cropping, the temptress of eroding capitalism, is revolutionizing traditional agriculture. Massive mines (designed to relieve the Australian tax-payer of the burden of subsidising their former colony) are thrusting isolated communities into the industrial age. Swamps, intact from the Pleistocene, are being drained; land, never formerly occupied, is being settled in Government-sponsored re-settlement schemes. The face of Papua New Guinea and the people who live in it are being altered irretrievably by development.

To most adult Papua New Guineans, change within their lifetime has been so rapid that the immediate past is already dim. The present is so demanding of new skills and new attitudes, the future so uncertain, that the past is irrelevant. For the majority of younger Papua New Guineans the brave new world of transistors, Toyotas and bulldozers is already a reality; the national currency, the *kina*, is overtaking all other traditional values, surpassing, indeed even suppressing the recently adopted Christian values.

The ownership of things from the past

It is important to distinguish between ownership of 'things' from the past and ownership of the past itself. The things from the past (cultural property) fall clearly into the authority of Roman and international law. Things can be precisely defined and legislated for; there is no doubt who 'owns' the things from the past in Papua New Guinea. The *National Cultural Properties Act (1967)* clearly defines the state's ownership of all material culture and archaeological sites within Papua New Guinea. The responsibility to administer and enforce this Act (which among other things attempts to control the flow of artefacts and art out of Papua New Guinea) lies with the National Museum. Unfortunately, as with so many institutions hurriedly founded and funded by the departing colonial power, lack of funds and trained personnel makes the task difficult. Papua New Guinea artefacts and cultural property are still entering the world markets, although one hopes that the trade is diminishing.

At the moment there is only one (expatriate) archaeologist at the National Museum with a partly qualified assistant curator and one or two (unqualified) helpers. The administration of the National Site Record files alone could occupy their time fully. Yet they are charged not only with this, but also with the development of educational displays, curation of the unique collections, as well as the watch-dog role of monitoring development projects. Proper research, except opportunistically as threats develop, is virtually impossible.

The University of Papua New Guinea, the senior academic institution in the country, once had a flourishing prehistory section within the Anthropology and Sociology Department. Changing priorities, internal academic politics and financial pressure saw this promising start (with a custom-built archaeology laboratory, several laboratory assistants and the possibility of several academic positions) confined to a single academic post, with virtually no laboratory funding, no laboratory assistants and a single teaching course with neither adequate introduction nor the possibility of effective development. The university's primary responsibility, to train a new generation of national archaeologists and develop a rigorous tradition of archaeological excellence for the new nation, has been abandoned. On my arrival four years ago prehistory had been reduced to a service teaching role for the arts faculty, supplying in miniscule doses a little titillation from the pre-colonial past within existing courses in other departments and disciplines.

The situation has now been retrieved, with a small but adequate programme, considerable student support (current enrolments in the introductory course are thirty seven), and some university sympathy (particularly from the science faculty). Yet there is still only one teaching position, and inadequate financial and logistic support. The foresight of the university fathers in providing for the future requirements of a new nation, to know and understand their past, has not yet been realized; with the return of the first two New Guinean post-graduate students in archaeology from the Australian National University next year, it may be possible for this objective to be achieved.

The university can play little role in the administration of the 'things' from the past; it can only develop an interest in, and devotion to, these things. At the moment, teaching courses concentrate upon field training, producing the practical field-workers for the new nation. Museology, curation, and many aspects of artefact and laboratory analysis cannot be taught within the constraints of current staffing and courses. These must be studied overseas through the generosity of our more prosperous neighbours.

Despite being surrounded by evidence of their past, visible in the astonishing diversity of peoples and languages in the university itself, despite the powerful impact of magnificent folk art displayed in the National Museum, despite, indeed, the words of the Papua New Guinea Constitution (see p. 55), most students show little interest in the past. Indeed sometimes they even display positive antipathy to the idea of the past and to its study. This attitude is embedded in the recent (colonial) history of Papua New Guinea and in traditional values.

Attitudes to the past

In many traditional societies the past was never a separate, divisible entity; it was firmly in the present. Some languages, indeed, do not have a separate tense for past events; there is only a present and a future; the past can only be referred to indirectly (Panoff 1968). In most traditional societies, no matter how altered, the past has imposed a pattern on the present; attitudes towards people both within and without the immediate group, attitudes towards marriage, children, pets, towards land, conflict, loyalty and so on have come from the past. Thus, for every language, ethnic or cultural group in Papua New Guinea there is a different past determining a wide range of attitudes and actions in the present. There is no single past for Papua New Guineans; no single code or charter; the past is as diverse as, or even more so, than is the present.

Yet there is place in this 'past-present' for change, for change is now part of the way of life of most Papua New Guineans. To many, traumatic change is within the recall and common experience of parents or grandparents; the change has been so fast and so total that there is no time to look back, for the risk of tripping up in the future is ever present. To groups with a longer history of colonial and missionary contact, the change has been so pervasive that the past has already been discarded, like a chrysalis, never to be revisited. Many individual Papua New Guineans, as well as the traditional societies, have experienced a change of state as total as that from a caterpillar to a butterfly. As the butterfly never revisits the shell of its former self, so most citizens of this new nation are indifferent to the fate of their recently discarded 'other-selves'. For this no one can be blamed; they have been thrust with such speed into the twentieth century that nostalgia, or even common curiosity, have little place.

It is easy to find part of the cause for indifference to the past with the missionaries, many of whom (particularly in the early years of colonialism) deliberately created an opposition to the past – the period of cannibalism, promiscuity, infanticide, warfare, headhunting and the like – a period best forgotten, banished, the *taim bipo*. Many of the symbols of this 'wicked' past (stone 'idols', 'indecent' carvings, sacred stones and other 'superstitious' objects) were confiscated, smashed or buried. Sacred groves were cut down, traditional symbols were desecrated (or consecrated). The tender links with the traditional past were deliberately severed. To the missionary, barely surviving in the malarial coastal missions, there seemed little sense in prolonging a past which, inevitably, with the new colonial governments, was doomed.

It seemed barely conceivable that this sort of destruction, involving the systematic denial of traditional values on the part of some of the missions, was genuinely inspired by fear of idolatrous objects or superstitions. It was clearly a pragmatic policy of cutting the continuity of the past with the present. It was a policy also which usually had the support of the new converts; the suppression of constant warfare, headhunting and cannibalism came as a relief to everyone. The effect of missionary attitudes on the loss of cultural property in Papua New Guinea is not well documented. The writer is currently researching the loss of material culture in the Southern Highlands opened up to contact only thirty years ago. This work has already exposed considerable mission impact. The results (largely from Huli informants) will be published after thorough checking. The story is a sad one.

Yet for some Papua New Guineans the past did not die with the discarding of a few objects and the coming of *pax Australiensis*; it was merely transferred deeper into the mind, to become part of their attitudes, personalities and motives. Thus for them the past is private, individual and secret, not public property or the object of curiosity by outsiders. It is in the present. The eternal contradiction exposed by T.S. Eliot:

> Time present and time past
> Are both perhaps present in time future,
> And time future contained in time past.
> If all time is eternally present
> All time is unredeemable.
> ('Burnt Norton' 1)

These lines could have been written for modern Papua New Guinea. The past, eternally present for so many, has merely been pushed underground where no outsider can have access. Unfortunately many modern Papua New Guineans are themselves becoming outsiders in their own communities, separated by profound cultural and educational differences from earlier generations. For them the past is irretrievably lost, eternally unredeemable.

Even administrators, traders and kiaps, although not so openly zealous in conversion, were also anxious to see the old ways go. Through coercion, force and sometimes brutality, a new present was forged, new technology was introduced, new values, morals and laws replacing the old. The independent state of Papua New Guinea has inherited this urge for change, this policy of banishing the past. The National Broadcasting Commission, which penetrates into the most remote villages in Papua New Guinea has replaced the colonial *mastas*; a constant barrage of (modern) Western music, vulgar advertisements, sport and news urges all to join the new money economy. The most important single word in politics, in the press and over the radio is 'development'. No matter how carefully monitored, development means only one thing; the past must give way to the present. Politically the past is inconvenient, often troublesome and therefore expendable.

More important perhaps than the colonial pioneers of change or the political catch cry of 'development' in forging attitudes to the past, was that generation of Australian colonial administrators and teachers, who reluctantly (but with efficiency) set about preparing the country for independence after the Second World War. These people belonged to a generation to which history was irrelevant, influenced by a new Australian nationalism, forged and tempered in the Second World War, which was abandoning a recent colonial past. To young and optimistic Australians the colonial past was merely an embarrassment which the symbolic disaster of Gallipoli did little to alleviate. Beyond those dim days of the First World War was an even murkier period peopled by convicts, bushrangers and the ghosts of thousands of dead Aborigines. It was a past conveniently forgotten.

Thus Papua New Guinea inherited through its modern school syllabus, from which history was conveniently expunged, the pragmatic Australian tradition of living for the present. The new generation of Papua New Guinean administrators, teachers and businessmen, who were shaping the attitudes of this new nation, were schooled in a colonial ahistoricism which still permeates every government department as well as the University of Papua New Guinea. It is a pity that the present generation of Australians (who are far more sensitive and alert to their past) did not help to frame the laws and constitution of the new independent state. Perhaps history, tradition and respect for the past would have a more prominent place in the fabric of the nation.

It is only in the preamble to the Constitution (of doubtful legal impact) that we see acknowledgement of the past of Papua New Guinea:

WE THE PEOPLE OF PAPUA NEW GUINEA
pay homage and respect to the memory of
our ancestors

WE THE PEOPLE OF PAPUA NEW GUINEA
acknowledge the worthy customs and
traditional wisdom of our people.

Despite the worthiness of these principles they play little further role in the legal framework of the new nation. Only in the fourth national goal, which directs the government to conserve the sacred and historical qualities of the land, and in the fifth national goal, which asks for 'recognition that the cultural, commercial and ethnic diversity of our people is a positive strength', do we see an echo of these principles. The fact that 'commercial diversity' is interposed between cultural and ethnic diversity, suggests that this apparently bold statement might be a well disguised plea for the sanctity of private enterprise and the continuation of Australian commercial interests, for no matter what view one has of the precolonial past of Papua New Guinea it was never commercially diverse. The fifth national goal, however, does go on to direct 'the fostering of a respect for and appreciation of traditional ways of life and culture, including language in all their richness and variety'. Instead of fostering respect, the national government has denied the National Museum adequate funds; provincial governments have banned and bullied anthropologists (the only trained recorders of traditional life and culture) and barely tolerated archaeologists. Linguists, many under the banner of mission enterprise (Summer Institute of Linguistics), are better received. Most study or research which is not promoting development, or the problems emerging from it, receives little support. For the moment the *kina* and not culture dominates the objectives of the nation.

The ancient diversity of cultures, languages and local histories which makes Papua New Guinea such an important region for study, has been further complicated by recent history. There are few unifying threads in the colonial period around which a National History can be woven; there was no War of Liberation, no major military disaster like Gallipoli, and little imported history (apart from Biblical history) to fill the gap. The colonial experience was very different throughout the country, shared between German and Australian *mastas* and between the League of Nations, the United Nations and paternalistic Australia. The education policies in the north and south were markedly different while development and investment policies also took different routes.

Experience in the Second World War also varied between regions. For most of the highlands this war, which had enmeshed the Pacific, was evident only in the appearance of a few Japanese, American or Australian aeroplanes. In Rabaul or Madang, by contrast, the trauma of Australian withdrawal, Japanese occupation and the savagery and brutality of liberation, was a quite different experience. For 'Papuans' on the south coast the continued Australian presence was yet another experience.

Other recent experiences are equally divisive; none more so than the impact of the imported divisions of Christendom. Almost every Christian sect (except the racially sensitive Mormons) can be found somewhere in Papua New Guinea, preaching, converting and consciously or unconsciously eroding past values. Extreme Fundamentalist and Evangelist churches, barely tolerated in their home countries, flourish in the jungles of Papua New Guinea. Language groups, ethnic groups and even villages are divided between competing denominations. At the university, lonely students are snapped up by opportunistic sects. On Friday nights the howling of the Pentecostals echoes across the campus, on Saturday the disciplined prayers of the Seventh Day Adventists replace them, and on Sunday, the remainder, the Uniting Church, the Catholics, the Lutherans and others may join in. Despite the apparent strength of these competing denominations, loyalty to church and creed is not well entrenched in many Papua New Guineans. Many cynical (or bored) students drift from church to church seeking the best Sunday feast or the most entertaining pastor. Others are deeply committed, accepting course advice from their church leaders, walking out of, or withdrawing from, courses where 'evolution' or 'Darwin' is mentioned. The minds, if not the souls, of Papua New Guineans are subjected to a diversity of imported morals and religions: many of these impinge upon attitudes to the past.

In addition to these imposed ideas are the 'nativistic' cults (e.g. cargo cults) which emerge from time to time, combining both traditional and Christian values, sweeping like mini bushfires through the minds and morals of isolated communities.

A new and ominous divisiveness is the growing inequality of wealth and opportunity. Cash is hard to come by, and many traditional redistribution systems (such as bride price) are coming under considerable stress. Despite the efforts of national and provincial governments to distribute the small national income evenly, there is a growing elite who alone have ready access to money and good schools.

Compounding the tragic colonial divisions of 1884, which split the Island of New Guinea and Island Melanesia into politically separate colonies of European powers is the political divisiveness of 'provincialism' in modern Papua New Guinea. Loyalties must now be shared between village, ethnic and language group, province and nation. Many of the new provinces merely subdivide the old colonial boundaries of New Guinea and Papua. The basis of the subdivisions is sometimes ethnic/linguistic, sometimes administrative convenience, but always following the former colonial administration structure which is permanently embedded in the landscape in the form of towns grown out of former patrol posts and mission centres, roads linking these and the cities whose very existence is the accident of colonial enterprise.

The depth to which all these ancient and modern divisions are etched into the fabric of Papua New Guinean society is nowhere more evident than on the university campus, where the student body is divided into dozens of provincial/ethnic associations. A few academic societies which cross-cut these loyalties struggle to survive. Denominational loyalties, however, transcend regional and provincial societies, and party political groupings, often strongly allied with regional/provincial boundaries, emerge with strength as elections approach. There is no doubt, however, from the student's first inauguration to the university, that the dominant divisions in the student body after creed are ethnic/provincial, a mixture of traditional and modern loyalties.

Whose past?

The obvious question which emerges in this diverse and divided nation is not who owns the past but *whose past*? Competing loyalties today merely build upon the loyalties of the ancient and recent past, each of which has its own history. The unifying history belongs in the distant past, long before the emergence of the present ethnic, regional, religious and political divisions. It is a unity which encompasses far more than the political boundaries of Papua New Guinea or even 'Greater Melanesia', Australia, Asia and the Pacific. To understand it requires such a mental transformation of the world as we know it, both geographically and culturally, such faith in the inductive historical method, and ability to conceive and handle time on such a grand scale, that few people can cope with it. After twenty years of immersion in Pacific and Melanesian prehistory, I am aware that the very language of my profession, the models through which I filter the evidence, are inadequate. In the same poem quoted above, T.S. Eliot expresses this dilemma of attempting to encompass and understand time:

Words strain,
Crack and sometimes break, under the burden,
Under the tension, slip, slide, perish,
Decay with imprecision, will not stay in place,
Will not stay still.
('Burnt Norton' IV)

But whose words? The answer to this question is actually the central theme of this volume: Who owns the past? The real owners of the past of any nation, state or province are not the people today, nor the land-owners who are the guardians of the evidence, but the manipulators of that past, the historians, prehistorians and archaeologists who transform the past into words. However inadequate these words, however weak the models, the handful of historians who attempt to understand and write about that past assume a control which approaches ownership. To understand this one need go no further than the Pacific, the prehistory of which, redolent with romance, has been more thoroughly investigated than that of Melanesia or Papua New Guinea.

The past of the Pacific peoples became the concern, by the late nineteenth century, of a few hardy 'scholars' and romantics. Their evidence (the increasing volume of (written) oral traditions and genealogies) formed the basis of an exciting view of the history of the Polynesians. Fornander's monumental *An Account of the Polynesian Race* (1878–85) was eclipsed twenty years later by Percy Smith's *Hawaiki: the whence of the Maori* (1910), the influence of which was to permeate the work of many later scholars such as Sir Peter Buck (1938, 1952) or Roger Duff (1956). A gradual shift to a new form of evidence, ethnological and archaeological, could not erode the impact of these early words until the advent of an independent arbiter, the beta particle, with radiocarbon dating. Today, despite the vast energy of Polynesian prehistory, the impact of these pioneer manipulators of words has not left us; we are still monopolized by a view of Pacific prehistory dominated by the Polynesians. Papua New Guinea and Melanesia have become woven into the story.

Thus, when oral historians in New Zealand failed to find traditional (oral) evidence supporting the archaeological demonstration that man had hunted and exterminated the giant flightless bird the moa, a permanent taint (anticipated by others such as Fornander), was cast upon the past of the Pacific. The absence of reliable mention of the hunting and extermination of the moa could mean only one thing; they had been exterminated by earlier arrivals. By dint of cunningly concealed leading questions, accounts of an earlier 'pre-fleet' population, the *tangata-whenua* (aboriginals) or *Moriori* were soon recovered (Sorrenson 1979: 43–44). In an infamous book (Smith 1913–15) these earlier people, described as lank, lazy and addicted to sitting around the fire, were identified as 'Melanesians' (Smith 1913–15; cf. Buck 1952: 10–19; Sorrenson 1979: 43–44). Although capable of hunting and exterminating the moa, they could not resist the 'superior' Hawaiki Polynesians who overwhelmed them in the Fleet migration. Thus was born the 'Melanesian myth' which has become over the years a convenient form of social Darwinism to rationalize the nearly successful disappearance of the Maori and the ruthless acquisition of their land (Skinner 1923; Simmons 1969 and 1977). Its echoes are still heard in New Zealand farming communities today.

The hypothetical Melanesians, concocted in a heady era of white supremacy in New Zealand were credited with all the less attractive features of Maori society: warfare, cannibalism and infanticide. In contrast the Polynesians were eulogized, their myths extolled and their cultures viewed sympathetically and romantically. Wonderment was expressed at their feat of courage and skill in colonising the vast Pacific Ocean (Buck 1938). It was obviously a relief to Europeans that this tremendous act of daring and maritime skill was that of a 'lighter-skinned' people. From first contact vain efforts were made to seek their origin in Egypt, from amongst the Jewish tribes, to see them as wandering Phoenicians or (when all else failed) as coming out of India (Sorrenson 1979: ch. 1). That they could have no relationship to their nearest neighbours, the black-skinned Melanesians, was taken for granted.

From the 'race'-dominated search was born the 'Polynesian Problem' – the whence of the light-skinned, curly-haired Polynesians – into which so much energy has flowed, so many hair-brained theories devised, and upon which so many academic reputations have been built (Sharp 1956: 11; Macmillan-Brown 1907; Heyerdahl 1950; Langdon 1975).

Unfortunately the story does not stop with the shift from oral history to other forms of evidence. When the quest finally passed into the hands of archaeologists in the 1950s they were delighted to discover in western Polynesia evidence that the earliest Polynesians had possessed a distinctive pottery, now known as Lapita ware (Golson 1959; Groube 1971). They were as excited as had been the readers of the *Journal of the Polynesian Society* forty years earlier when it was announced that the Maori had indeed possessed a Supreme God called Io (=Jehovah?). This finally removed the Maori and most Polynesians from the sullied ranks of the Polytheists.

In the two decades following the discovery of pottery in Polynesia the highly decorated (but poorly fired) Lapita pottery has been viewed with all the emotional sympathy and enthusiasm once reserved for the Polynesians themselves. It is, perhaps, inevitable that archaeologists should eulogize pottery rather than people, but as a 'superior' ware (with fine geometric designs) it reaffirmed the superiority of the Polynesians, despite the fact that it was more widespread and had been discovered first in Island Melanesia. It was rapidly assumed that this pottery documented the movement of the Polynesians into the Pacific, with each station marking their progress through darkest Melanesia.

A more rational argument that the Polynesians had *become* Polynesians after separation from Island Melanesia (a case strongly supported by linguistic and archaeological evidence) met with a mixed reception (Groube 1971). Some who disputed the primacy given to Tonga as the Polynesian 'homeland' (a position supported by the subsequent discovery of Lapita pottery in Samoa), nevertheless took up the spade and demonstrated the richness of Lapita sites in Melanesia (Green 1972, 1976, 1979). Others, ignoring the archaeological and linguistic evidence, sought Lapita origins (and thus Polynesian origins) beyond the boundaries of the Pacific. Today, the most influential versions of Polynesian prehistory, replacing Sir Peter Buck's *Vikings of the Sunrise* are those of Bellwood (Bellwood 1975, 1978a, 1978b, 1980). He firmly claims that the Polynesians were Mongoloids who entered the Pacific by avoiding the numerous populations of Melanesia:

Within the past 600 years these populations of Mongoloid ancestry . . . have gone on to settle the empty areas of Micronesia and Polynesia . . . the long-established residents [of Melanesia], in particular those of New Guinea, may have been able to hold out against the newcomers . . . The implications of early horticulture in Melanesia are great. It is possible to hypothesize that the Melanesians of New Guinea . . . had become large, fairly sedentary populations sustained by horticulture more than 5000 years ago. If future archaeological work supports this hypothesis then the failure of the Austronesian-speakers to overrun Melanesia may be attributable to their not having the numerical and economic superiority they had once had over the scattered hunter-gatherers of Island South East Asia.
(Bellwood 1980: 177 and 180, cf. 1978a: 49 and 238)

Although this version refers not to Polynesians but to 'Austronesians' (the speakers of the widespread language family of which Polynesian is a minor branch) it clearly implies the Polynesians; the dates for what is merely pottery, but has been transformed by verbal sleight of hand into 'Lapita culture' and now even 'Lapita people' (Green 1979; cf. Fagan 1980: 218) are close to those claimed by Percy Smith in his *Hawaiki: the whence of the Maori*. Polynesian prehistory has all the earmarks of a self-fulfilling prophecy.

That there are many archaeologists (including myself) who find it inconceivable that the Polynesians were derived from other than the diversity of Melanesia, and the credit for their achievements need not be sought beyond the energy of this complex region, is not very apparent in modern literature. Our failure to take up the cudgel and challenge the fruitless pursuit of an Asian or southeast Asian homeland is not only due to the flagging fortunes of archaeological research in Island Melanesia and lack of evidence, but to the inadequate models with which we view the past, our inability to understand the nature of change within the time-depth now allowed by the remorseless honesty of the radiocarbon clock. I will return to this problem in the final section of this paper.

What has this tale to do with 'the ownership of the past'? Throughout 150 years of enquiry into Polynesian origins, the past of the Pacific has been firmly owned by a handful of highly productive scholars, initially oral historians, then ethnologists and latterly, archaeologists. They are the real owners of the past of the Pacific peoples, not the Maori, Hawaiians, Tongans or Samoans. So successful has been their 'authorized' version that the Polynesians themselves are the most reluctant to accept a humble Melanesian origin: the myth of Polynesian superiority is now firmly entrenched in the Pacific (see Wendt's comment in Mulvaney's paper, p. 96). Thus in answer to the question 'whose past?' a genealogy of scholars rather than of Pacific ancestors would be closest to the truth.

Before looking at the words and ideas which are now forming the past of Papua New Guinea it is necessary to examine the ideas generated in Australia, Papua New Guinea and Melanesia are as intimately associated with the past of Australia as they are with that of the Pacific. In Australia a different, but also racially concerned, view of the past has held sway for many generations. Here the problem was not to explain the presence of a 'superior' people with surprising accomplishments – for it was evident to the white colonists that the reverse was true – but to account for the presence of the Aborigines at all. The problem was that, as an island, Australia could only have been settled out of Asia (the nearest source of placental mammals, including of course man) by a sea journey. With the much advertised poverty of reliable sea-craft on coastal Australia (Jones 1976; Lampert 1981), except in the area nearest to maritime Melanesia, there were only two possible explanations.

One, favoured until quite recently, was that the settlement of Australia was recent (i.e. Holocene) when efficient water craft had been developed in Asia. This was supported by the failure to demonstrate the association of man with other than modern mam-

malian fauna (White and O'Connell 1982: 24). The analogy to the
European Palaeolithic implied in this sort of reasoning was persuasive because of the prevailing view, which has an eminent
genealogy from Tylor, Lubbock and Darwin and had been immediately applied by the white settlers (White and O'Connell 1982:
23; cf. Daniel 1962), that the Aborigines were a relict Palaeolithic
population, a fossil of an earlier stage of development. Particularly
unfortunate in being labelled in Tylorean terms were the recently
extinct Tasmanians, who, with their odd hair style and apparent
technological backwardness gave rise to a different 'two-strata' theory; the Tasmanians were seen as remnants of a truly Palaeolithic
stage, while the mainlanders (possessing ground-stone tools) were
given a Neolithic status (White and O'Connell 1982: 28).

As with the contemporary Melanesian myth in the Pacific, the
view that the Aborigines were some sort of fossilized remnant of
an earlier stage of cultural development served as a convenient
excuse for appalling treatment and land-grabbing. It also tended
to denegrate interest in Aboriginal history: as an unchanging, un-
important relict of the distant past they warranted little mention
in Australian history books (e.g. Clark 1963). This view of the pre-
European past of Australia was transferred to Papua New Guinea
by missionaries, administrators and school teachers. It underlies
the current ahistoricism of the education system.

The second theory, slowly emerging from studies of the physical
anthropology of the Australian Aborigines and adjoining peoples
and from the discovery of some apparently ancient skulls (Keilor,
Cohuna), was that the settlement of Australia belonged to the
Pleistocene when low sea-levels may have made the passage from
Asia to Australia feasible. This view was most forcefully developed
by Birdsell (1949, 1957, 1967), who put forward a three-wave explanation of the settlement of Australia: the first wave (represented
by the Tasmanians and some rainforest Aborigines) comprised
'Oceanic Negritos', related according to his theory to the Anda-
manese (Indian Ocean) and Semang (Malaya). These were followed by the stocky 'Murrayians' (cf. the Ainu of northern Japan)
and then the 'Carpentarians'. This is a classic model of multiple
origins, versed entirely in racial terms but based upon apparently
secure measurements of living populations. Such models have had
a major impact upon Papua New Guinea.

From further complex mensuration data, including skeletal and
cranial measurements, others have built upon or modified Birdsell's claims. Abbie (1975) was able to identify the Tasmanians as
Melanesians, an entertaining revival of the Melanesian myth of the
Pacific. Howells and Giles (Howells 1973 and 1976; Giles 1976)
from comparison with a much-used sample of Tolai skulls from

West New Britain made similar claims; even the much debated Keilor skull has been identified with the Tasmanians (Macintosh and Larnach 1976; Howells 1976: 156 and Fig. 10). The prospect of Melanesians lurking around in early Australia, however, has more foundation than the similar claims from New Zealand in the nineteenth century.

The post-Second World War period, in fact, saw a vast industry of blood analysts, geneticists, tasters, prodders and measurers taking to all the peoples of the Pacific. Despite the apparent scientific basis of their investigations and the plethora of resultant publications which led to the foundation of a new academic journal *Archaeology and Physical Anthropology in Oceania*, the result, as Simmons admits, was disappointing: 'Our 35 years of blood group genetic research have unfortunately failed to provide us with any clues, at least obvious to us, as to the Biological Origin of the Australians' (Simmons 1976: 319). It is ironical that the new journal mentioned above has now expunged 'physical anthropology' from its title and a vast stockpile of statistics of every conceivable measurement of Australians, Papua New Guineans and Asians is mouldering in the archives. The simple categories of skin colour, hair form, teeth, stature and skull shape so beloved of Polynesianists have been transformed by human biologists into masses of figures and genetic symbols. Yet from these data come only the obvious generalisations which could have been intuitively derived from consideration of proximity: Australians are most like their nearest neighbours in New Guinea and Melanesia, although each is genetically distinguishable (Howells 1976: 155).

Fortunately for Australian prehistory, which could have become bogged down in the same sort of simplistic racial thinking which has plagued Polynesian prehistory, independent evidence supported by new approaches from a different type of scientist-historian, notably geomorphologists, has rescued Australian archaeology. Unfortunately the multiple origin hypotheses are not yet dead: a new breed of human palaeontologist, clutching their recently recovered skeletons are keeping the tradition alive (Thorne 1971; 1976).

The new evidence from geomorphology, from a new generation of professional archaeologists and from the precision of radiocarbon dating, is too well known for review here. That man was in Australia by at least 40 000 years ago, and at that time and for the next 30 000 years Australia and New Guinea were one land, has great implications for Papua New Guinea. This new vision of the past, peopled by stone tools and carbon-dates rather than mythical 'races', has not yet had time to affect Papua New Guinea; an earlier, Australian-derived vision of the past still dominates.

Unfortunately the widening cultural and political gap between Australia and Papua New Guinea since the latter's Independence appears to be as profound as the rising of the Arafura sea 10 000 years ago. With the notable exceptions of a few (for example, J.P. White and J. Golson), most Australian archaeologists show little interest in the archaeology of Papua New Guinea. Few Papua New Guinean students accept that it was theoretically possible to walk from Madang to Hobart only 12 000 years ago. Most students are derisive, indeed insulted by the claim that the Australian Aborigines and Papua New Guineans have a common ancestor. They are equally sceptical that Papuans and Highlanders may be related, or that any of the major ethnic groups share a unity in the past. Some are angered that Asia is claimed as the ultimate homeland of Papua New Guineans.

Much of this reaction arises from the natural difficulty, shared by most people in the world, of transforming the present into the past:

> What might have been is an abstraction
> Remaining a perpetual possibility
> Only in a world of speculation.
> ('Burnt Norton' I)

Such speculation in the case of Papua New Guinea, against the ever-present backdrop of immense diversity, requires a mental leap which even professional archaeologists, versed in millennia, find difficult. An Asia without Asians is inconceivable; the 'Old Melanesia' espoused by Howells (1973), or even the existence of Sahuland itself, demand considerable faith in the words of archaeologists. And there are many other rivals for the faith of Papua New Guineans.

Some of the opposition to these ideas, however, comes from another source, from an earlier generation of writers on the pre-European past of Papua New Guinea, whose views have been carried through the missions and schools to most of the country. They are views which fit comfortably with and complement the ethnic sense of separateness and divisiveness of modern Papua New Guineans. Typically, these views are also based upon casual assessments of skin colour, hair, stature and the like; they are very European views of history and diversity.

On the question of diversity there seems to be little doubt: even modern authors fall back on the multiple origin explanation:

. . . the probabilities are that the big island and its smaller neighbours were colonized by successive waves of migrants from lands to the north and west. (O. White 1965: 10)

For centuries Papua New Guinea slept: undreamt of by the expanding nations of Europe . . . They were never one people. They appear to have come as the result of several migration moves spanning thousands of years . . . (Woolford 1976: 1)

A major source of perpetuation of this view has been the accumulation of evidence from linguistics. The geomorphologist Löffler says 'There must have been several different migrant groups because many of the present languages are not related to one another' (1979: 24). This explanation, repeated in so many books, I would call the 'rubbish dump theory'. It envisages the island of New Guinea as a sort of cultural dumping ground, accepting migrant populations from a more turbulent Asia. It satisfies a strange European prejudice (despite the many examples to the contrary) to favour continents for all important developments and to assume that isolation on an island implies cultural stagnation (cf. Crete, Malta, Easter Island). It also shifts the burden of explaining the diversity of Melanesia to the unknown complexities of Asia. The 'rubbish dump' theory is obviously closely allied to the multiple origin hypotheses of an earlier generation of Australianists such as Birdsell, and like them is inevitably expressed in pejorative terms of flesh colour, stature and race:

The first men in New Guinea may well have been ethnic cousins of the Aborigines of Australia, the Dravidians of India and the Sakai people of the Highlands of Malaya . . . the pioneers were woolly-haired Negrito or pygmy type believed to have originated in Malaya or Indonesia . . . The next wave of migrants are thought to have been tall dark-skinned, curly-haired negroid people with prominent noses who were classed 30 years ago as 'true Papuans'.

The third migratory wave were the Melanesians – a vigorous sea-faring people who . . . had picked up a confusion of physical traits including a wider range of skin-tints and some resemblance to the mongoloid races of South east Asia and the Negroes of West Africa.

(O. White 1965: 10)

This confused complex explanation, which combines the Polynesian elitist model with Birdsell's three-wave hypothesis, with a generous lardering of what can only be called a 'christmas pudding' approach to the diversity of Melanesia, is typical of many explanations of Melanesian prehistory. There is a consistent pattern to these views of the past of Papua New Guinea:

1. A number of migrations out of Asia with relationships sought amongst a variety of populations in East Asia, ranging from India to northern Japan, the exact number of migrations varying according to the whims and sensitivities of the reviewer.

There was, in the early years of speculation, only reluctant admission that the earliest migrants may have been related to the Australian Aborigine; the persuasion of the distinctive 'woolly' or 'frizzy' hair of New Guinea and Melanesia and other superficial differences as well as the absence of agriculture in Australia, combined with the prevailing view of the Aborigines as a palaeolithic remnant made comparisons difficult. When they were made, it was with the interior, Highlands populations (invariable labelled with the pejorative term 'pygmy' (and nowadays 'dwarf', see below). Most of the views linking the interior populations of New Guinea with the Aborigines of Australia or the 'pygmies' of interior Malaya were made before the Highlands had been fully explored, from superficial and unscientific descriptions from first contact. The cosmetic similarity of the Tasmanian hair style with that of some Highlands groups had excited Birdsell in his promotion of the 'oceanic negrito' hypothesis. Of such is history written in this region.

2. There is widespread concurrence that a final 'wave of immigrants', the vigorous, sea-faring people of the above quotation, resettled the coast of New Guinea and Island Melanesia. These people were invariably seen as superior, vigorous, expert seafarers and so forth, thus echoing the Polynesian model. It was ironical that these same people, the 'Melanesians' were seen as inferior to Polynesians from the distant Pacific. In the New Guinea context, despite the irritating difficulty of inability to identify them as a single physical type (hence the christmas pudding model above), they were in turn superior to the interior populations. Underlying this view was a strong European (maritime) prejudice to favour coastal peoples.

Lurking beneath this view of the past of Melanesia is a barely stated but clearly consistent hierarchy of 'races': at the top the lightskinned Polynesians, then the darker-skinned (mixed) coastal populations of Melanesia (the 'Melanesians'), followed by the (Neolithic) interior 'Papuans', then the mainland Aboriginal, with the unfortunate (and extinct) Tasmanians at the bottom of the pile. Permutations and variations of this theme, with its heavy racialist undertones, dominate an earlier generation of books on Papua New Guinea. Unfortunately, in the guise of 'scientific archaeology' and versed in new terminology, it still monopolizes the words on the past.

How do Papua New Guineans react to this 'European eye-view' of their past? The tension between Highlanders and 'coastals', apparent in the administration, politics and the university, is amply fed by the coastal/interior contrast, although Highlanders reverse the priorities. Most Papua New Guineans, whatever their ethnic groups, taught by an earlier generation of Australian school-teachers and with only a dim knowledge of Australia, are happy to accept the inferiority of the Australian Aboriginal. The strong reaction of many students to the idea that Papua New Guineans and Australian Aborigines have a common ancestry is evidence of the impact of this view on current attitudes. A growing sense of solidarity with the Australian Aboriginal (evident at least amongst the student body) may erode this racialist attitude, but the natural sense of superiority with which every ethnic group in Papua New Guinea views other groups (exacerbated by the divisiveness described above), will probably ensure its survival for many generations. It is also likely to be fed by a new phenomenon, urbanisation, which is bringing together the immense diversity of the nation: anthropologists are not the only ones aware of the physical variation of Melanesians. Questions such as 'Why are Bougainvillians so black?' and 'Why are Highlanders so short?' recur annually in tutorials with each new student intake. With a growing sensitivity to variation, in language and appearance, this view will find a sympathetic response in future decades.

It is a convenient explanation, also, for the more extreme missionary persuasions. Clinging on to pre-Darwinian chronology for the world, with its miniscule time span of 6000 years, a multiplicity of migrations is the only satisfactory explanation of the diversity of languages and people. In a land which favours feelings of ethnic superiority and fed by Fundamentalist propaganda, the ownership of the past of Papua New Guinea is securely in the hands of those who view the world in terms of skin colour, hair form and stature.

The arch-exponent of this position, whose views are now as widely disseminated as were those of Percy Smith or Sir Peter Buck in earlier generations, is Peter Bellwood, who although approaching the prehistory of this region from the direction of Polynesia has some firm comments on the origin of Melanesians (1978b: 44–45):

1. Using as his principal source of inspiration the writings of Carlton Coon, Bellwood lumps together the populations of the region under the label 'Australoids'. He detects three varieties:
    a) the tall Australian Aborigines
    b) the dwarf Australoid populations, 'The negritos of the Andaman Islands, central Malaya (Semang), the Philippines and the pygmies of Highland New Guinea'
    c) the tall Melanesians ('generally darker and taller than the Highlanders [with] less rugged features' who 'are a very diverse population phenotypically as befits their multiple phylogenetic origins'.
2. 'The people of the New Guinea Highlands are probably the

most direct descendants of the original Australoid settlers of Western Melanesia.'

3. Following Coon and Weidenreich, 'the Australoids are lineal descendants in the South East Asian area of *Homo erectus* population represented by the Javanese remains . . . [this] seems to me to be the most acceptable [hypothesis] for Australoid evolution'.

The linking of the settlement of Papua New Guinea/Melanesia with *Homo erectus* is a current theme in Australian archaeology, based upon new fossil discoveries (Thorne 1971; cf. Macintosh and Larnach 1976: 117). The recognition that a skull from Niah cave in Borneo is 'Australoid' and similar to Tasmanian skulls completes the thin circle of evidence, which is based primarily on physical appearance (Bellwood, pers. comm. and Brothwell 1960) with a thin bolstering from (selected) often quite ancient data from physical anthropology.

An alternative, but vigorous promotion of multiple migrations, comes from the linguists, particularly the prolific pen of Wurm. In many academic papers spanning two decades he has advocated 'migrations' of grammar and words to account for the complexities of language variation in Papua New Guinea. Pronouns march, like Napoleonic armies, through the Sepik to the highlands. In his latest publication no less than eight separate migrations are claimed to account for current relationships (Wurm et al. 1975: 935). The linguists, however, despite their efforts, can disinter only a fraction of the past of Papua New Guinea; the rate of (random) language change, as discussed below, is too great for their evidence to be persuasive beyond 10 000 years. They are also not immune to injecting skin colour into their arguments: 'As a non-linguistic factor, the interesting point may be mentioned that speakers of Austronesian languages in Melanesia are generally melanid, i.e. more dark-skinned that speakers of other Austronesian languages' (Wurm 1982: 8). It is not surprising that this observation comes in the context of a 'christmas-pudding' model of linguistic diversity in the Austronesian languages of island Melanesia.

That skin colour or even physical attributes should enter the arena of linguistics is surprising when it is considered that within the Indo-European language family (of approximately the same antiquity as Austronesian) there is a much wider range of skin hues, from the blue-eyed blondes of Aryan mythology to the dark-skinned Indians. This fact hardly warrants mention in European history books and was an issue delicately avoided by the bleached historians of the Third Reich.

Thus, currently, the real owners of the past of Papua New

Guinea must be identified with writers such as Bellwood who have inherited the Victorian addiction for writing history in terms of skin colour and race. The tiny rumblings of the archaeologists (except for the well-publicized work of Golson (1976, 1977, 1981, 1982) at Kuk, in the Wahgi valley) can be barely heard. Yet it is with the discoveries of archaeology that we see the first signs that the 'authorized' view may be very wrong, and that we must sit down and rethink our basic models before leaping into the past of this diverse country.

The claim for some form of swamp manipulation for agricultural purposes at Kuk as set out by Golson does not fit comfortably with the prevailing views of the backwardness of the region. We have already seen how Bellwood adroitly exploits this evidence to account for the failure of the invading (Neolithic) Austronesians to penetrate New Guinea (above p. 67). The emergence of an independent centre of plant exploitation and manipulation in the highlands of New Guinea fits neither Pacific, Australian nor international models of the past. Long-sanctified words like 'Neolithic', 'the agricultural revolution' or 'hunter-gatherer' require re-examination in the light of this possibility. A long hard look must be taken at the importance of tropical forest environments in the development of intensive food-production.

A review of the hints and the possible explanations of some of the archaeological evidence from Papua New Guinea is premature; it will only add to the present confusion. One thing is clear, the settlement of New Guinea was, as the Australian evidence testifies, extremely early (more than 40 000 years ago) and coming from this early period are large stone tools which strongly suggest that even the earliest inhabitants were more accomplished forest manipulators than any current views suggest (White et al. 1970; Groube et al. 1981; Groube 1982 and forthcoming). The implications and explanations of these discoveries are for the future.

The ownership of the past in the future

The owners of the past of Papua New Guinea in the coming decades will, one hopes, be prehistorians who have learnt to avoid the simple pitfalls of equating present diversity with past events such as migrations from Asia, or expressing those views in the prevailing terms of race. To do this, however, there must be a long, careful look at our models of the past, which it is becoming embarrassingly clear, are quite inadequate to cope with the slowly emerging facts, particularly the long antiquity of settlement in the country.

Viewed against other major populations in the world the peoples of New Guinea, Melanesia and Australia have a long pedigree. Apart from the Americas, where dates so far do not match in antiquity those from Australia and New Guinea, most of the world's populations are relatively recent, springing from large-scale expansions and reshuffling during the Holocene. If, as is highly probable, the diversity of Australia and Melanesia is largely the result of single initial colonization (White and O'Connell 1982: 46–49), the people of this region have the longest continuous history of human breeding in the world; taking the widely quoted figure of 60 000 years for the settlement of Sahuland, at least 2400 human generations. If, as is generally assumed, the majority of Europeans are descended from the first farmers who moved up the Danube about 8000 years ago, then the diversity of Europe comes from a continuity of only about 320 human generations. A similar figure could be claimed for the majority of the Bantu-descended populations of central, East and South Africa and, according to most authorities in dating the expansion of the modern Mongoloids, only a little more for the millions of descendants of this great population expansion. If the conservative figure of c. 18 000 years ago is accepted for the settlement of the Americas, the natives of those countries have a much longer history of about 720 human generations. We have neither the imagination nor the models to cope with such long periods, particularly with the remorseless effect of random genetic drift, exacerbated by the probable small size of the colonizing units and resultant isolation between founding groups across a diverse and rugged sub-continent.

Thus if I were to give an answer for the future to the question with which this conference is concerned, 'Who *will* own the past of Papua New Guinea?', I would argue it will not be the archaeologists whose words and models have already been found wanting. Nor will ownership lie with the linguists whose evidence decays too rapidly for the time span of settlement in Papua New Guinea, but with the mathematicians who can build the models to demonstrate the scale of change, biological, linguistic and cultural which can take place in isolation and over the enormous time span now allotted to man in New Guinea. It is ironical that historians, fond of seeking explanations in terms of events, geological, ecological or cultural, may have to seek the real solution to the past of this country from the behaviour of dice or a deck of cards. Thus time, which makes the effects of drift and isolation so important, will be the real owner of the past of Papua New Guinea, a solution anticipated by Eliot in 'Burnt Norton': 'Only through time time is conquered.'

References

Abbie, A.A. (1975), *Studies in Physical Anthropology II*, Australian Institute of Aboriginal Studies, Canberra.

Bellwood, P. (1975), 'The prehistory of Oceania', *Current Anthropology* 16, 19–28.

—— (1978a), *Man's Conquest of the Pacific: the Prehistory of Southeast Asia and Oceania*, Collins, Auckland.

—— (1978b), *The Polynesians: Prehistory of an Island People*, Thames and Hudson, London.

—— (1980), 'The peopling of the Pacific', *Scientific American* 243(5), 174–185.

Birdsell, J.B. (1949), 'The racial origins of the extinct Tasmanians', *Records of the Queen Victoria Museum* 2, 105–22.

—— (1957), 'Some population problems involving Pleistocene Man', *Cold Spring Harbour Symposium on Quantitative Biology* 22, 47–70.

—— (1967), 'Preliminary data on the trihybrid origin of the Australian Aborigines',*Physical Anthropology and Archaeology in Oceania*, 2, 100–55.

Brothwell, D.R. (1960), 'Upper Pleistocene human skull from Niah Caves, Sarawak', *Sarawak Museum Journal* 9, 323–49.

Brown, J. Macmillan (1907), *Maori and Polynesian: their Origin, History and Culture*, Hutchinson, London.

Buck, P.H. (1938), *Vikings of the Sunrise*, Lippincott, Philadelphia.

—— (1952), *The Coming of the Maori*, 2nd edn, Whitcombe & Tombs, Wellington.

Clark, C.M.H. (1963), *A Short History of Australia*, New American Library, New York.

—— (1975), *The Constitution of the Independent State of Papua New Guinea*. Port Moresby, 16th September 1975.

Daniel, G.E. (1962), *The Idea of Prehistory*, C.A. Watts, London.

Duff, R. (1956), *The Moa Hunter Period of Maori Culture*, Government Printer, Wellington.

Eliot, T.S. (1947), 'Burnt Norton', in *Collected Poems: 1905–1935*, Faber & Faber, London.

Fagan, B.M. (1980), *People of the Earth*, 3rd edn, Little Brown, Boston.

Fornander, A. (1878–1885), *An Account of the Polynesian Race*, 3 vols, Trubner, London.

Giles, E. (1976), 'Cranial variation in Australia and neighbouring areas', in Kirk, R.L. and Thorne, A.G. (eds), *The Origin of the Australians*, Australian Institute of Aboriginal Studies, Canberra, 161–72.

Golson, J. (1959), 'Archeologie du Pacifique Sud: resultats et perspectives', *Journal de la Société des Oceanistes* 15, 5–64.

—— (1976), 'Archaeology and agricultural history in the New Guinea highlands', in Sieveking, G. de G., Longworth, I.H. and Wilson, K.E. (eds), *Problems in Economic and Social Archaeology*, Duckworth, London, 201–20.

—— (1977), 'No room at the top: agricultural intensification in the New Guinea Highlands', in Allen, J., Golson, J. and Jones, R. (eds), *Sunda and Sahul: Prehistoric Studies in Southeast Asia, Melanesia and Australia*, Academic Press, London, 601–38.

—— (1981), 'Agriculture in New Guinea: the long view', in Denoon, D. and Snowden, Catherine (eds), *A History of Agriculture in Papua New Guinea: a Time to Plant and a Time to Uproot*, Institute of Papua New Guinea Studies, Port Moresby, 33–41.

—— (1982), 'The Ipomoean revolution revisited: society and the sweet potato in the upper Wahgi valley', in Strathern, A. (ed.), *Inequality in New Guinea Highlands Society*, Cambridge Papers in Social Anthropology 11, Cambridge University Press, Cambridge, 109–36.

Green, R.C. (1972), 'Revision of the Tongan sequence', *Journal of the Polynesian Society* 81(1), 79–86.

—— (1976), 'Lapita sites in the Santa Cruz group', in Green, R.C. and Creswell, M.M. (eds), *Southeast Solomon Islands Cultural History: a preliminary survey*, Royal Society of New Zealand, Wellington, 245–65.

—— (1979), 'Lapita', in Jennings, J.D. (ed.), *The Prehistory of Polynesia*, Australian National University Press, Canberra, 27–60.

Groube, L.M. (1971), 'Tonga, Lapita pottery and Polynesian origins', *Journal of the Polynesian Society* 80(3) 278–316.

—— (1982), 'Recent discoveries on the Huon Peninsula, Moroke Province', in Eaton, P. and Chambers, M. (eds), *Environmental Education Series* 1, University of Papua New Guinea, Port Moresby, 8–14.

—— n.d. 'Waisted and stemmed axes from Asia, Australia, and New Guinea'. (Preliminary report on research on the Huon Peninsula, forthcoming.)

Groube, L.M., Mangi, J. and Muke, J. (1981), 'Recent discoveries on the Huon Peninsula', unpublished paper presented to the 51st ANZAAS Congress, Brisbane, 1981.

Heyerdahl, T. (1950), *The Kon Tiki Expedition*, George Allen & Unwin, London.

Howells, W.W. (1973), *The Pacific Islanders*, Scribner & Sons, New York.

—— (1976), 'Metrical analysis in the problem of Australian origin', in Kirk, R.L. and Thorne, A.G. (eds), *The Origin of the Australians*, Australian Institute of Aboriginal Studies, Canberra, 141–60.

Jennings, J. (ed.) (1979), *The Prehistory of Polynesia*, Australian National University Press, Canberra.

Jones, R.M. (1976), 'Tasmania: aquatic machines and off-shore islands', in Sieveking, G. de G., Longworth, I.H. and Wilson K.E. (eds), *Problems in Economic and Social Archaeology*, Duckworth, London, 235–63.

Kirk, R.L. and Thorne, A.G. (eds) (1976), *The origin of the Australians*, Australian Institute of Aboriginal Studies, Canberra.

Lampert, R.J. (1981), *The Great Kartan Mystery*, Terra Australis 5, Australian National University, Canberra.

Langdon, R. (1975), *The Lost Caravel*, Pacific Publications, Sydney.

Löffler, E. (1979), *Papua New Guinea*, Hutchinson, London.

Macintosh, N.W.G. and Larnach, S.L. (1976), 'Aboriginal affinities looked at in world context', in Kirk, R.L. and Thorne, A.G. (eds), *The*

Origin of the Australians, Australian Institute of Aboriginal Studies, Canberra, 113–26.

Panoff, M. (1968), 'The notion of time among the Maenge people of New Britain', in *The History of Melanesia*, Second Waigani Seminar, University of Papua New Guinea, Port Moresby, 443.

Sharp, C.A. (1956), *Ancient Voyagers in the Pacific*, Polynesian Society, Wellington.

Simmons, D.R. (1969), 'A New Zealand myth: Kupe, Toi and the Great Fleet', *New Zealand Journal of History*, 111(1), 14–31.

—— (1977), *The Great New Zealand Myth*, A.H. & A.W. Reed, Wellington.

Simmons, R.T. (1976), 'The biological origin of the Australian Aboriginals', in Kirk, R.L. and Thorne, A.G. (eds), *The origin of the Australians*, Australian Institute of Aboriginal Studies, Canberra, 307–328.

Smith, S.P. (1910), *Hawaiki: the Whence of the Maori*, 3rd edn,Whitcomb & Tombs, Wellington.

—— (1913–1915), *The Lore of the Whare Wananga*, 2 vols, Polynesian Society Memoir 4, Wellington.

Skinner, H.D. (1923), *The Morioris of the Chatham Islands*, Bishop Museum Memoirs, 9(1).

Sorrenson, M.P.K. (1979), *Maori Origins and Migrations in the Genesis of Some Pakeha Myths and Legends*, Auckland University Press, Auckland.

Thorne, A.G. (1971), 'Mungo and Kow Swamp: morphological variation in Pleistocene Australians', *Mankind* 8(2), 83–89.

—— (1976), 'Morphological contrasts in Pleistocene Australians', in Kirk, R.L. and Thorne, A.G. (eds), *The Origin of the Australians*, Australian Institute of Aboriginal Studies, Canberra, 95–112.

White, J.P., Crook, K.A. and Baxton, B.P. (1970), 'Kosipe: a late Pleistocene site in the Papuan Highlands', *Proceedings of the Prehistoric Society*, XXXVI, 152–70.

White, J.P. and O'Connell, J.F. (1982), *A prehistory of Australia, New Guinea and Sahul*, Academic Press, Sydney.

White, O. (1965), *Parliament of a Thousand Tribes*, Heinemann, London.

Woolford, D.M. (1976), *Papua New Guinea: Initiation and Independence*, University of Queensland Press, Brisbane.

Wurm, S.A. (1982), 'The linguistic point of view', in May, R.J. and Nelson, H. (eds), *Melanesia: Beyond Diversity* I, Research School of Pacific Studies, Australian National University, Canberra, 7–10.

Wurm, S.A., Laycock, D.C., Voorhoeve, C.L. and Dutton, T.E. (1975), 'Papuan linguistic prehistory and past language migrations in the New Guinea area', in Wurm, S.A. (ed.), *New Guinea Area and Language Study*, I, *Papuan Languages and the New Guinean Linguistic Scene*, Pacific Linguistic Series, C-38, Australian National University, Canberra, 935–60.

4
Art Objects and Historical Usage

Bernard Smith

Question invites question. 'Who owns the past?' invites 'What is the past?'. Is it a class of one or of many members? An abstract universal of but one instance, or a dying god whose sole obsession is to devour the future, its children. 'What is time' said Augustine: 'when I do not ask myself, I know.' If the past then, like time, is so difficult to conceive of, our question looks like one that does not admit of an answer.

So perhaps we should try a psychological rather than a metaphysical approach. We listen to a melody anticipating notes still to be played, even if we have never heard it before, while others fade away into memory. All perception seems to be like that; not an instant of time but a duration, filled and experienced, an irreducible mix of memory, sensation and expectation. Out of such experiences I become aware of my identity; a possessable past, built out of memories. And though my memory selects and distorts the things remembered, and also forgets, it is the only direct access to the past I possess.

But if we should substitute for this subjective and fragile, yet direct, access to the past, an indirect approach, we may construct quite complex pictures of the past. By observing the behaviour of perceptible things we may construct accounts of the past in terms of events. Yet it is almost as difficult to talk about an event as to talk about the past. The problem is this. An event not only possesses a beginning and an end, it also possesses a middle that does not necessarily occur half-way through. Although events are located in time they're not purely temporal structures, like days and years, but conceptual units constructed by historians and others to give the past a kind of visibility. Built out of sensory perception they stand in, as it were, for time. To envisage the past, therefore, in terms of events, is to adopt a metaphorical approach to it.

Now metaphors gain their colour from their components, but in this case only one is visible. So the pictures of the past we construct for ourselves will be determined by the nature of the objects chosen to stand in for the past. So it is that the sun, moon and stars have been observed and a sidereal past constructed, measured in light years and populated with events such as the creation and dissolution of stellar universes. The nature of this sidereal past is cyclical, regular, like the behaviour of the bodies perceived and the mathematical methods used in constructing it. The geological past, derived from the study of rocks, is also of a highly recurrent character, consisting of Ice and other kinds of Ages, but more attention in that case is now given to linear processes such as the cooling of the earth and the story of life contained in the fossil record. The biological past again stresses cyclical behaviour, but with a new interest in identity, mutation and conflict. When, however, we turn to the study of the human past less attention is given to recurrent behaviour as we move from the archaeological record towards history in the generally accepted sense, the art of using written records to construct a past. Should historians reveal a degree of regularity, even a low degree, their discipline experiences a kind of parturition and a new social science is born: economic theory, demography, sociology, and so forth. The study of recurrent human behaviour, it seems, is for others.

In this passionate preoccupation with the particular the historian affords an interesting parallel with the fine artist. I stress the word 'fine' because I shall introduce a broader definition of art in a moment. The fine artist also possesses this passion for the particular. Unlike the craftsman and the industrialist who seek to maintain a regularity of quality and form in their productive sequences, the fine artist tries to ensure that each unit is as original as it can be made (Smith 1976: 143–145). The fine artist, one might say, constructs original works, the historian constructs original events.

I shall not press the parallel, beyond noting that the historian's struggle with originality is just as difficult as the artist's. It was none other than von Ranke who wrote, 'the event in its human intelligibility, its unity, and its diversity; this should be within one's reach. One tries, one strives, but in the end it is not attained' (von Ranke 1885: 57). What a *cri de coeur* from one of the most confident of historians! Well, what's the problem with events?

They're constructed, we might agree, from selected facts linked in causal networks. Palaeontologists and prehistorians, more often than not, suffer from a paucity of them: inorganic traces of a human presence, bone fragments and the like. The historian, on the other hand, selects facts largely, though not exclusively, from objects constructed by human beings, and, as he or she moves towards the study of the present, may be embarrassed by a surfeit of them.

Human productions have long been described, and, I suggest, are best described, as art objects. Art objects, that is, whether of a physical or mental character, as distinct from natural objects. 'Nature hath made one world and art another', wrote Sir Thomas Browne. Some of the more specific distinctions, such as that made between art and science, need not detain us. Because for our purpose all human productions that embody an element of conceptualisation, purpose and skill may be classed as art objects. The natural sciences, for example, would be viewed as arts developed for the purpose of revealing truths – or must I say falsifiable hypotheses – about the natural world. Nor need we concern ourselves unduly with that conventional distinction between fine art, craft and industrial production, for all three demand high degrees of conceptualisation, purpose and skill, either from individuals or from groups.

Now it is to art objects, in this broad sense, that historians turn mostly for their sources. To the primary usage of art objects historians add a secondary usage, an historical usage. But because such objects are constructed for purposes and by skills that differ from those of the historian, methods of interpretation must be developed that take cognisance of the original skills and purposes. It is in this sense that all historians are art historians; they must learn to interpret and understand art objects. To take an obvious example: those historians who must direct their attention mainly to written sources, will often need to satisfy themselves as to the nature and age of the paper and ink of their documents – as we have been reminded recently in the affair of the so-called 'Hitler' diaries. And in dealing with a written text an historian confronts a linguistic art form of great complexity, the techniques of interpretation of which, themselves, possess a history reaching back to the earliest successful distinctions between myth and legend on the one hand, and history, as an objective enquiry, on the other. There is a latent artistry in the historian's sources that lies in wait to trap the unwary.

At this point it will be useful to recall the well-known ambiguity of the word 'history'. We say 'that's all history', or 'that's past history', referring to something that's happened. But we also describe as 'history' what historians produce. The two views are complementary rather than contradictory. One describes the whole field of historical enquiry, the other, the process of enquiry. But there is a significant difference. The first view assumes that history, as the perceptible presence of the past, is accessible without mediation. The second assumes that the past is mediated for us by historians; those artists whose skill it is to tell us the truth about a chosen event or a chosen portion of the past.

Artists, however, who undertake to tell the truth must work within the limitations of their *genre*, their medium and their technique. A novelist usually undertakes to tell a typical kind of truth. 'Everything is copied from the Book of Nature', wrote Henry Fielding, in his preface to *Joseph Andrews*, 'and scarce a character or action produced that I have not taken from my own observations and experience, yet I have used the utmost care to obscure the persons by such different circumstances and colours, that it will be impossible to guess at them with any degree of certainty'. A portraitist may seek a higher degree of specificity than is available to the novelist. William Dobell portrayed the philosopher, John Anderson, at a particular time of life, yet even then there was an opportunity for summary generalisation; for not everything can be said even about the life of a face. As Lord Macaulay put it: 'No picture, then, and no history, can present us with the whole truth: but those are the best pictures and the best histories which exhibit such parts of the truth as most nearly produce the effect of the whole' (Macauley 1828: 76).

Macaulay's judgement is in the nature of an aesthetic one, and I believe he is right in this. For the effects of a whole are not something that can be falsified. They can only be assessed by personal judgement. This is one of the paradoxes of historical writing. The more the historian conceptualises, and conceptualisation lies at the heart of the art, the less the work becomes available to tests of falsification. It should be possible to exchange most of the facts in a fine historical work, such as Huizinga's *Waning of the Middle Ages* for a parallel set, and for them to sustain similar conclusions, the main events of the book, remaining relatively unimpaired. Yet it wouldn't be the same book, for though facts tend to be typical and events unique, they do much, linked as they are, in an intricate network of causation, to determine the character of the whole. The historian is involved in what has been called a hermeneutic circle.

Yet there is much in the historian's art that is falsifiable. Unitary occurrences, such as when and where a death occurred, are readily falsifiable. 'It's a duty not a virtue', someone said, 'to get the facts right'. A causal relation can be disputed and shown to be false. Yet historical works that are more than annals of events resist falsification. We would not be likely to say that Joseph Needham's *Science and Civilisation in China* is true; we might want to say it's the best book on the subject. Because, although a history is a work whose purpose it is to tell the truth, it's also a work of art; and we do not judge a work of art wholly in terms of its intentions. It might be more honest to say that we judge it in terms of our intentions or, less cynically, by its value for us and others.

The problem of truth and history brings us close to the question 'Who owns the past?'. For it is precisely those who would claim that an historical work, such as the *Authorized Version* or the *Short History of the Communist Party of the Soviet Union* (Bolshevik), contains the whole truth, who are inclined to lay proprietorial claims upon the interpretation of the past, in the hope of thereby controlling the future, with the aid of their history.

But I must leave that question with you and turn to one distinction in the arts that may further help us clarify the historian's relation to the past. This is the distinction between art objects that exist in material form, such as a building or a battleship, and art objects, like a poem or a scientific theory, that transcend material form. These latter cannot exist wholly in the minds of their producers, or at least not for long; yet neither do they exist wholly in the texts, scores, and performances in which they are recorded or by which they are reenacted. They survive in a transcendant form between the mental and physical worlds, like an electric current between two terminals.

Transcendant works elude possession. A poet cannot physically possess his poem after he has written it down, though he may have some claims on its subsequent use. It will begin a transcendant life in its readings, as indeed anything written down may. But a painter does possess his painting and may sell it. Destroy it and something essential is destroyed. Yet I would not want to make a sharp distinction between transcendant and physical art. Both may and do take on both physical and transcendant aspects in order to survive. If Warsaw is destroyed it can be built much as it was; if the Francois Vase is smashed to pieces it can be put together again and reproduced in innumerable books and reproductions. If Courbet's *Stonebreakers* disappears in the Dresden raid we have at least reproductions, so that something is preserved. Increased technological power in the replication of art has weakened the distinction between its physical and transcendant forms, so that they are better seen as two aspects of art rather than as two kinds of art.

Now these two aspects of art may help us understand the secondary usages to which historians put works of art in the process of creating their own.

For the historian, the transcendant reveals itself in tradition; which is what is left after all the listening and learning, the looking and the reading has ended. It is a kind of perception in which the past is perceived in the disguise of the present. When Gibbon heard the friars singing he heard the past in the present, which is a different thing from going to the past for one's sources. Gibbon's awareness of the past became immediately available to him in the act of perception. In one respect it was like any other act of perception in which concepts acquired in the past are associated with sense impressions in the order to plan a course of action. And it is to tradition that the historian turns to plan his or her kind of action; that is to say, it is the conceptualising, generative, side of the art. In a formal sense only is the historian's medium language, which is shared with several other kinds of literary artist. In a substantial sense the historian's medium is tradition, an inchoate apprehension of the past in the present that has to be worked in order to provide the insights, inspirations, intuitions that mould and shape the history. I don't want to suggest that it's homogeneous. It may be perceived as sacred, to be defended against heresy; as tribal or national, to be defended against the intruder or foreigner; as the triumph or decline of order and good government; as the oppressive hegemony of a dominant class, or as a kind of communion with heroes and liberators. To put it simply tradition provides the historian with a point of view and it cannot be avoided any more than the air he or she breathes. As William Blake might have put it: the potter, clay; the historian, tradition.

But you can't prove a thing with a point of view. In order to assemble those networks of causation that provide the scientific groundwork of the art, the historian must turn to the physical aspects of the art objects available, to what has come to be called heritage; to texts, statistical tables, pictures and monuments, that can be used as evidence and quoted in the footnotes. It is to heritage that the historian turns for the facts. Myth and legend may be evolved entirely from tradition; to write history one has recourse to heritage.

With these distinctions in mind let us return to the question, 'Who owns the past?'. Consider tradition. Traditions are normally perceived as corporate and integrated structures; so that claims on a traditional past are rarely made by individuals. But groups, tribes, sects, nations, international organisations do claim the right to own or protect particular traditions. A sect may claim sole right to the performance of certain rituals and cermonies and proscribe their performance by outsiders as profanation or blasphemy. A nation may perceive itself to be the god-selected protector of freedom and liberty and condemn other nations possessed of different political systems as tyrannous. But traditions because of their transcendant character are difficult to withhold from others. It's like trying to own the wind. So all technologically advanced societies have tended to transform their traditions into possessible entities, largely through the establishment of institutions, of which law is perhaps the prime example. By means of codes, case-law, constitutions, legislation and so forth, law as an institution transforms tradition into art objects, which in their totality, become potent rationalisations of past behaviour, by means of which, it is possible both to predict and, in some measure, control future behaviour. In this law is the archetypal human institution. All other institutions whether political, cultural or religious, are engaged, in accord with their own practices, in similar activities. Seen in this light, 'Who owns the past?' is another way of asking 'Who makes claims to order and control the future?'.

At this point we might consider the question whether the writing of history exercises an influence upon the future. Some years ago Sir Karl Popper developed an influential argument to show that it is impossible on logical grounds to predict the course of history. This has been taken in some quarters to mean that history can exercise little or no influence at all, or even make rough but useful guesses at to what might occur in the future. Popper argued that 'if there is such a thing as growing human knowledge, then we cannot anticipate today what we shall know only tomorrow' (1957: x). Put in that way the statement is not so much a truth as a tautology. But there is also an implicit assumption that innovative knowledge operates uniformly over the whole field of knowledge. But this is not so, and where innovative knowledge does not operate there lies the possibility for recurrent human behaviour. Furthermore, innovative knowledge is itself often inspired and promoted in order to forestall and block undesired predictables. Much social history in alliance with medical science and social legislation could be explained in this way; as in the health control of socially related diseases. It was this application of new knowledge to undesired recurrent behaviour that Marx, surely, had in mind when he talked about progress from the realm of necessity to the realm of freedom (1975, III: 296–97).

Popper's arguments are not to be taken as proof that history cannot influence events but as a salutory warning to historians that they should not allow their hopes and fears for the future to affect the quality of their judgements. This is a question of honesty or dishonesty in the workplace. But if they possess no hopes or fears for the future I doubt whether their work will ever be worth much. Both the Day of Judgement and the Golden Age are buried deeply in most traditions; and the historians who catch an occasional glimpse of them write the influential and powerful histories.

Some historians, it is true, believe that historical writing should be confined to the explanation of unique events, avoid long-term trends and recurrent social behaviour; that this is the sociologist's, or some other social scientist's, concern. But as I hinted earlier I do not take these opinions seriously. They sound to me like demarcation disputes between the members of rival trade unions.

Historians cannot predict the future and should not attempt to. Nor should they deny that their work will affect the way the future is perceived and planned for, and possible occurrences confronted if they do occur, with the knowledge of the past that historians provide. We don't know precisely when wars or revolutions will occur; but we can expect them to occur. And it would be hopelessly naive to imagine that military strategists and revolutionaries do not study the histories of war and revolution in an attempt to mould the course of new ones. They are doing it all the time.

Existing is to a very large extent predicting. When I wait on the pavement for the traffic to pass I predict what will happen if I don't, automatically. Most historians begin writing history by predicting that if they do it well a university will give them a higher degree. Between that kind of prediction and the influence of Augustine's *City of God* on the course of European history there is a great gulf, but it is a matter of degree not of kind. The reason, I suspect, why this question of the historian's influence is so misunderstood is because history is not a blueprint for the future, like an annual budget. The work enters tradition and becomes a part of it; and, as I said earlier, you can not quote tradition in the footnotes.

It is interesting to survey historical explanation in terms of the competing claims of tradition and heritage. Explanations embodied in myth, legend and epic are sustained largely by oral transmission in which physical objects play a smaller role. Which is not to say that sacred sites and sacred objects are not of the greatest importance in the reinforcement of belief. But in such cases tradition does not appeal to heritage to prove the truth; both are bound within a common belief structure. By contrast, written history depends upon a heritage of written records to sustain its veracity. This is not surprising, because throughout written history most historians have preferred, following the potent example set by the compilers of myth, legend and history, to tell the story of man as actor: as warrior, ruler, legislator or powerful cleric; and such men of action characteristically leave written records. Records that record their actions. Indeed this has remained the dominant kind of historical writing down to the present day.

During the Enlightenment however some historians began to write history not as the history of greatness and power, but as the history of production. There may well have been a liberation ethic at work here, if not a certain narcissicism, for historians were themselves artists and producers rather than actors on the world stage. These new historians began to write economic and social history, archaeologists began to study the material remains of the past, becoming historians of production, *faute de mieux*, and others began to write the history of literature, philosophy, the arts, and so forth. In consequence a much more representative account of the human past came to be assembled. For in a world in which the vast majority were illiterate, historians who had depended exclusively upon written records, had tended to write histories for the literate and, more often than not, about the literate.

It was the economic historians who first effectively broke through this linguistic monopoly by making effective use of mathematics, that most precise of arts, in their investigations. And the colour of their accounts began to take on the colour of their techniques. Like the astronomers, who found cyclic behaviour in the economic past; trade cycles and long term trends. It began a new phase of predictive social investigation that continues.

For the economic historian, however, production is a means to an end. Indeed, someone defined economics as the study of ends and scarce means. The events of economic history are expressed in terms of market forces within a framework (a grammar if you like) of production, exchange and distribution. Neither the formative or imaginative design aspects of production nor its technical aspects *per se* are of central concern to the economic historian. The economist's approach to production is instrumentalist: things are produced because they are needed. It was left to the historians of the arts to approach the act of production aesthetically, as a pleasant activity, a shaping and forming activity, of value and interest as human behaviour apart from the fulfilment of needs. To take acts of production themselves as historic events was something of a novelty.

But their model, it could be claimed, lay in an archetypal event of some historic significance, if indeed it is true that *Homo erectus* became human in the long process of learning to make things and teaching himself and herself to speak.

There's so much misunderstanding, however, about the use of art objects as historic events, that a few comments may be helpful. It's not the art historian's business to worship the icon or even to admire it. It's not the art historian's business to frame set pieces of art criticism within a loose chronological framework, though such hybrids between history and criticism may possess some pedagogical value. It is because of such misunderstandings that art historians are sometimes viewed as philistines devoted to unweaving human rainbows. But historians in general have always at their best maintained a tough-minded attitude to their material ever since they began to distinguish the practice of their own art from that of myth-making. As with all historians, the art historian's values are implicit in the choice of events and the facts advanced in their construction. If the art historian's values as a whole are in question they are best discerned in their choice of art objects, as distinct from other forms of human activity, from which to construct events and write their histories.

This is not to say that the activities of production that end in art objects are any more admirable in themselves than other kinds of human activity. One does not avoid moral issues by focussing on the production process. Art is what art is for. For even in the very processes of production the purpose remains visible in the design though sometimes one must look hard and long for it; the function gives rise to the form in nuclear warheads as in Renaissance *cassoni*.

The extension of historical interest from men as warriors, rulers and legislators to a wider interest in human kind as producers has provided a more representative and diverse picture of human activity. But with this benefit has come attendant cost. History studied as a scientific pursuit and history as production have greatly increased the need for collecting art objects of all kinds because it is from heritage, as we noted, that historians derive their evidence. In the process an increasing reification of tradition and of morality has set in. Art historians, archaeologists, anthropologists and others who make universalist claims can and do destroy the traditions of technologically weaker societies. The traditional history of one society is thus absorbed into the universal heritage history of the more powerful society.

I have argued – when I have not simply asserted – that through memory we possess direct access to a personal past. That tradition provides an indirect and metaphorical means by which that personal past may be extended into a social past, by means of which we become aware of that sociality we share with others. It is by means of tradition that we commune with the myths of our society – or must I say the social formations from which we emerge and to which we adhere. But it is only through heritage that myth is provided with the acceptable scientific face that modern societies demand. By means of heritage as our field and history as our process of enquiry we set out to construct coherent and more or less testable accounts of the past.

Historians need access to heritage in order to write their histories. But as modern society becomes increasingly conscious of its historic past the art objects that constitute heritage undergo a strange transformation, a transformation that takes place at the moment of displacement from art object to historic object. That is why aesthetic valuing appropriate to the primary act of production is so often confused with the historian's secondary usage of art objects. In the cause of their secondary usage art objects are removed from the temporal flux and every attempt is made to retain them in their condition at the moment of their displacement from art to heritage – like a foetus taken from a womb and put in ice. Curators and conservators are then employed to guard the objects in their acquired, timeless conditions.

At this point accessibility, so essential to historians, begins to become problematic. Sometimes the historic objects will be removed from the eyes of laymen because the dirt in their fingers or the warmth in their bodies might damage the objects. They become available only in their replications or in the artfully and historically devised settings created by their guardians. Safeguarded by thermostatic controls and high security provisions they approach the new sanctity of pricelessness. In such situations the writing of history becomes increasingly the history of sacred and timeless property. The heroic traditions of myth are exchanged for the priceless heritage of history, an art that in its turn becomes increasingly a function of the laws relating to property.

I would not want to make too much of these encroaching dangers but they are worth noting. One of my most cherished memories is of a fine, still morning of late autumn in the Dordogne when my wife and I – mere tourists – were conducted around the Lascaux Caves by its two young discoverers. But I expect that if I wanted to return today I should have to attempt to establish the fact that I too have a right to be numbered among the Guardians.

I've not attempted to comment on the specific problems outlined in our brief to contributors because it seems to me that the relative claims of the sacred versus the secular, the needs of science and of tradition, the national versus the international, and so on, are empirical matters that cannot be decided by general principle but can only be resolved after a careful consideration of particular contexts and circumstances. Tact, caution, the effort to understand is needed on both sides.

References

Macauley, Lord (1828), 'History', *Edinburgh Review*, May 1828, in Stern, F. *The Varieties of History: From Voltaire to the Present*, Meridian Books, London, 1956, 71–89.

Marx, K. and Engels, F. (1975), *Collected Works*, vol. 3, International Publishers, New York.

Popper, Karl (1957), *The Poverty of Historicism*, Routledge and Kegan Paul, London.

Ranke, L. von (1885), Preface to *Histories of the Latin and Germanic Nations from 1494–1514*, 3rd edn, in Stern, F. *The varieties of History: from Voltaire to the Present*, Meridian Books, London, 1956, 54–62.

Smith, Bernard (1976), 'Art and industry: a systematic approach', in *The Antipodean Manifesto: Essays in Art and History*, Oxford University Press, Melbourne, 140–56.

5

A Question of Values

Museums and Cultural Property

John Mulvaney

The dedicatory inscription at the entrance to Mexico's imposing National Museum of Anthropology symbolizes the official Mexican understanding of its past and of its relevance to the present.

The Mexican nation erects this monument in honor of the great cultures that flourished during the pre-Columbian era in regions that now form part of the Republic of Mexico.

In the presence of the vestiges of those cultures, contemporary Mexico pays tribute to indigenous Mexico, in whose expression it discerns the characteristics of its national identity.

In the museum's guidebook, its director elaborated this concept with his affirmation, 'that modern day Mexico is the result of a fusion of two old and diverse cultures, and that it is this indissoluble mixture which gives Mexico its unique national character' (Vazquez 1968: 12–13). To judge from the importance of museums in Mexico City, it seems evident that the Mexican government assumes that *all* Mexicans are heirs to and owners of their past 'cultural property' (to adopt UNESCO terminology).

The plan for the Museum of Australia, which was released this month, proclaims a comparable philosophy (Museum of Australia 1983: 2). Its purpose is to be 'a museum with which every Australian can identify'; it should exhibit 'with vigour and objectivity, using our collective heritage to promote the consciousness and self-knowledge which foster a mature national identity'. My personal commitment to this unitary museological conception of our multicultural inheritance has been stated previously (Mulvaney 1980 and 1981). I suspect, however, that it might not gain immediate acceptance by all Australians, whether of Aboriginal or of European descent.

In order to provoke you meanwhile, I remind you of the thoughtful comment of American historian, Robin Winks, when contributing to a symposium on 'the future of the past'. 'The ways in which people view their past', he observed, 'are to a considerable extent reflected in those objects that they choose to preserve as reminders of themselves' (1976: 141). What objects have Australians preserved? Until recently, mementos of war rather than peace? Of pastoral mateship which excluded foreigners and Aborigines? Of minority rural sheepmasters rather than majority urban workers?

Certainly, the 1974–75 Inquiry on Museums and National Collections found Australian governments to be largely uncaring about museums and the preservation of the material evidence from the past. Although there have been impressive changes during the past few years, the significance of preserving the past remains a question of values and of priorities. If, a generation ago, 'Whelan the Wrecker' typified urban attitudes towards 'development', the same drive for 'progress' – despite the cultural costs – still attracts popular support today, whether in the cause of demolishing a rare Martin Place building or in drowning the Franklin valley.

Bernard Smith investigates in his contribution the meaning of 'the past'. My emphasis is upon the implications of its 'ownership'. Quite separate from any legal title to real estate or to chattels, a wide spectrum of emotional ties and subjective but compelling concepts may link people with places or objects. The complexity of 'ownership' and the claims urged to substantiate it, are evident in the current debates about southwestern Tasmania. In what sense does the region 'belong' to the world community, or to the Australian nation, to the Tasmanian state or to its majority of voters, to a statutory authority, to all Australian Aborigines or to the Tasmanian Aboriginal people?

Cultural property began leaving Australia in 1623, when Jan Carstenz collected ethnographic items on a Cape York beach; significantly, he also shot some of their owners (Mulvaney 1977: 263). During the last century and the early twentieth century, Aboriginal artefacts left the colonies in quantity, either in private collections or as government gifts or museum exchanges. Of the thousands of artefacts which left Australia, possibly only one major collection was returned. This large assemblage of wooden artefacts was sent from Beechworth to the Paris Exhibition of 1878, with the unusual condition that it was only a loan (Cooper 1975). It is probable that no Aboriginal artefact of wood or other perishable material in any Australian museum pre-dates about 1840, while they are rare even up to 1870. This means that traditional life was extinguished in many areas before Australian museums were able to collect representative specimens. However, some specimens from these areas do survive overseas from these early contact periods and the case for the repatriation of some of them seems strong.

The fact should be remembered, however, that these items only survived because they *were* transported overseas. Our museums were established later, while even the Australian Museum, now over 150 years old, lost its ethnographic collection in a fire in 1882. Lack of conservation techniques, low budgets and sporadic interest during the early years of other museums did little to amass ethnographic collections. It is relevant, also, that museums are a Western institution. Aboriginal society held different values, and rather than collecting and storing artefacts, these often involved the destruction of creative works immediately following their use in ceremonies, or upon the deaths of their owners. It is worth noting that the first bark paintings to be collected in Arnhem Land in the nineteenth century were simply drawings on the walls of impermanent bark shelters (Groger-Wurm 1973: 4). Except for the case of certain sacred items, therefore, preservation of the material past for the instruction of future generations was not a feature of Aboriginal culture. Consequently, Aboriginal people may come to acknowledge the good fortune that European collectors preserved fragments of their cultural heritage.

I have emphasized these Australian factors in order to highlight the parallels between the history of Aboriginal relics and that of European archaeology. There is not the time to trace how the trickle of classical treasures to Western Europe in the seventeenth century become a flood of antiquities from all parts of the world during the nineteenth century. It is epitomized by two authors. Seton Lloyd described the Mesopotamian scene during the last century as 'a scramble for antiquities' (1947: 145–61); Brian Fagan simply titled his recent study *The Rape of the Nile* (1977).

The British Museum appears beleaguered today as the citadel of expropriated colonial cultural heritage, as exemplified by demands for the restitution of the Elgin marbles, the beard of the sphinx and Benin bronzes. Perhaps its isolation is unfortunate, because other European bastions appear to have escaped major siege. Surely the Louvre's Venus de Milo, the Code of Hammurabi and Southeast Asian sculptures are equally redolent of cultural colonialism?

It is easy to blame the destructive giants of early archaeological discovery and to condemn the concentration of the cultural patrimony of other nations in European cities. It is understandable that righteous demands are made for the repatriation of relics. Yet it also is fair to acknowledge that, in many instances, their preservation depended upon their removal. This familiar argument is advanced by the British Museum in defence of the Elgin Marbles.

It is evident that a high proportion of these archaeological depredations, including most of the renowned masterpieces, are exhibited to the public, or are available for research, under conditions of security and reasonable conservation. Left in their countries of origin they may have suffered destruction, or been housed quite unsuitably and so ensured the same end.

These realities may not justify their retention by such institutions today, but it does distinguish them from relics on today's rapacious investment market. This aspect largely seems to be overlooked by many ardent nationalists who direct their attention to past symbols rather than to ongoing depredations. Modern looting is facilitated by contemporary greed and technology, ranging from bulldozers to electronics, and it is fuelled by the poverty of depressed indigenous peasants for whom grave robbing provides a means of existence. The likes of Indiana Jones today destroy sites more ruthlessly than the reviled enthusiastic but misguided early archaeologists.

It was observed recently of Central America that 'not since the . . . Conquistadors ravaged these countries . . . have the Maya been so plundered' (Torres de Arauz 1982: 136). Ecuador's officials recently discovered smuggling on a massive scale, which included the activities of a foreign diplomat (Zaldumbide 1982: 132). Karl Meyer's *The Plundered Past* is a brilliant exposé of the scale of rackets in this nefarious antiquities traffic (1973). The point to emphasize is that, unlike nineteenth-century appropriations, most of these relics remain in the hands of private collectors or dealers. The mode of their acquisition requires secrecy and the destruction of their spatial and stratigraphic context; such objects may remain uncatalogued, unresearched and unseen.

Over the last three decades, the response to this pillage of the past has been evident at both the national and the international levels; it coincides with a conscious search for national or cultural identity by third and fourth world peoples. It is appropriate first to consider the international response and its rationale, in order to set national or sectional attitudes into perspective.

The Hague Convention of 1954, for the protection of cultural property in the event of armed conflict, established the conceptual basis for subsequent UNESCO conventions, when it affirmed that 'damage to cultural property belonging to any people whatsoever means damage to the cultural heritage of all mankind since each people makes its contribution to the culture of the world'. Its definition included movable property.

The 1960 UNESCO recommendation concerning the protection of cultural property endangered by public or private works expressed similar sentiments (quoted *Report on the National Estate* 1974: 25). These were given specific application during that year over moves to rescue Abu Simbel from the waters of the Nile. In launching an appeal for funds, UNESCO's director-general anticipated a dilemma facing Australians today in the dispute over another proposed dam. How should the Egyptian government, he asked, 'choose between the needs and welfare of their people and the treasures which belong not only to their country but to humanity as a whole?' (*UNESCO Courier* February 1960: 3). 'It is not easy to choose between temples and crops', he stated elsewhere, 'These monuments . . . do not belong solely to the countries which hold them in trust. The whole world has a right to see them endure. They are part of a common heritage which comprises Socrates' message and the Ajanta frescoes . . . Treasures of universal value are entitled to universal protection' (Chamberlin 1979: 178).

This philosophy, as applied to immovable property, was embodied, in 1964, in the International Charter for the Conservation and Restoration of Monuments and Sites (the Venice Charter of ICOMOS), and later the supreme cultural and natural heritage properties were embraced by the 1972 World Heritage Convention. It was the turn of movable objects in 1970, when UNESCO adopted the Convention on the Means of Prohibiting and Preventing the Illicit Import, Export and Transfer of Ownership of Cultural Property (Burnham 1974: 184). It emphasized 'that the interchange of cultural property among nations for scientific, cultural and educational purposes increases the knowledge of the civilization of Man, enriches the cultural life of all peoples and inspires mutual respect and appreciation among nations'.

A positive attempt to halt looting and illegal traffic in relics was initiated during the same year. The Pennsylvania University Museum and Harvard University took the lead in declaring that their institutions would purchase no items in future, unless they were provided with a pedigree of legal ownership, details of context and other data (Meyer 1973: 254–59). The Pennsylvania Declaration piously urged effective national legislation, the policing of sites and the control of trade in relics. It concluded that, despite its significance for the world community, 'the preservation of the cultural heritage for mankind as a whole is, in fact, a domestic problem for all nations' (Meyer 1973: 255).

The doctrine relating to cultural property at the international level embodies three notions. Firstly, that at one level of 'ownership', the relics of the past belong to the heritage of all people. Secondly, that international understanding and mutual tolerance can be promoted through this common inheritance. The final concept, however, accepts that a national cultural identity is desirable and that it can be fostered through the influence of the individual national inheritance.

Consequently, despite the pan-world sentiments of these conventions in respect to movable property, there is an assumption that any nation may be placed at disadvantage if its cultural property has been dispersed, so that it is unable to promote its own cultural identity through their exhibition (Lewis 1981: 4–7). Indeed, in November 1978, UNESCO established an Intergovernmental Committee to promote and advise on the return of cultural property to its country of origin, or its restitution in cases of illicit appropriation.

High-sounding sentiments also are expressed at the national level, and it is necessary to examine their implications. Not surprisingly, philosophies differ between nations holding rich museum collections and those which do not; the 'have-nots' also refer cynically to the 'very liberal interpretation' of UNESCO codes, adopted by some museums who nominally subscribe to them. They also point to the contradiction that developing countries, who seek the return of heritage items, simply cannot afford to bid for them on the commercial market. The more that 'primitive art' and ethnographic items become fashionable to collect, or become useful tax-evasion investments, the more difficult it becomes for the donor country (Edwards and Stewart 1980: 167, 171, 181–82). Even a country such as New Zealand cannot afford to compete on the world market. The recent adverse decision in the Ortiz case, where the British High Court judged that smuggled archaeological material should not be returned, does not encourage optimism (Edwards and Stewart 1980: 173).

The alternative to open purchase of private collections, is to negotiate for the repatriation of public collections. This naturally involves a conflict of loyalties amongst those museologists sympathetic to third world needs, but conscious of the cultural and scientific importance of their holdings (see Wilson's discussion pp. 99ff) and Gathercole 1981). The British Museum has been forced to enunciate its case for retaining its collections intact. Although the Trustees favour ratification of the 1970 UNESCO Convention, it may be significant that the United Kingdom has not done so; neither has it become a signatory nation to the World Heritage Convention.

Proponents of the *status quo* in the British Museum (but the same applies to all major Western institutions), urge the better prospects for conservation, their superior curation, storage, security and research facilities and the enormous public visitation. It is understandable that some donor countries see the irony of these realities. As one of them stated recently at a symposium entitled *Lost Heritage*: 'If you, the formerly predominant powers, instead of helping yourselves to these objects and taking them to your own countries, had provided the facilities and the specialists locally, those objects could have been preserved in our countries and that is where we would now find them' (Stétié 1981: 9).

An African has noted that scholars who are trained in Europe may return home with a knowledge of just how valuable certain objects are to the culture of their country of origin. An Indian critic observed that visitor numbers to see key Indian artefacts could prove even higher in populous India than in Europe – 'and they would have a greater meaning as well' (Kumar 1981: 18).

Other British arguments rely upon legal status, for it requires an Act of Parliament to deregister material (see Wilson's discussion, p. 100). Some question the legality of returning material to a modern state, given that state boundaries and regimes have changed since the item was removed. Obviously, such problems are real, but they should not prove beyond solution. Another standard case, concerns the 'universal heritage' contained within great museums (Lewis 1981: Gathercole 1981a: 2). 'To us', a British Museum curator claimed, 'the museum is not a mirror of national identity but a reflection of the universal heritage of man' (Rankine 1981: 18).

David Wilson, its embattled director, claims that the British Museum is a custodian for the heritage of many peoples; that to alienate collections and to return them under present UNESCO undertakings is dangerous, because UNESCO policies or national agreements may be reversed in the future. Perhaps his chief concern, however, is precedent: 'If you start to nibble at the . . . collection by taking away even one or two objects there would soon be a flood of applications for the return of materials . . . This would create a situation which would be sad for universal institutions and for the concept of universal culture . . .' (Wilson 1981: 18).

But universal culture appears an abstract and specious subterfuge to those for whom the artefacts possess a deeper emotive significance. Mr Michael Somare expressed his feelings as a New Guinean in his message to a Canadian symposium on Oceanic art:

We are people. We do not like the way in which we have been regarded as passive objects of research and study by experts. We view our masks and our art as living spirits with fixed abodes.

I would ask you to co-operate with us in returning our ancestral spirits and souls to their homes . . . (Edwards and Stewart 1980: 175)

The Chairman of the UNESCO Intergovernmental Committee expressed similar sentiments:

For a cultural artifact . . . is not merely something which is more or less dead, beautiful and scientific; something which is put in a showcase in a marvellous museum . . . It is something that, for a particular people, is a living thing which enables a people to achieve confidence in itself . . . (Stétié 1981: 8)

Would the flood gates really open if key items were returned? In my opinion the moral case is so strong for the return of some objects, that the major institutions will be unable to ignore the precedents already established by some lesser museums. Prominent amongst these is the Cambridge University Museum of Archaeology and Anthropology, which has drawn up comprehensive, but firm, guidelines for considering any request for repatriation (see *Coma*, Bulletin of the Conference of Museum Anthropologists 8 (1981): 23–24). It is relevant that some Australian museums have repatriated ethnographic objects to Papua New Guinea and the consequences have proved mutually beneficial. Aboriginal communities also have received back specified items of great ritual significance. There has been no sign of flooding to date. It would be unrealistic, however, not to assume that those artefacts selected for return will constitute the supreme and unique treasures. With the development of improved techniques of replication, however, retention of a replica by the institution which returns cultural property under guidelines such as those referred to above, goes some way towards answering a number of the problems posed. It would not solve the problem of the Elgin Marbles.

Neither can it resolve the vexed issue of human skeletal remains. In the face of demands for the return of excavated human bones for burial, it is necessary to apply comparable guidelines to those mentioned for cultural property. It is necessary to emphasize the scientific importance of ancient bones of any race, and of the medical, dietary and cultural inferences which may flow from their analysis. It also is a matter of elementary ethics that persons of known historic identity should not be disinterred without the permission of kin. The barbarity perpetrated upon William Lanne's corpse cannot justify the retention of his head in any museum under any code of ethics. Because ancient bones may need to be re-examined as the passage of time brings new investigative techniques, the custodians to whom such remains are entrusted should be made aware, before final disposal, of their own potential responsibilities to future generations of their own people. Total destruction of human remains now, for example by cremation, may come to be regarded as vandalism by future generations of the custodians; careful reburial may prove a more appropriate practice.

Like the Mexican National Museum of Anthropology, the Director of the Papua New Guinea Museum, Mr G. Mosuwadoga, envisages his institution as playing a key function in the cultural heritage of his nation:

> . . . to provide adequate facilities to review the material culture and arts for the village people and scholars; to look upon the museum as a united cultural institution for all the ethnic groups; to establish it as a monument to the past and a source of inspiration for the future culture of Papua New Guinea. (Edwards and Stewart 1980: 157)

It is more challenging to attain a similar goal for our museum in Canberra, or any other Australian museum. It can be achieved if non-Aboriginal Australians give sympathetic and serious consideration to the position of Aborigines in Australian society. I emphasize that, apart from international and national models of the past and of its present uses, there exist also sectional versions. The creation of the Museum of Australia could foster the development of mutual respect for the *positive* achievements of the two cultures which interacted so tragically, by recognising the special involvement of Aborigines with their own past.

The attitude of some Aborigines was stated forcefully over a decade ago by Paul Coe, and its relevance to our present concerns is evident.

> On the platform with me were people from Mozambique, FRELIMO as well as other Southeast African liberation movements. There were also American Indians. I explained to them that the Aboriginal movement should be classified as a liberation movement rather than a civil rights movement or a land rights movement and that in fact we had been colonized just as forcefully and arrogantly as anyone else in Africa or in the States. The only difference between us and the African people is that they happen to be in the majority. Therefore it is regarded as a civil rights movement. This is a point that is not clearly understood by most people and it should be emphasized. The reason why Papua New Guinea is becoming an independent nation is that they retained their culture and identity, and more importantly, they are still the majority. (Gilbert 1973: 111–12)

Bernard Smith grasped the importance of such perceptions in his 1980 Boyer lectures, when he referred to 'a stubborn and courageous, though usually quiet and passive refusal, maintained for two centuries, to allow their own culture and spirituality to be absorbed completely into the white culture of Australia' (1980: 40). Simply because the majority of Australians do not perceive of Aboriginal society and its aspirations in that manner does not make it any less real (Compare the situation in the United States of America,

Nason 1973: 1–3 and Viola 1978: 143–8). Museologists and those in related academic disciplines must win acceptance from Aboriginal communities on equal terms; they must convince them that, not only are their interests positively safeguarded from amalgamation into European culture, but that they are involved in all facets of museum activities, in their role as custodians of their cultural material. If their custodianship is acknowledged, I believe that many confrontationist situations will disappear; comprehension of the international and national value of their cultural heritage can come only with mutual respect and positive educational activities. I agree with Bruce Trigger that, as in America, archaeologists should be wary of converting the Australian field into one whose justification is the testing of models or the search for analogues, which assist reconstruction of other people's prehistory. The existence of possible evidence for symbolic and cognitive systems or spiritual values within past Aboriginal societies needs prime emphasis. The study of prehistoric rock art, which may encapsulate such data, merits a higher research status than that accorded by most Australian prehistorians. Ironically, the other crucial source for insights into such conceptual aspects is the analysis of mortuary practices and grave goods, matters which find little favour with Aborigines today.

Eric Willmot develops the theme of Aboriginal custodianship in this symposium, so I will not do so. I direct your thoughts, however, to this theme in other countries. Resonga Kaiku gave a comparable assertion of Papua New Guinean cultural identity, when he claimed, that foreign scholars when involved in future research in his country 'should stress that Papua New Guineans are the rightful custodians of their cultural heritage' (in Edwards and Stewart 1980: 180).

In reference to written records of American Indians, W.T. Hagan made an observation which is applicable to the totality of the evidence relating to the Aboriginal past across much of Australia: 'But think of the damage we can do the Indians. The historical Indian may be the captive of the archives, but the key to those archives is in the hands of non-Indian historians . . .' (Hagan 1978: 138–9). 'But, for the Native American this is more than just some intellectual game', he continued, again echoing the Australian scene:

What is at stake for the Indian is his historical identity, and all that can mean for self-image and psychological well being. At stake also is the very existence of tribes, and the validity of their claims to millions of acres of land and to compensation for injustices suffered in earlier transactions with the federal and state governments.

No Aboriginal person has stated the present problem more directly than did Ros Langford, when addressing the Australian Archaeological Association meeting in Hobart last year, which passed a resolution which 'acknowledges Aboriginal ownership of their heritage' (Allen 1983: 7–10).

The Issue is control. You seek to say that as scientists you have a right to obtain and study information of our culture. You seek to say that because you are Australians you have a right to study and explore our heritage because it is a heritage to be shared by all Australians, white and black. From our point of view we say – you have come as invaders, you have tried to destroy our culture, you have built your fortunes upon the lands and bodies of our people and now, having said sorry, want a share in picking out the bones of what you regard as a dead past. We say that it is our past, our culture and heritage and forms part of our present life. As such it is ours to control and it is ours to share on our terms. (Langford 1983: 2)

I conclude this survey of 'ownership' of the past, by reflecting that 'custodianship' is a much more appropriate term, because it allows for the concept of universal culture. It is salutary to close with the reflections of the Samoan scholar Albert Wendt. Although having a specific meaning for modern Samoa, they also have direct application to the Australian situation.

It will not do to over-glorify the past. The present is all that we have and we should live it out as creatively as possible. Pride in our past bolsters our self-respect which is necessary if we are to cope as equals with others. However, too fervent or paranoid an identification with one's culture – or what one deems to be that culture – can lead to racial intolerance and the like. This is not to claim that there are no differences between cultures and peoples. Or to argue that we abolish these differences. We must recognise and respect these differences but not use them to try to justify our racist claims to an imaginary superiority. (Edwards and Stewart 1980: 27)

References

Allen, J. (1983), 'Aborigines and archaeologists in Tasmania, 1983', *Australian Archaeology* 16, 7–10.

Burnham, B. (1974), *The Protection of Cultural Property*, International Council of Museums, Paris.

Chamberlin, E.R. (1979), *Preserving the Past*, Dent, London.

Committee of Inquiry on Museums and National Collections, *Museums in Australia 1975*, Australian Government Publishing Service, Canberra, 1975.

Committee of Inquiry into the National Estate, *Report on the National Estate*, Australian Government Publishing Service, Canberra, 1974.

Cooper, C.P. (1975), The Beechworth Collection of Aboriginal Artefacts, unpublished honours thesis, Department of Prehistory and Anthropology, Australian National University, Canberra.

Edwards, R. and Stewart, J. (eds) (1980), *Preserving Indigenous Cultures: A New Role for Museums*, Australian Government Publishing Service, Canberra.

Fagan, B.M. (1977), *The Rape of the Nile*, MacDonald and Jane's, London.

Gathercole, P. (1981) 'British University museums and the problems relating to restitution', *Lost Heritage*, Commonwealth Arts Centre and the Africa Centre, London, 11–14.

—— (1981a), 'The repatriation of ethnographic objects', 'Comment', *RAIN-Royal Anthropological Institute News* 46, October 1981, 2.

Gilbert, K.J. (1973), *Because a White Man'll Never Do It*, Angus & Robertson, Sydney.

Groger-Wurm, H.M. (1973), *Australian Aboriginal Bark Paintings and their Mythological Interpretation*, Australian Institute of Aboriginal Studies, Canberra.

Hagan, W.T. (1978), 'Archival captive – the American Indian', *The American Archivist* 41, 135–42.

Kaiku, R. (1980), 'Restoration of national cultural property: the case of Papua New Guinea', in Edwards, R. and Stewart, J. (eds), *Preserving Indigenous Cultures: A New Role for Museums*, Australian Government Publishing Service, Canberra, 175–183.

Kumar, C. (1981), panel discussion reported in *Lost Heritage*, Commonwealth Arts Centre and the Africa Centre, London, 18.

Langford, R. (1983), 'Our heritage – your playground', *Australian Archaeology* 16, 1–6.

Lewis, G. (1981), 'Lost heritage – some historical and professional considerations', *Lost Heritage*, Commonwealth Arts Centre and The Africa Centre, London, 4–7.

Lloyd, S. (1947), *Foundations in the Dust*, Oxford University Press, London.

Meyer, K. (1973), *The Plundered Past*, Hamilton, London.

Mulvaney, D.J. (1980), 'The proposed Gallery of Aboriginal Australia', in Edwards, R. and Stewart, J. (eds), *Preserving Indigenous Cultures: A New Role for Museums*, Australian Government Publishing Service, Canberra, 72–78.

—— (1981), 'What future for our past?', *Australian Archaeology* 13, 16–27.

—— (1977), 'Classification and typology in Australia', in Wright, R.V.S. (ed.), *Stone Tools as Cultural Markers*, Australian Institute of Aboriginal Studies, Canberra, 263–68.

Museum of Australia (1982), *The Plan for the Development of the Museum of Australia*, National Capital Development Commission, Canberra.

Nason, J.D. (1973), 'Finders keepers?', *Museum News*, March 1973, 1–3.

Rankine, J. (1981), panel discussion reported in *Lost Heritage*, Commonwealth Arts Centre and the Africa Centre, London, 18.

Smith, Bernard (1980), *The Spectre of Truganini*, ABC, Sydney.

Stétié, S. (1981), 'The view of UNESCO's Intergovernmental Committee', *Lost Heritage*, Commonwealth Arts Centre and the Africa Centre, London, 8–10.

Torres de Arauz, R. (1982), 'Museums and the containment of illicit traffic', *Museum* 34, 134–136.

Vazquez, P.D. (1968), *The National Museum of Anthropology, Mexico*, Alexis Gregory, New York.

Viola, H.J. (1978), 'American Indian cultural resources training program', *The American Archivist* 41, 143–48.

Wendt, A. (1980), 'Reborn to belong: culture and colonialism in the Pacific', in Edwards, R. and Stewart, J. *Preserving Indigenous Cultures: A New Role for Museums*, Australian Government Publishing Service, Canberra, 25–34.

Wilson, D. (1981), panel discussion reported in *Lost Heritage*, Commonwealth Arts Centre and the Africa Centre, London, 18, 24.

Winks, R. (1976), 'Conservation in America: national character as revealed by preservation', in Fawcett, J. (ed.), *The Future of the Past*, Thames & Hudson, London, 141–49.

Zaldumbide, R.P. (1982), 'Return and restitution of cultural property', *Museum* 34, 132–34.

6

Return and Restitution

A Museum Perspective

David Wilson

The purpose of this short paper is to put the case for the great international museums against claims for the return or 'restitution' of cultural property. In many ways claims for return are seen by the uninitiated as a battle between the third world and developed countries in which loaded terms – 'colonialism', 'loot' and 'booty' – are bandied about by the claimants and ostrich-like silence is maintained by those against whom claims are made. Journalistic sieving and selectivity do not help either side, whilst the strident tones adopted by some countries in international institutions (chiefly in UNESCO) cause rifts and divisions which are fuelled by politicians for home consumption or by career civil servants on international gravy trains.

A *cause célèbre* occasionally fans the embers into flame; an unthinking legal decision, a loosely worded professional statement, a ministerial witticism, or simple misreporting, can relight the beacon for a few sad days. All involved make mistakes. In the recent brouhaha concerning the Elgin Marbles, the Greek Minister of Culture played into the hands of the museum authorities by asking the British 'to make a sentimental and political gesture' by returning the Parthenon frieze to Athens. In an unconsidered moment – one in a series of interviews – I once asked why the Greeks concentrated on the Elgin Marbles and not on the Venus de Milo. I have had reason to regret that rhetorical question ever since.

There is so much that must be left unsaid. The museum curator must protect his colleagues in foreign countries, many of whom are only too well aware that the case that could be put by the old museums is substantial: they realize the political, commercial and venal background to some of the claims, but echo them so as not to put their careers, or those of their political masters, at risk. The diplomat fans the flames in public, while despising the arguments in private. On the other side the museum director in the developed world will keep his head down when his colleagues are attacked because he doesn't want to draw attention to his own problems. Sometimes in blowing his own top he blows other people's cases. Statements about inadequate conservation or control of the smuggling of antiquities are counter-productive, leading to pleas for cash or to accusations of patronizing colonial attitudes.

If I may intrude a personal note, I should say that it is impossible for me to write dispassionately on this subject. I have been at the receiving end of much strident criticism; I have been personally vilified and caricatured; I have had to give a great·deal of time and emotional energy to this problem and I foresee that for the rest of my active career I shall be involved increasingly in troublesome debate on this matter. I must also make it clear that the governors of my institution – who are rightly labelled 'Trustees' – and the government of my country have said that on no account will they return objects held by the British Museum to their country of origin, save under the terms provided for the British Museum Act of 1963. These terms allow the Trustees to dispose of duplicate material, or to lend objects.

The museum is in no way dog-in-the-manger about its holdings: there is absolutely free access to any part of the museum's collections by any person who can show that he needs it. The museum does not recognize any academic *Prioritätsrecht* in relation to its material and has never, to my knowledge, accepted any collection with conditions of restricted access. Further, as a government institution, its files, records and documents are available under the Public Records Acts of 1958 and 1967, so that within the limits of national security all documentation concerning the collections is open to any member of the public. Last, I should stress that the international service rendered by the British Museum to the academic world through its open-handed service to scholarship and to the general public through its loans system is practically unique. No museum publishes more widely or allows the scholar from outside to publish its material more freely. No museum services more international institutions with aid. The ideals expressed in a statement of the founding Trustees in 1753 remain at the core of the museum's belief today: 'The said Museum or Collection may be preserved and maintained, not only for the Inspection and Entertainment of the learned and the curious, but for the general Use and Benefit of the Public.' When idealists criticize the British Museum let them remember the British Museum's own ideals and measure them accordingly.

I have written at some length about the British Museum as it is one of the museums most under attack at the moment. It is worth pointing out what the British Museum is, does and means. It was founded under the will of Sir Hans Sloane in 1753, not as a museum of British antiquities but as a museum of universal knowledge in the spirit of the European Enlightenment and, although it has hived off two of its major sections (the library in 1973 and the natural history collections in 1880–83), it remains *au fond* true to this universal tradition. Established by Act of Parliament, it has been supported – at arm's length through its Trustees – by the British state ever since its foundation. It has been a major influence in world scholarship and remains to this day an enormously important reservoir of talent, material and knowledge in most fields of human endeavour. It has no oil paintings, little medieval or later Western sculpture, no Western furniture and no historical collections of the industrial revolution and later. Otherwise it collects all material culture. It represents a considerable investment of national resources, but in its turn attracts revenue to the country in the form of invisible tourist earnings. Its publications are without parallel in the museum world: its catalogues stretch in an unbroken tradition back to the eighteenth century and its publishing house has in the last few years strengthened that tradition. The museum has taken the computerization of its collections seriously and is, through this medium, already providing a unique service to scholarship. It is a great international institution.

There are other such institutions of which the Smithsonian Institution in Washington is perhaps the nearest in scope. But the Louvre, the Metropolitan Museum in New York and the State Hermitage Museum in Leningrad must also be ranged alongside it. The Berlin Museums, if reunited, would also be included. Whilst other museums (those in Peking, for example) may have more visitors, the museums named here have universal collections, actively curated and constantly growing. These are the museums which are truly international in scope and which service scholars throughout the world. Other museums and countries have big international collections: Rome, Copenhagen, Philadelphia, Budapest, Leipzig, Cleveland, Vienna and Stockholm for example. Others, Brussels and Amsterdam for example, have specialist collections of international importance. Many smaller museums in the developed world have important collections of material from foreign countries – the Benaki Museum in Athens, for example, has large Islamic collections originally formed in Egypt, the Topkapi Museum in Istanbul has the largest collection of Chinese ceramics outside China, whilst the ethnographic collections of the National Museum of Ireland include remarkable material from Africa and the Pacific. All over the developed world from Malibu to Moscow, from Florence to Oslo are important collections of comparative material with an origin outside national boundaries. These collections have many functions – to educate, to provide material for scholarly study and international understanding, to provide a comparative cultural yardstick. But it is the large international, *universal*, museums which concern me here for they must be treated as special cases in discussions concerning the return of cultural property.

First, let us examine such emotive words as 'loot' and 'plunder' which are used with abandon by the protagonists of 'restitution'. Throughout history man has been brutal to man, taking booty as a result of war. From the second century BC onwards we have records of booty taken by Romans, who carried it in triumph on their return from the wars: later, the Arch of Titus celebrates the sack of Jerusalem, portraying the objects brought to Rome. The Romans looted for wealth and for art. Cicero inveighed against such plunderers:

In our most beautiful and highly decorated city what statue, or what painting, is there which has not been taken and brought away from conquered enemies. But the villas of those men are adorned and filled with the spoils of our most faithful allies. Where do you think is the wealth of foreign nations, which they are now all deprived of, when you see Athens, Pergamos, Cyzicus, Miletus, Chios, Samos, all Asia in short, and Achaia, and Greece and Sicily, now all contained in a few villas. (*Verrine Orations*, Part II, V, 127)

At least the Romans appreciated what they collected. Less so did the migrating hordes that followed – the Goths, the Vandals and Germanic tribes of the north – who wanted precious metals and weapons and only occasionally appear to have collected out of curiosity. Not until Charlemagne, in an attempt to revive some of the spirit of the Roman Empire, did the collection of works of art start again as the new emperor embellished his cathedral at Aachen with sculptures and architectural fragments.

Looting on a grand scale started again in the Middle Ages. The Venetians led the sack of Constantinople in 1204 and a survival of the raid still stands – almost as a symbol of Venice – the four horses of Lysippus placed above the west door of St Mark's (horses which were themselves taken for a short holiday by Napoleon as part of another triumph). The material lost by the Burgundians to the Swiss in their flight from Grandson in 1476 was military booty *sensu strictu*, but it did include a considerable art collection as well as jewels and religious plate. The sack of Rome in 1527 was but the most remarkable and closely documented of the looting of the religious wars of the sixteenth century and provided booty as rich as that taken from Constantinople by the Venetians and the Crusaders, although the Raphael tapestries were returned as an act of piety by Anne de Montmorency: '*Urbe capta partem aulaeorum a praedonib. distractorum conquistam Annae Mommarancius Gallicae militae praef. resarciendam atque Julio III P.M. restituendam curavit, 1553*'. This inscription is on the border of the tapestry of St Paul at Athens in the Vatican.

Already the avid collector was making his selection of booty. Charles VIII of France in 1495 took much loot in Italy, including the famous library of the kings of Naples. In 1541 the Turks took Ofen and removed part of the famous library of Matthew Corvinus. But it was the seventeenth century which showed the world what looting meant. The Thirty Years War enriched the cultural holdings of the Swedish nation incredibly, not only in works of art and treasures (like the reliquary of St Elizabeth from Würzburg), but also in books and manuscripts which enriched not only private libraries, like that of Skokloster, but also the library of the great protestant university of Uppsala, which received books from Munich, Würzburg, Prague, Riga, Mainz, Fraucenburg and Braunsberg. The booty of Prague – pictures, coins and medals, objects of art – was enormous, perhaps, as one writer has suggested, never equalled as booty until the Second World War.

The French were the next to pillage on a grand scale, first looting the treasures of their own aristocracy as a result of the Revolution, and then adding more and more to the national treasure chest as a result of their foreign wars. Napoleon organized the plunder of the conquered nations with a thoroughness typical of that archetypal administrator. He appointed commissions of *savants* and particularly Dominique Denon, *l'emballeur*, who was but one of many who pillaged consistently for the glory of France. Much of the most famous loot was eventually returned – the horses of St Marco for example (to Venice, of course, not Constantinople) – but much remained in France, twelve of the finest Aachen columns are still today in the Louvre. But it is clear that the Revolution and Napoleonic wars stirred up an unparalleled mobility among European treasures. It was thus, for example, that the Rosetta Stone came to London – captured from the French after their Egyptian defeat. At the same time the great public collections of Paris provided a popular audience for art in a way never paralleled before.

This was also the period of the first great colonial wars in which loot was taken from India and the Far East. The treasure of Tipoo Sahib came to London, whilst in 1860 the sack of the Summer Palace in Peking by the French and British, joined in a destructive fury by Chinese rebels, reduced to nothing part of the great treasure of the Emperor of China. This was the period also of the plundering of Abyssinia and of various punitive expeditions in Africa (for example, Asante, Benin) which indirectly enriched further the European and American museums.

But consciences were stirring. The Hague Convention, national self-restraint, treaties and agreements, succeeded in keeping the loot of the First World War to a minimum. The behaviour of the *Einsatzstab Rosenberg* during the Second World War is, one trusts, the last example of official looting during war, although it must be admitted that Vietnam, Cambodia, Biafra and other countries have lost valuable material as the result of casual military looting, which one assumes can never be completely eradicated.

Who then owns what? As a result of European wars and pillage, the European heritage has been distributed more than once. There is little that one would wish to see returned to their original owners (who are they in any case?) or redistributed among the European treasuries and museums. But this self-satisfied attitude causes pain when one turns to the real feelings of ex-colonial people who feel a need to establish their national identity. Much of the material from Third World countries was not collected as a result of war or pillage. Much came as a result of gifts and barter, and of a genuine spirit of scientific enquiry by Europeans eager to know more about the people with whom they came into contact. Much was of no more value to the original owners than were the trinkets which they received in exchange from the collectors. According to the lights of the collectors of the period the material now housed in museums all over the world was acquired legally and with the full – even eager – permission of their owners. This is as true of the Elgin Marbles as of spears from Fiji. It is difficult to adjust modern terms to the morality of the past. Is the status of an eighteenth-century explorer (Captain Cook, for example) sent out with the best scientific credentials so different from the art dealer in the nineteenth and twentieth-century marketplace, creating collections for public and private enjoyment and consequently moving collections across continents and later oceans? If the scientific collection of the material culture of the vanishing primitive societies does not proceed, how can we even understand these societies? If the countries which govern these societies will not or cannot fund such collection, who can or should do it? If collections are made by foreigners, should the foreign museum be the ultimate depository, or should there be *partage* – and if there is *partage* where do you store the material? These are the simple and the unanswerable questions.

First, it should be emphatically stated that no museum should countenance looting in the modern world. Nor should they encourage in any way the illicit export of cultural objects. It is easy to condemn the illegal traffic in cultural objects, but it is impossible

Fig. 1

The Franklin River, southwestern Tasmania, entered on the list of World Heritage Areas in December 1982. Controversy over the future of this area with its intense beauty and vital natural and cultural resources dominated the Australian conservation, political and legal arenas for the first six months of 1983. Above the limestone cliffs bordering the river at this point lies Kutikina Cave. (Photograph: D.J. Mulvaney)

Fig. 2

The rich archaeological deposits in Kutikina Cave (formerly known as Fraser Cave) attest to occupation of the Franklin River area in the late Pleistocene, at a time before the rainforests colonized the region. At that time the environment would have been dominated by glacial activity, with the local vegetation predominantly of grassland and open forest. (Photograph: Rhys Jones)

Fig. 3

Symbol of the Hellenic past, the temple of Athena Parthenos on the Acropolis of Athens, completed under Pericles. Unrivalled as symbol and as an architectural masterpiece, it shows in this view from the northwest the ravages of the last three centuries. Of the sculptures of the pediment few survived the explosion of 1687, or the attentions of subsequent collectors; the metopes and frieze have suffered similar depredations. Natural hazards from acid rain and the cracking of the fabric from expansion of unshielded metal clamps used in earlier restorations, as well as the attentions of thousands of admiring tourists, all put this monument at risk. (Photograph: Isabel McBryde)

Fig. 4

Universal cultural heritage: officials and guests at the unveiling of a plaque to commemorate the entering of the Willandra Lakes Region, New South Wales, on the
list of World Heritage Areas, listen to Dr Jim Bowler, geomorphologist, explaining
the sequence of Pleistocene deposits on the Walls of China, context for finds of
early Australians. The circle includes Mr Neville Wran, Premier of New South
Wales and Professor Ralph Slatyer, Chairman of the UNESCO World Heritage
Committee, staff of the National Parks Service and Australian Heritage Commission with the editor of this volume as Acting Chairman of the Heritage Commission. (Photograph: Australian Information Service, print supplied by the
Australian Heritage Commission)

Fig. 5

'The issue is control': at the ceremony for the unveiling of the plaque to commemorate World Heritage listing at Lake Mungo, members of local Aboriginal communities discussed with the Premier control and 'ownership' of Aboriginal sites in the region. (Photograph: Wilfred Shawcross)

Fig. 6

Image: This illustration from the cover of John Richardson's *Wacousta*, published in Montreal 1867, embodies the stereotype of the Indian as a satanic figure. Despite significant earlier differences in the actual relations between Europeans and native people in Canada and the United States, during the nineteenth century American stereotypes became continental. (Print: Department of Rare Books, McGill University Libraries, Lawrence M. Lande Collection)

Fig. 7

Reality: Blackfoot 'brave' near Calgary, Alberta, 1889. Despite demographic loss and the disappearance of the bison, unbiased white observers attested the continuing dignity of native life. (Print: Notman Photographic Archives, McCord Museum, McGill University)

Fig. 8

Reality: Indian Women in Vancouver, British Columbia, 1901 – on the wharf to greet an official party during the Royal Tour. (Print: Notman Photographic Archives, McCord Museum, McGill University)

Fig. 9

Bennelong, an Aboriginal of the Sydney district forcibly brought into the settlement by Governor Phillip in 1790 as part of his attempts to establish relations with the Aborigines and to 'reconcile them to live amonst us'. Bennelong's adoption of some of the trappings of the intrusive culture made him a character about early Sydney town recorded in many contemporary accounts and in this engraving of the time. (Print: National Library of Australia, Rex Nan Kivell Collection (NK 4777))

Fig. 10

Members of the New South Wales National Parks and Wildlife Service Aboriginal Sites Committee discuss management issues with NPWS staff at an engraving site near Gosford. The decking walkway allows visitors to see the engravings at close hand with minimum risk of damage to the rock surfaces. This committee, composed of Aboriginal community representatives and archaeologists, advises the Service on policy and management, so acknowledging the vital interests of both Aboriginal people and researchers in the protection of Aboriginal sites. (Photograph: Isabel McBryde)

Fig. 11

The past in the landscape, 40 000 years of Aboriginal prehistory: the New South Wales Sites Committee on a field inspection of sites on the Walls of China, the lunette of Lake Mungo, April, 1981. To Aboriginal members of the committee this field visit was an experience of deep significance, much more than an exercise in solving heritage management issues. (Photograph: Isabel McBryde)

Fig. 12

James Stuart's illustration of the Parthenon portico with the exterior columns removed to show those of the pronaus and the western end of the great frieze of the
Panathenaic Procession. This drawing published in 1787 was based on the work of
Stuart and Revett in Athens 1751–1753. (*The Antiquities of Athens*, measured and
delineated by James Stuart (FRS) and Nicolas Revett, 4 vols, London, 1762–1816:
vol. 2 (ed. W. Newton, 1787), Chapter 1, Plate IV)

Fig. 13

Detail of the frieze recorded by Stuart and Revett showing sculptures on the north-
ern side of the building. (*The Antiquities of Athens*, measured and delineated by
James Stuart (FRS) and Nicolas Revett, 4 vols, London, 1762–1816: vol. 2 (ed. W.
Newton, 1787), Chapter 1, Plate XIV)

to stop it. The British Museum, for example, never knowingly buys illegally exported material and goes to considerable lengths to establish the origin of every piece that is purchased. But this is a two-edged weapon. Because of this policy the museum has lost much material – and the international community much knowledge – by turning down the opportunity to acquire for a public collection material smuggled out of African or Asian countries in the last twenty years, material which has disappeared onto the mantle-pieces of a multitude of curio seekers and casual collectors and investors. Governments with long land boundaries cannot police the activities of smugglers, so there is a fine market. Some governments have told the museum fraternity that they would like to be offered material which appears on the fine art market, but would prefer that, if they cannot purchase these objects, this material be placed in public collections elsewhere. Museums bear the brunt of the attack by the proponents of restitution because their collections are easily identifiable and well known. Collections in the private or semi-private sector are less well published and not so accessible.

Second, as objects come onto the market, either from illicit or legally defensible sources, the developed world should help and encourage the countries of origin to acquire them. In this way, for example, the British Museum has advised Nigeria in building up a national collection and been instrumental in identifying and re-turning various stolen objects to countries of origin. At the same time the developed world should – and does – support research, excavation and collection in countries of the Third World, giving freely of their curatorial and conservation experience.

The Third World and other countries bent on return and 'res-titution' should, however, realize that they are themselves in dan-ger of being considered vandals if they persist in their course with regard to the great international collections. The universal mu-seums have looked after their collections for many years – they are great monuments to man's achievement. They have saved much from oblivion. They provide expertise and comparative material: only in them can we grasp some ideas of the totality of man's mind, its possibilities, its weaknesses, its similar or different reactions. To demolish these major monuments of culture would be unforgivable.

I find it strange – in a period when great international agen-cies are established to foster international understanding – that the international knowledge enshrined in these long-established, major institutions is under threat. Narrow nationalism, isolationism and the consequent misunderstanding which they produce must not be allowed to bring down the shutters on a major field of human endeavour. Such a plea may be politically naive, but it is at least intellectually honest.

Museums can still be founded in countries which have no museums, collections can still be built up, staff trained, excavations undertaken, material borrowed, books and photographs acquired, 'spot' objects purchased. A national museum should outshine an international museum in its own particular area. But the international museums are needed to provide stimulus and knowledge. One Asian country recently requested the return of all the European holdings of its own material. But apart from one or two important pieces practically everything on the list was capable of duplication in that country and indeed a vast archaeological project has been started with European co-operation which has already produced exciting new and duplicate material. Surely that country's scholars can see that there is value in having its culture represented in foreign institutions? As recently as 1969 a Greek Director of Antiquities said that the Elgin Marbles were the best ambassadors abroad for the Greek nation.

Politicians often say that their case is 'special'. But then every case is 'special'. If once a group of objects were returned, then there would be a continual and increasing demand for return from all over the world: each one a 'special' case. This 'flood-gates' argument is rejected rhetorically by supporters of return, but it is a fact: this is a bandwagon which could result in wholesale cultural destruction for the sake of narrow nationalism. Such demands can only lead to cultural isolationism and mutual misunderstanding.

Those of us who work in the international field and believe in an international ideal – those of us not on the gravy train – should support the great universal museums of the world. They are worth fighting for.

7

Law and the Cultural Heritage

Alice Erh Soon Tay

I

Public concern and agitation, or rather sectional concern and agitation, tend to focus on one problem at a time. It is easy, but also valuable, for them to highlight new problems while the law is still grappling with the old.[1] Until recently, and to some extent still today, the primary problem in liberal democracies has been and is to preserve and protect antiquities in a society that readily permits them to pass into or remain in private ownership and that recognizes the great complexities that surround just and equitable interference with ownership. As we shall see, legal and administrative provisions in all countries have found it easier to interfere with immovable property than with chattels, except by way of export controls. Legal systems have not tackled such thorny questions as whether owners of manuscripts or carriers of secret traditions – whether Masons or Aborigines – should have power to veto the study and publication of these traditions or of relics associated with them, except on the basis of traditional legal principles such as breach of confidence. What is new is the amount of public discussion of such questions and the attention being paid to them in principle by political groups, legislators and administrators. What is often forgotten is that the whole concept of protecting the past is fairly recent and that legal systems, especially in common-law countries, are still seeking to make room, primarily through legislation, for laws and regulations protecting the past. The importance of group interest and claims is manifesting itself not by bringing new concepts of group ownership into the law, but by more traditional legislative provisions that nevertheless reflect the social recognition of such groups and their interest. Museums and other institutions, too, going beyond their legal duties, are taking to much greater consultation with and publicly displayed respect for the peoples whose traditions, customs and artefacts they exhibit.

Even the concept of a public or national interest in the past, like the concept of a public national interest generally, in a fully developed sense is largely an eighteenth-century invention, for Europe at least. Both concepts have a significant and often interesting history in European and other civilizations. Before the French Revolution, however, with exceptions for the Commonwealth in England and republics or constitutional monarchies elsewhere, the *chose publique* was seen not as a national or public interest. It was a personal and in that sense private concern of the king; the public function was *his* function just as other functions were those of parliaments, estates, guilds or feudal lords. There were relics, monuments, symbols, things seen as having historical meaning and importance for which respect was demanded. They were known quite early in the embryonic international law of the Middle Ages as *res sacrae*, but by no means successfully protected from destruction or plunder in war. The national enforcement of such respect was largely informal and extra-legal, supplemented by the provision of temporal sanctions to enforce religious norms against desecration, and by the law of sacrilege and *lèse-majesté* which protected the manifestations of feudal and imperial power. The latter operated in quite a real and effective way to protect the heritage and enjoyment of the king and many of his family against anyone but themselves.

Leaving aside the notable activity of the Church (many of whose powerful leaders began from the fifteenth century to collect antiquities and enjoy classical art) there was little general protection in any European law before the French Revolution of historic relics as such, on the grounds of their historical importance. There could be, and was, protection of specific monuments and appreciation of cultural achievement, especially aesthetic achievement. For example, in 1425 Pope Martin V ordered the demolition of new buildings which were liable to cause damage to ancient monuments, and in 1464 Pius II forbade the export of art works from the papal states. Legend, partly based on fact, abounds in many countries with instances of rulers killing or physically constraining great artists and craftsmen to prevent the duplication of major cultural achievements. The valuing of the past for its own sake (and not for aesthetic qualities or connection with present problems, authority or power) was, in Europe, again a comparatively modern phenomenon. It emerged in the sixteenth and seventeenth centuries and reached fruition in the nineteenth. In 1534, Pope Paul III established an Antiquities Commission with broad powers for the protection of ancient structures. The edict of Cardinal Aldobrandini of 15 October 1624 forbade excavation without prior authorization and required a land-owner to report the discovery of any object of historical interest within twenty-four hours of its being found. The edict of Cardinal Pacca, 1802, went further and gave the Holy See a choice between purchasing the excavated objects or returning them to the finder. In the latter case, the finder still had a duty under the edict to protect the objects as listed items and the state had a first right of purchase. Against such specific acts of legislation, however, stand other seventeenth century actions such as that of Pope Urban VIII who declared the Colosseum a public quarry. Kings, too, had developed antiquarian interests. In England, as early as the sixteenth century, an office of the King's Antiquary was created, but there was only one incumbent (John Leland 1533). A society for the preservation of national antiquities formed in London in 1572 was suppressed by James I on his succession in 1603 (Daniel 1975: 18). Developments in Scandinavia had more lasting influence in both Denmark and Sweden. For example, in 1630 Gustavus Adolphus of Sweden appointed a state antiquarian and later, in 1666, a proclamation forbade the destruction of ancient monuments and relics whether on public or private property. In 1684, a Swedish decree protected archaeological material 'found piecemeal in the ground, ancient coins of all varieties, and finds of gold, silver, and copper, metal vessels, and other rarities, many of which are at present being discovered and secretly hoarded'. All such finds were to be sent to the King, a reward being payable to the finder. An Antiquities College in Uppsala University ensured that such finds would not be dispersed (Klindt-Jensen 1975: 16–17, 27). In 1807 a Danish Royal Commission was established for the preservation and collection of national antiquities. Other nations developed a similar appreciation of antiquity as part of Romantic nationalism and legislation followed slowly in the wake of the strengthening interest in archaeology.

The common law is a thirteenth-century creation – like Roman law, remarkably modern for its time, capable of great flexibility and expansion and yet focussing attention on aspects of human intercourse and human relationships that persist through the centuries. Like most legal systems, it has taken more time than people generally recognize to work from particular and segmented grappling with specific abuses and problems to general principles. Modern demands, to an extent which is also not often recognized, are driving it back to a renewed particularization and segmentalization. Legislation often introduces as many new problems, to be resolved by the common law, as it solves old ones. The great merit of common law has been its sense of continuity and complexity and its consequent ability to draw on a vast social and temporal range of carefully considered and digested experience. For this ability the political legislator and the political administrator are not especially noted. The common law's chief defect, in modern times, has been its structural and procedural discomfort with the concept of the public interest and with the requirements of an administratively-minded approach to areas as a whole. In Australia, and in other common-law countries, the common law governs us from the past for both good and ill. Legislative reform or innovation to overcome its defects is often a much more complex problem, intellectually as much as practically, than simply removing anachronisms or substituting 'modern legislation' for traditional rules. Laws passed by Parliament rarely, if ever, cover all the ground and never exhaust all the possibilities. Common law, and often ancient common-law conceptions, come in not only to interpret what Parliament has enacted but also to afford alternative bases of defence or claim to contesting parties. Total and allegedly rational administration by the State requires a degree of interference with citizens' property, rights and independence that goes much further than at first envisaged and that has not been acceptable in any Western country.

The common law characteristically developed around the paradigm of trespass, of the unjustified invasion of another human being's person, property, possession or enjoyment. It saw ownership, possession, enjoyment and other rights as profoundly individual in nature and those individual rights, not state or public policy, as providing the fundamental ground of legal claims. The fact of rightful possession, rather than title conferred by the state, was central to the development of common law in a way it was not to Roman law.

The law of finding, developed from the thirteenth century onward, focussed primarily on the question whether things were secreted, lost or abandoned: title was retained by the owner and his heirs if he had not abandoned. The occupier of the land where the object was found obtained title only if the object had been abandoned or had passed unchallenged into the occupier's control. Only in the case of treasure trove and wrecks – both technical concepts in early and present common law – was another interest allowed to intervene. Ownership in these cases, it was held from early times, lay in the king. In the absence of other legislation intersecting with this – and there has been no general legislative intervention in the case of treasure trove – that is still the position today, in England and in Australia. In England finds have been so frequent, and legislation covering such finds so notable for its absence, that cases seeking to establish a Crown interest under the law of treasure trove persist to the present day. The Home Office in the 1930s issued a memorandum on the subject, stating the circumstances in which the Crown claimed title as treasure trove. In Australia, though the law of treasure trove applies, no important cases have come before the courts; there is however a statutory duty to report finds of value to the police to assist in tracing possible owners.

The law of treasure trove is a peculiarly common-law institution. It is probably derived from an ancient Germanic or Scandinavian source having no parallel in ancient or later Roman law. Where it was any treasure discovered by chance, and remaining unclaimed, it then went to the sovereign. By the Jutish laws, codified in 1241, 'If any man should find gold or silver in a barrow or turned up by his plough or in any other way, it must be handed over to the King.' The same conception existed in Swedish law, though it was abolished in 1684. The Danish law of treasure trove (*danefae*, or dead man's property) was incorporated into the Danish constitution in 1683 and is the law today as it stood then. The French civil code has a different concept of treasure trove (Art. 716) – 'everything hidden or buried in the earth which no one can prove belongs to him and which is discovered by mere chance'. Such finds in France belong to the finder if he finds them on his own property and must be shared equally with the property owner, if found on another's property. The common law concept of treasure trove confines it specifically, as Sir Edward Coke said, to 'any gold or silver in coin, plate or bullyon . . . of ancient time hidden, wheresoever it be found, whereof no person can prove any property' (3 *Coke's Institutes* 132). In such cases Coke says categorically, 'it doth belong to the King, or to some lord or other by the King's grant or prescription'. The limitation of treasure trove to gold and silver – it has been extended by the courts beyond coin, plate or bullion – makes it clear that the royal prerogative was not exercised on behalf of an historical interest in the materials. Blackstone thought the law was not based solely on the king's desire to enrich himself, but meant rather to protect his right of coinage. For a long period, treasure trove successfully claimed by the king went into the exchequer to help defray the cost of government. In the last century the Crown prerogative has indeed been claimed in order to protect and preserve the finds as interesting antiquities for the benefit of the nation as a whole. But the Home Office has had to accept and confirm that the Crown claim can be sustained only in respect of gold and silver (Palmer 1981; Yales 1980).

In England, important historical finds have been frequent and by no means confined to gold and silver. In 1972, a farm worker hoeing a field found a twelfth-century statuette of St John the Evangelist which fetched 35 000 guineas at Christie's; bronze tools and weapons 2500 years old were found at Occold in Suffolk in 1980; and other finds include a whole Iron Age settlement, Roman lamps made of lead, Roman coins of base metal, a leaden pot and a 'splendid' haul of Roman treasure consisting of thirty-three silver spoons, a quantity of finely worked jewellery, and deeds to title. All attracted attention but could not be claimed by the Crown as treasure trove except for the items composed of silver.

Of course, litigation arose and continues over borderline cases, though the traditional requirement that treasure trove should have been hidden is now presumed. In Quarry Field at Coleby in Lincolnshire in 1975, a searcher armed with a metal detector unearthed 7811 coins of the third century AD. The coins were an alloy of base metal and silver. A coroner's inquest, required by English law when possible treasure trove is found, resulted in the matter being transferred to the Chancery Division of the High Court, which found that the coins did not contain sufficient silver to make them treasure trove. Title to them therefore lay, according to established common law principles, in the owner and occupier of the land (a company) and not in the finder. The court recognized that the Crown's claim was being pursued to protect and preserve the coins for the benefit of the nation, but held that 'the Crown cannot unilaterally extend its prerogative rights. That is a matter for the Parliament.' The learned judge, Dillon. J, added:

> The position however in which the preservation for the nation of recently discovered antiquities depends on a prerogative which originated for quite different purposes is not satisfactory and the topic is one which could well merit the attention of Parliament so as to adopt criteria in keeping with modern thinking and the ways of modern life. (*Attorney-General of the Duchy of Lancaster v. G.E. Overton (Farms) Ltd*, (1980) 3 *All England Reports*, 503 at p. 506)

Despite this, in England, Parliament has been reluctant to interfere across the board with the liberties of finders, or especially owners or occupiers, even taking into account the spate of new national and international legislation to be discussed below. Earlier, in 1971, the Brodrick Committee appointed by the United Kingdom government to review the powers of coroners had recommended in its report, *inter alia*, that coroners should continue to carry out their functions in regard to treasure trove 'until comprehensive legislation is introduced to deal with the whole question of the protection of antiquities' (1971, Cmnd. 4810, para. 13.22). Nothing happened to improve the protection of antiquities, however, until 3 December 1981 when an Antiquities Bill was introduced in the House of Lords by Lord Abinger. It received the second reading on 8 February 1982 and went into the committee stage on 4 March 1982 where it was substantially amended. It was brought from the Lords on 5 April and read the first time in the House of Commons on 5 May where it did not receive a second reading. The Bill thus did not pass through both Houses and never became law. The Bill itself, though 'the fruit of much archaeological experience' (Sparrow 1982: 201) was a comparatively modest measure. It sought to redefine the concept of treasure trove without abolishing it. An earlier Private Member's Bill which proposed the abolition of the concept of treasure trove failed to win the support of the British Museum on this as well as other grounds.

The Antiquities Bill dealt with 'small' or 'portable' objects; it aimed to remove 'the present highly artificial and absurd division between articles which have been hidden for retrieval and those which have been lost or abandoned' (Lord Abinger on the second reading) by removing the requirement of *animus revertendi*; it perceived all alloys to which gold or silver had been deliberately added as within the scope of treasure trove (thus reversing the effect of the *Overton* decision) and gave protection to 'associated objects' along with the principal objects of gold or silver (or alloy), including a container or coins in a hoard which were not of gold or silver; it also provided power for the Secretary of State to bring other classes of objects within the protection of treasure trove in the future, by statutory instrument. The law of treasure trove is thus not dead legally or practically, and it could easily surface in Australia – more not less probably, as time goes by.

The common law of wrecks is more extensive in application, and consequently more complex and technical, than that of treasure trove. Early common law, as enunciated by Blackstone (1 *Blackstone's Commentaries* 290–4), provided that ships which perished on the sea and goods lost at sea, which *reached shore* and were therefore wrecks belong to the Crown as part of the king's prerogative. The Statute of Westminster, 1275, had recognized this right and required that the vessel must have been abandoned by all living creatures and that no owner had come forward to claim title within a year and a day of the finding of the wreck. Traditionally, wreck did not include items found underwater on the seabed, unless perhaps these had been accidentally raised, as by being hauled up by the cable of a ship. Since whole populations, including those of parts of Cornwall, supplemented their income by finding or creating wrecks, the common law is rich with cases. Many of them are criminal, based on the recognition that abandoning ship and contents is not necessarily abandoning title to ship and contents. Underwater exploration and discovery have added new problems of definition to the concept of wreck. This is on top of the traditional three-cornered competition between those who claim title, those who claim salvage and those who claim wreck. Even in national law, including common-law systems, international problems concerning the definition of territorial waters abound. So do problems of distinguishing land derelict from derelict at sea, abandonment of title from abandonment of possession, dead ships from not truly dead ships, title to ship from title to cargo. 'In private law, nothing offers such a bewildering maze, an intricate spider's web, as the law relating to wrecks. Unfortunately, to a great extent, the law on submarine antiquities is entangled with the law on Receiving of Wrecks' (Korthals Altes 1974: 132).

To appreciate any particular situation in its full and often international context, one must grasp what law is to govern and what kind of object is involved. The object may be *res nullius* either in the sense that it never had an owner or in the sense that it became one through being *res derelicta* (truly abandoned). It may be an object of which the owner is not known but which could, in principle, still be private property. This could be so even after a long lapse of time since an owner who has never formally abandoned in principle transfers title to his heirs. The object may be *bona vacantia*, which escheats to the Crown at common law because all *ayants droits* (interested parties) are known to be dead. The very complexity of the law in this area has encouraged and is encouraging legislative intervention both in wrecks generally and the control of wrecks as archaeological sites and part of mankind's cultural heritage. As a result, the Crown's claim to wrecks has been greatly strengthened and extended, in England and in Australia.

II

The law of treasure trove and wreck was concerned with these as objects of value, not as objects having historical or cultural significance as part of antiquity or of the national heritage. With the French Revolution, however, monuments began to be appreciated for their artistic, historical and scientific significance, as the 'cultural heritage of a nation, evidence of historical traditions, a historical identity card' (Zaryn quoted in Niec 1976: 108), thereby conferring on art a new function. A decree of the French National Assembly of 26 May 1791 converted the Louvre from a Royal Palace into a National Palace, and vested in the National Assembly the right to decide the ways in which it would be used and the means to be employed 'to make this group of monuments worthy of its designation'. In 1793 the Louvre was proclaimed the 'Museum of the Republic' and in 1803, soon after the Napoleonic Code, the Musée Napoleon was opened, more than fifty years before the founding of the Victoria and Albert Museum in 1857. The

Napoleonic civil code already provided for the protection of cultural property; by 1887 France had the strictest and most elaborate provisions of any European country. A law of 1887 made objects in public collections inalienable, and laws of 1909 and 1913 adopted the principle of classification which is the hallmark of protective legislation on the French model. Thus French legislation protected all movable and immovable property whose 'preservation is in the public interest from the point of view of history, art and science'. It provided that such property, whether owned by the state, the departments or the communes (roughly, counties and municipalities), by legal personalities under public law, corporate bodies or individuals, should be classified by the Ministry of Cultural Affairs. Once an object is registered as cultural property it is protected by provisions of the decree which forbid its destruction or unauthorized sale abroad and throw on the owner a responsibility for preserving the object. After registration, no one can acquire title by adverse possession (contrary to normal French and, for that matter, English law). The owner of a classified object can bring an action to recover possession at any time and against anyone, even against a *bona fide* purchaser. Registered cultural property which is publicly owned is inalienable. The state has a pre-emptive right to purchase all cultural properties put up to auction, throwing a duty on the auctioneer to inform the Minister of Cultural Affairs of objects to be sold and providing procedures for fixing a price. A law of 1920 restricted export of all property of cultural interest including relics recovered from excavations in France; but in 1921 this was restricted to export only of such objects as were classified. Since 1944, the French government has issued lists of cultural property requiring an export licence. Objects of art must have either a certificate of exemption issued by the Professional Committee of Art Galleries or an export licence which the Customs Office is to issue only after it has consulted the Central Administration of National Museums in France.

Among democratic societies, France is perhaps the state-centred society *par excellence*. The French approach can also be found in the legal systems of Italy, Spain, Austria, Belgium and Switzerland, though the two latter countries do not impose export restrictions. The British, as one might expect, have been much slower to interfere directly and generally with private property and with the rights of the individual citizen. Compared with France's strict regime, Britain has what we may call a soft regime. Britain's legal protection of cultural property by legislation began in 1882 with the passage of the *Ancient Monuments Protection Act* (45 & 46 Vict. C.73). It was supplemented by the *Ancient Monuments Consolidation and Amendment Act* of 1913, the *Ancient Monuments Act* of 1931, and the *Historic Buildings and Ancient Monuments Act* of 1953. The British define ancient monuments as:

> any monument specified in the Schedule to the Ancient Monuments Protection Act of 1882; monuments reported by an Ancient Monuments Board as being 'monuments the preservation of which is of national importance'; and any other monument or group of monuments and any part or remains of a monument or group of monuments which the Minister [of Public Buildings and Works] considers to be of a like character or of which in the opinion of the Minister the preservation is a matter of public interest by reason of the intrinsic architectural, traditional artistic or archaeological interest attaching thereto. (Committee of Enquiry into the Arrangements for the Protection of Field Monuments, August, 1966–68, at 68 (1969))

The British regime lays stress on a more limited concept of scheduling as opposed to the French interest in principle, if not really in practice, in classifying and recording all cultural property in the country. It was limited, unlike the French, to immovable property. Once scheduled, a monument in England acquires a legal status, and the ownership of such protected monument, in England as in France, is encumbered with restrictions. In England, however, the legislation on ancient monuments specifically excludes from its provisions occupied dwellings and ecclesiastical buildings which are still in use.

With movable cultural property, the legal protection afforded by Britain lies mainly in the export control of art which has special importance to the British national heritage. Thus, works of art valued at £2000 or more, more than one hundred years old, and in Britain for at least fifty years are subject to an export permit necessary for them to be taken out of the country (*Export and Customs Powers (Defence) Act*, 1939 and *Export of Goods (Control) Ordn. 1981* (S.I. 1981, No. 164)). If an expert is of the opinion that the work of art is of such importance that licence should be refused, the case is sent to the Reviewing Committee on the Export of Works of Art which applies three tests: '(1) Is the object so closely connected with our history and national life that its departure would be a misfortune? (2) Is it of outstanding aesthetic importance? (3) Is it of outstanding significance for the study of some particular branch of art, learning or history?' (Reviewing Committee on the Export of Works of Art, 16th Report Comnd. No. 4244, at 4–5 (1969).) If the committee decides that the work should not be exported, an export licence will not be granted if an offer to buy the work is forthcoming from any public institution in the United Kingdom during a stated period at a stipulated price. If no such offer is made, the export licence will be granted despite the committee's recommendation. The British regime, as opposed to the French, has been followed in Finland, the Netherlands and Sweden.

In 1979, a new *United Kingdom Ancient Monuments and Archaeological Areas Act* extended protection of a sort to movable historical relics and archaeological finds in a curiously indirect and limited way. It gave the relevant Secretary of State power to designate areas of archaeological importance which appear to him to merit treatment as such, to appoint competent persons to undertake archaeological investigations in them and to prohibit the use of metal detectors on such sites or the removal of any object of archaeological or historical interest discovered on a proclaimed site by a metal detector. The Act also provides for the compulsory acquisition of ancient monuments for the purpose of securing their preservation under the normal procedures for the compulsory acquisition of land by the State. It gives the Secretary of State the right of entry to scheduled ancient monuments for the purpose of carrying out work necessary for their preservation, and it further gives specific power to acquire by agreement any ancient monuments. It gives to local authorities the same power in respect of ancient monuments situated in their area.

In comparison with European legal systems, the American way of protecting monuments is unusual. It reflects the fact that when the first legislation protecting cultural property was adopted, vast territories were owned by the federal government, especially in the west and south, where most of the protected monuments were located. The lack of antiquities explains why only monuments received protection under national law. Because most lands belong to federal and state authorities, interest focused only on the monuments situated on public land (Niec 1976).

The original United States statutes protecting cultural property in that country are an Act for the Preservation of American Antiquities, enacted in 1906, and an Act to Provide for the Preservation of Historic American Sites, Buildings, Objects, and Antiquities of National Significance and for other Purposes, passed in 1935. There is no definition of protected objects in these acts, though criteria for protection can be deduced. The important factor distinguishing any object as a national monument is its historical value. Such an object may be an estate, an architectural construction, or a movable object. The 1906 Act was devoted to the protection of any historic or prehistoric ruins or monuments or any object of antiquity situated on lands owned or controlled by the Government of the United States. Some states followed with legislation of their own (for example, Illinois in 1907 and Michigan and North Carolina before the Second World War) but the vast majority of state legislation appeared in the 1960s. It varied in the degree of thoroughness of protective measures and the energy with which it was enforced. In some states legislation only applies to lands owned or controlled by the state governments, so that excavations and finds on private land are not controlled.

The validity of the 1906 Act – where it came within federal powers – was tested for the first time in 1974 in *United States v. Diaz* (499 F.2d. 113 [1974]). Diaz was charged under the Act with appropriating 'objects of antiquity', namely face-masks made by an Indian 'medicine man' some three or four years earlier. There was expert evidence given that anthropologically an 'object of antiquity' could include something that was made just yesterday if it related to long-standing religious or social traditions, but the United States Court of Appeals, Ninth Circuit, held that the penal provisions of the Act were uncertain and therefore invalid. In 1979, in *United States v. Smyer* (596 F.2d 939 [1979]) the Court of Appeals, Tenth Circuit, reached the opposite opinion. This division of opinion between two courts whose jurisdictions covered areas rich in archaeological sites, and other considerations, led to the *Archaeological Resources Protection Act 1979* which has improved and strengthened enforcement provisions and implemented a clearer system of permit control. It still does not extend regulations to excavation on non-federal lands, but it does provide that it is an offence 'to sell, purchase, exchange, transport, receive or offer to sell, purchase, or exchange, in interstate or foreign commerce, any archaeological resource excavated, removed, sold, purchased, exchanged, transported or received in violation of any provision, rule or regulation, ordinance, or permit in effect under State or local law'.

The United States Federal Act of 1935 enlarged the range of protected objects. Its introduction declared: 'It is a national policy to preserve for public use historic sites, buildings and objects of national significance for the inspiration and benefit of the people of the United States'. The Act vested in the Secretary of the Interior wide authority in the area of cultural protection. Among the secretary's duties is the responsibility for making 'a survey of historic and archaeological sites, buildings, and objects for the purpose of determining which possess exceptional value as commemorating or illustrating the history of the United States'. Character of ownership is irrelevant to the act of classification, which carries no legal implication, and does not diminish the right of the owner of an historic monument to do as he pleases with it. Nevertheless, the federal authorities can secure wide surveillance over monuments through a system of agreements concluded by the

Secretary of the Interior with states, municipal subdivisions, corporations, associations, or individuals. These agreements may contain provisions regarding the protection, maintenance, or preservation of monuments. Furthermore, the secretary has the power to 'acquire in the name of the United States by gift, purchase, or otherwise any property, personal or real, or any interest or estate therein, title to any real property, if it is done to implement a national policy of protection of historical monuments'.

The increasing concern at the federal level with the protection of cultural property is well illustrated by a set of statutes passed by by the 89th Congress (see Prott and O'Keefe 1983, I: 65). These included the Act to Establish a Program for the Preservation of Additional Historic Properties throughout the Nation and for other Purposes, which empowers the Secretary of the Interior to expand and maintain a national register of districts, sites, buildings, structures, and objects significant in American history, architecture, archaeology, and culture, and to grant funds to states for the purpose of preparing comprehensive state-wide historic surveys and plans for the preservation, acquisition, and development of such properties. The President's Advisory Council on Historic Preservation was created for the purpose of preparing recommendations for the President and the Congress on all matters relating to the protection of cultural property. Federal agencies were required to consult with the council if their proposed activities might adversely affect a site or district that was listed on the national register.

Under the federal legislation there is no body having the right to control or supervise export of American cultural property. But the United States is one of a rather small group of nations which forbids, in respect of some countries, the importation of cultural property illegally exported from the country of its origin. Following a treaty concluded with Mexico in 1970, President Nixon in 1972 signed legislation prohibiting the importation into the United States of pre-Colombian monumental and architectural sculpture and murals illegally removed from the country of origin. A recent Bill prohibits the importation of illegally exported objects not only of Mexican origin but also those coming from Central America and South America or the Caribbean Islands.

European and American legislation was initially concerned mainly with monuments and art works. It has been extended in recent times to pay more attention to archaeological and prehistoric relics. Historical significance is now more readily accorded to aspects of folk cultures. During the 1975 debate in the Canadian House of Commons on the Canadian Cultural Property Export and Import Bill, enacted in 1977, a speaker said:

Canada, of course, does not have many archaeological sites which yield valuable treasures, except those the Minister mentioned in terms of our native peoples. There is not a hoard of Canadian material which the world museums are hungry for. The Canadian problem is to protect the fragile and meagre evidence of our prehistoric past and to save the evidence of the cultures of our native peoples and to preserve in Canada the works of art and art materials which have accumulated during our short history.

The same might well be said of Australia.

Japan – a country that has perhaps the strongest sense of the importance of tradition to be found in any modern country – has indeed extended the protection of its legislation beyond cultural property consisting of immovable or movable objects. Legislation covers 'art and skill employed in drama, music and applied arts, and other intangible cultural products, which possess a high historical or artistic value for the country,' and extends to 'manners and customs related to food, clothing and housing, to occupations, religious faiths, festivals, etc., clothes, implements, houses and other objects used therefore which are indispensable for the understanding of changes in our people's mode of life' and to 'gardens, bridges, gorges, seashores and mountains and other places of scenic beauty . . . '. It is in this spirit that we find, in Japan, great artists, potters and architects honoured by the title 'Living National Treasures'. And in Japan, if an historic monastery whose 700-year-old ritual is valued throughout the country should decide to change that ritual, such an alteration may not be allowed, though the monastery might claim a state subsidy to carry on.

By now, some 150 states have at least one piece of legislation dealing with at least one class of antiquities. The majority of these legislative Acts date from the 1950s, though as we have seen there were significant early moves for protective legislation: for example, Hawaii in 1898, El Salvador in 1903, India in 1904, the United States in 1906 and Argentina and Spain in 1911. Prior to this, a Treasure Trove Act was enacted in British India in 1878, followed ninety years later by the Pakistan *Antiquities Act* of 1968. Sri Lanka, then Ceylon, also enacted a Treasure Trove Ordinance, extending the concept, in 1888. French Tunisia's Decree of 7 March 1886, regarding ownership and conservation of antiquities and art objects was followed by the Decree of 8 January 1920 covering ruins and antiquities. In 1918 Soviet Russia – then the *Rossiiskaya Sotsialisticheskaya Federativnaya Sovetskaya Respublika* (Russian Socialist Federal Soviet Republic) – protected all cultural property in the new regime through the law of 4 October 1918, by confiscating and nationalizing all cultural property (i.e. monuments, art objects and collections) including objects in private possession and all such objects owned by persons leaving the state. Much of it was later sold abroad by the state. All communist countries now control such objects and especially their export rigorously. The Middle Eastern countries, some with the help of UNESCO experts, have legislated to protect archaeological sites and to control the export of antiquities. They generally define these as objects of cultural interest or historic value made before 1700.

The older established states of the Mediterranean world with its immense wealth of cultural properties and antiquities also have a long history of legislative attempts to control their exploitation. Such legislation was one of the first enactments of the independent Greek government in 1834. Italy, Egypt (1835) and Iraq (1926) also made such moves well in advance of the mid-twentieth century display of legislative concern.

III

International law has both followed and influenced national law. Since the eighteenth century, theoreticians of international law have condemned wanton destruction and looting of cultural property during war (Williams 1978: 15–28). Outrage over Napoleon's looting of Europe, the destruction of Rheims Cathedral and the burning of the library of Louvain University in the First World War, and the horrendous acts of the Nazis in the Second World War, all contributed to the demand for international law and agreement.

The earliest attempt to codify such feelings was in the Lieber Code of 1863 – a code of instructions for the government of armies of the United States in the field, executed by order of the Secretary of War. It stipulated (by Art. XXXI) that the victorious army may take full title to publicly owned movable property and use it as it sees fit, but title to immovable property is held in abeyance during occupation until conquest is complete. Certain forms of public property, however, such as churches, hospitals, establishments of education, foundations for the promotion of knowledge, schools, universities, academies of learning or observatories, museums of fine arts, or of a scientific character, are not to be treated as public property under the above Art. XXXI with regard to title or right to occupy. They acquire the status of private property when they are not involved in the war effort. Special protection is granted by Art. XXXV to 'classical works of art, libraries, scientific collections, or precious instruments such as astronomical telescopes as well as hospitals': 'they must be secured against all avoidable injury, even when they are contained in fortified places whilst besieged or bombarded'. The Lieber Code also provides that works of art in the war zone may be removed where this can be done without injury; they may not be sold, given away, privately appropriated, injured or destroyed but must be kept for their ownership to be determined through the treaty of peace (Art. XXXVI). In this way, the principle evolved that cultural property is inviolable and cannot be appropriated by a conquering state. Although the Lieber Code was a set of rules for internal American warfare, it did mark a significant step in the direction of protection of cultural property in war generally. It was the chief model on which the first international declaration on cultural protection in war, adopted in Brussels on the initiative of Emperor Alexander II of Russia in 1874, was based. This declaration itself was relied upon, and several of its provisions were used, in the Hague Peace Conference in 1899.

The 1899 and 1907 Hague Conventions continued the development of a principle of protection of cultural property, relying heavily on the Brussels Draft, which in turn relied on the Lieber Code. Their leading achievements were the doctrines that the occupying state had only a usufruct of property of the conquered state by right of occupancy, and as a usufructuary must safeguard the capital and take only the revenue (Art. 55).

The inadequacy of the Hague Conventions to prevent loss, destruction and damage and to restore missing property to their rightful owners is a long, complicated and sad story. New owners argue the claim of *bona fide* purchasers where dispersal took place through sale and exchange, or raise the defence of act of state where property had been confiscated. The Nazis themselves denied the applicability of the Hague Convention to seizures of Jewish property on grounds that 'the Jew and his property are outside the law' and therefore outside the protection of the rules of international law.

In the forty years since the end of the Second World War some international conventions have been adopted:
1. The UNESCO 1954 Hague Convention for the Protection of Cultural Property in the Event of Armed Conflict which seeks to give protection to all property, irrespective of origin or ownership, that is of importance to the cultural heritage of any people. This is the text which introduced the term 'cultural property', and it stresses that 'damage to cultural property belonging to any people whatsoever means damage to the cultural heritage of all mankind, since each people makes its contribution to the culture of the world';
2. The Council of Europe's 1969 European Convention on the protection of the Archaeological Heritage which urges that a

greater unity should be achieved between the member states of the Council of Europe, in particular, with respect to 'safeguarding and realizing the ideals and principles which are their common heritage' (European Treaty Series No.66 (1969) & Int. L. Mat. 736). This Convention is seen as having established the concept of a European cultural heritage. Currently the Council of Europe is engaged in drafting a Convention on Offences against Cultural Property and a Convention on the Underwater Cultural Heritage;

3. The 1970 UNESCO Convention on the Means of Prohibiting and Preventing the Illicit Import, Export and Transfer of Ownership of Cultural Property. This was the most comprehensive multinational agreement on cultural property to date. It was the first international treaty to seek to protect cultural property from destructive threats in peace time, by directing individual nations to protect the cultural property existing within its territory against the dangers of theft, clandestine excavations and illicit export (Preamble). The Convention considered it 'essential for every State to become increasingly alive to the moral obligations to respect its own cultural heritage and that of all nations' (Preamble);

4. The 1972 Convention Concerning the Protection of the World Cultural and Natural Heritage signed in Paris (with Australia as one of the signatories). It stresses in its Preamble that 'the deterioration or disappearance at any time of the cultural or natural heritage constitutes a harmful impoverishment of the heritage of all nations'. The Convention requires each state signatory to the Convention to recognize the duty of ensuring the identification, protection, conservation, preservation and transmission to future generations of cultural and natural heritage. It defines the cultural heritage as:

monuments: architectural works, works of monumental sculpture and painting, elements or structures of an archaeological nature, inscriptions, cave dwellings and combinations or features, which are of outstanding universal value from the point of view of history, art, or science;

groups of buildings: group of separate or connected buildings which, because of their architecture, their homogeneity or their place in the landscape, are of outstanding universal value from the point of view of history, art or science;

sites: works of man or the combined works of nature and of man, and areas including archaeological sites which are of outstanding universal value from the historical, aesthetic, ethnological or anthropological points of view. (Art. 1)

The states signing the convention undertake to endeavour to give the cultural and natural heritage a function in the life of the community; to set up services, if they do not already exist, to protect, conserve and present such heritage and to give them appropriate staff and means; to develop scientific, technical studies and research to counteract dangers threatening the cultural and natural heritage; and to take appropriate legal, scientific, technical, administrative and financial measures necessary for the identification, protection, conservation, preservation and rehabilitation of this heritage. In 1954, the term 'cultural property' was coined; by 1972, the concept of the common heritage of mankind had taken shape.

IV

To the sentiments expressed in and surrounding the international conventions, Australian governments, at least in principle, now subscribe. Popular feeling here is perhaps even stronger than official attitudes would suggest, though it has perhaps shown more interest in the natural than the cultural heritage.

Until the mid-1970s there was no comprehensive legislation dealing with the protection of cultural heritage. There were, of course, various Acts which dealt with (traditional) cultural institutions – museums, libraries, art galleries – and these inevitably had some impact on those select areas of cultural heritage. The National Library had the specific commission of acquiring in Australia and from overseas items of historical significance in the formation and growth of the Australian nation. The *Customs Act 1901* gave the Governor-General power to prohibit by regulation the export of goods from Australia. The current Customs (Prohibited Exports) Regulations prohibit, *inter alia*, the export without the consent of the Minister of archaeological and anthropological material, including articles of ethnological interest and biological material other than blood, derived from, or relating to Australian Aborigines or persons of Southeast Asian or Pacific origin other than Europeans, who were resident in or visitors to Australia before 1906. It similarly prohibits export, without consent, of any document that records the terms of a transaction or arrangement made between Aborigines in a particular part of Australia and an early settler or explorer in that part of Australia. Export of fossil materials and other geological specimens, of coins made or appearing to have been made in Australia or elsewhere or before 4 October 1901, or of a facsimile or imitation of or dummy representing such a coin also requires the Minister's prior consent. So do tokens made or issued in Australia before 1901 for use instead of coins, contemporary records or accounts (including books, diaries, newspapers, maps, sketches, paintings, photographs, manuscripts and other documents) of events or occurrences connected with the discovery, early settlement or early exploration of Australia, and goods that were or are represented to have been owned or used by a person associated with the discovery, early settlement or early exploration. There was also planning legislation, such as the Victorian *Town and Country Planning Act* 1944, that had an impact on the preservation of the built and natural environment. There was specific legislation concerned with particular items of cultural importance especially old homes and buildings – such as Acts establishing trusts for these properties. Thus, even though there was some law that could be used by those concerned to preserve the cultural heritage, there was no legislative regime which directly and comprehensively tackled the problems. On Aboriginal cultural heritage, there was virtually nothing in the way of protection.

One exception in this bleak landscape was *The National Trust of Australia (New South Wales) Act* 1960, which formally constituted the National Trust in New South Wales (the body itself had been founded in 1945). Its objects were set out in Section 4:

(a) to acquire, control, maintain, protect and preserve for the benefit of the public generally lands, buildings, works, structures and articles, of beauty or of national, historical, antiquarian, scientific, artistic, architectural or cultural interest (including aboriginal relics, aboriginal rock carvings and aboriginal rock paintings and archaeological sites);

(b) to protect and preserve the natural features of, and to conserve the fauna and flora on, any lands referred to in paragraph (a) and acquired by or under the control of the National Trust;

(c) to encourage and promote, by any means whatsoever, public appreciation, knowledge and enjoyment of, respect for, and interest in, any lands, buildings, works, structures or articles, referred to in paragraph (a);

(d) to provide and improve amenities on and access to any lands, buildings, works and structures referred to in paragraph (a) and acquired by or under the control of the National Trust;

(e) to co-operate with any corporation, body or society, either within or outside New South Wales, having objects wholly or substantially similar to the objects of the National Trust, in promoting the objects of such corporation, body or society or the National Trust.

Other states have adopted similar legislation and an active programme, especially one on the natural heritage side, has begun. These Acts, however, do not give the National Trust or its state branches power directly to regulate or control constituents of the natural or cultural heritage so declared by them except through acquisition, or where the items are on public land or in public ownership. The Trust has limited powers to impose by-laws and penalties in regard to property under its control (S.16). In the main it plays the role of propagandist and adviser. Thus, in listing items as deserving preservation, it can, and does, have moral influence on local councils, planning authorities and planning Bills, Acts and regulations, through which much can be and has been done. It now functions as a 'watchdog' of cultural heritage and often advises the New South Wales Heritage Council which does have coercive powers. Until the 1972 International Convention, however, it was assumed that there was no, or very limited, federal power to legislate in this area; hence the reliance on state acts.

Since the 1970s, legislation has proceeded in Australia very much under the influence of the 1972 convention. It has had a broad conception of cultural heritage and has accepted the desirability of listing, but has been wary of regulating buildings in private possession. The legislation has avoided the problem of classifying movable objects altogether. The Commonwealth Act establishing the Australian Heritage Commission in 1975[2] gave the commission power to list as part of the national estate a site, area or region, and buildings or structures, which may include equipment, furniture, fittings and articles associated or connected with such buildings or structures. The commission, *inter alia*, advises the Minister on action to conserve, improve and present the national estate, and on giving grants or financial or other assistance to the states, local government bodies, organizations or persons. It keeps a register but has no direct power to control anything registered except in so far as a minister, department or the Commonwealth has power to do so independently of the Act (S.7). The Act, in short, creates no new power but formulates policies and ways of making recommendations for which existing powers are to be used. It does, however, define the 'national estate' as consisting of those places, being components of the natural environment of Australia or the cultural environment of Australia, 'that have aesthetic, historic, scientific or social significance or other special value for future generations as well as for the present community' (S.4(1)). 'Place' is defined in S.3(1) as including:

1.   a site, area or region;
2.   a building or other structure (which may include equipment, furniture, fittings and articles associated with or connected with such building or other structure);
3.   a group of buildings or other structures (which may include equipment, furniture, fittings and articles associated with or connected with such group of buildings or other structures);

and, in relation to the conservation or improvement of a place, the immediate surroundings of the place.

Basically the commission has two crucial functions. First, it keeps a register of the national estate. Section 23 allows a 'place' to be entered on the register provided the commission has given the public an opportunity to object and provided it has considered those objections. Under S.25 the Minister can direct the commission to withdraw a place from or to enter it on the register. The Minister's direction is to be made after consideration of an 'environment report', under S.11 of the *Environment Protection (Impact of Proposals) Act* 1974.

Second, under S.30, government departments and authorities are required not to affect adversely 'places' entered in the register.

30. (1) Each Minister shall give all such directions and do all such things as, consistently with any relevant laws, can be given or done by him for ensuring that the Department administered by him or any authority of the Commonwealth in respect of which he has ministerial responsibilities does not take any action that adversely affects, as part of the national estate, a place that is in the Register unless he is satisfied that there is no feasible and prudent alternative to the taking of that action and that all measures that can reasonably be taken to minimise the adverse effect will be taken and shall not himself take any such action unless he is so satisfied.

(2) Without prejudice to the application of sub-section (1) in relation to action to be taken by an authority of the Commonwealth, an authority of the Commonwealth shall not take any action that adversely affects, as part of the national estate, a place that is in the Register unless the authority is satisfied that there is no feasible and prudent alternative, consistent with any relevant laws, to the taking of that action and that all measures that can reasonably be taken to minimise the adverse effect will be taken.

(3) Before a Minister, a Department or an authority of the Commonwealth takes any action that might affect to a significant extent, as part of the national estate, a place that is in the Register, the Minister, Department or authority, as the case may be, shall inform the Commission of the proposed action and give the Commission a reasonable opportunity to consider it.

(4) For the purposes of this section, the making of a decision or recommendation (including a recommendation in relation to direct financial assistance granted, or proposed to be granted to a State) the approval of a program, the issue of a licence or the granting of a permission shall be deemed to be the taking of action and, in the case of a recommendation, if the adoption of the recommendation would adversely affect a place, the making of the recommendation shall be deemed to affect the place adversely.

But notice here the 'unless . . .' clause in S.30(1) and S.30(2). These sub-sections and section 30(3) amount to very weak brakes on governmental action. This is all the 'bite' the commission has: it has no power other than 'moral power' over private persons.

Section 23(5) also effectively excludes Aboriginal sites and places from the ambit of the Act:

(5) The Commission shall not take any action under this section in relation to a place for reasons relating only to the association of the place with the history, culture or beliefs of Aboriginals unless
   (a) the place is a site specially protected under a law of a State or Territory by reason of its association with the history, culture or beliefs of Aboriginals; or
   (b) the action is taken in accordance with a direction of the Minister under section 25 or the recommendation of a person or organization approved by the Minister for the purposes of this sub-section.

Another Act that does have some provisions for protection of cultural heritage is the *National Parks and Wildlife Conservation Act 1975*. The Act provides for 'management plans' to be set out for proclaimed reserves. Among the objects of such plans shall be the preservation of the park or reserve in its natural condition and the protection of its special features, including objects and sites of biological, historical, palaeontological, archaeological, geological and geographical interest. In the Alligator Rivers Region, it shall also be the interests of the traditional Aboriginal owners of, and of other Aborigines interested in, so much of the land within the part or reserve as is within the region.

Part IV of the Act makes provision for the appointment of 'wardens' and gives them various policing powers and functions. Section 71 permits the Governor-General to make regulations dealing with parks and reserves. Once again, the Act is circumscribed by constitutional power. More important is the problem of the nature of the protection given to relics. If X takes a relic from a park he or she has committed an offence. But does the Commonwealth have title to the relic? That depends on whether it was movable or immovable, and on whether the Commonwealth can be said to have taken *possession* of the article. In the light of *Attorney-General of New Zealand v. Ortiz*[3], such questions may not be easily answered.

The New South Wales *Heritage Act* 1977 attempts a national (or State) approach to preservation of the cultural heritage. Focussing on the environmental heritage, which it defines as 'those buildings, works, relics or places of historic, scientific, cultural, social, archaeological, architectural, natural or aesthetic significance for the State (S.4(1))', it embraces both the natural and the built environment. But the Act is confined to non-Aboriginal relics, defining 'relics' as 'any deposit, object or material evidence relating to the settlement prior to 1st January, 1980, or such other date as may be prescribed of the area that comprises New South Wales, *not being aboriginal settlement* (S.4(1))'.

Aboriginal cultural heritage, both relics and sites, is dealt with largely under provisions of the *National Parks and Wildlife Act* 1974 (see below). The Heritage Council has wide investigatory and coercive powers. In making recommendations to the Minister in respect of interim or permanent orders relating to an item of the environmental heritage or a precinct, the council is required to apply the stringent criteria of 'necessity' (Ss 24, 31, 36, 37 and 38) though the Act does not elaborate on the basis on which necessity is to be determined: necessary for what purposes?

The main focus of the Act is the provision for interim conservation orders (S.26) and permanent conservation orders (S.44). Conservation orders may be made in relation to 'the environmental heritage' and interim orders in relation to precincts. 'Precincts' are areas containing buildings, works, etc. (S.4(1)). A conservation order may also deal with the 'curtilage' or surroundings of the building, work, etc. (S.26(2)).

An interim conservation order is an order of no longer than two years' duration, made by the Minister where immediate protection is deemed 'necessary'. Such orders are made to allow the Heritage Council to make investigations as to whether or not a permanent conservation order or an environmental planning instrument is necessary. The order is published in the Gazette. Section 57 outlines the effect of the interim order:

(1) A person shall not, in respect of a building, work, relic or place to which an interim conservation order or a permanent conservation order applies or any land (other than such a place) which is subject to an interim conservation order or a permanent conservation order –
(a) demolish that building or work;
(b) damage or despoil that relic, place or land or any part of that relic, place or land;
(c) excavate any land for the purpose of exposing or moving that relic;
(d) carry out any development in relation to the land on which that building, work or relic is situated, the land which comprises that place, or that land;
(e) alter that building, work or relic;
(f) display any notice or advertisement on the building, work, relic, place or land; or
(g) damage or destroy any tree on or remove any tree from that place or land,
except in pursuance of an approval granted by the Heritage Council under Subdivision 1 of Division 3.
(2) The Minister, on the recommendation of the Heritage Council, may, by order published in the Gazette, grant an exemption from subsection (1) or such of the provisions of that subsection as are specified in

the order in respect of the engaging in or carrying out of such activity or class of activities by such person or class of persons in such circumstances as may be so specified.

An interim order remains in force for two years except where it is replaced by a permanent order or an environmental planning instrument, or the order is revoked. An interim order is revoked by publication of a revocation in the Gazette.

The power to make a permanent conservation order lies solely with the Minister and there is no appeal from, or judicial review of, his decision. An owner, mortgagee or lessee can object to the proposed order, and in that case an enquiry under S.41 must be held. Section 41 sets out four possible grounds of objection:

Where an owner (not being an owner referred to in section 38(1)), a mortgagee or a lessee of a building, work, relic or place the subject of a proposal of which notice is given under section 39 makes a submission by way of objection on any one or more of the following grounds, namely –
  (a) that the building, work, relic or place the subject of that proposal should not be subject to a permanent conservation order by reason that it is not an item of the environmental heritage;
  (b) that the building, work, relic or place the subject of that proposal should not be subject to a permanent conservation order by reason that its permanent conservation is not necessary;
  (c) that the building, work, relic or place the subject of that proposal should not be subject to a permanent conservation order by reason that such an order would render the building, work, relic or place incapable of reasonable or economic use; or
  (d) that conservation of the building, work, relic or place the subject of that proposal could not be achieved without causing undue financial hardship to the owner, mortgagee or lessee,
the Minister shall appoint a person to hold an inquiry into that submission.

Once a permanent conservation order is made it can be revoked, after a public notice has been issued on the recommendation of the Heritage Council and after consideration of submissions from the public at large (Ss 48–55 set out the procedure in detail). Permanent orders are therefore not as easily rescinded as interim orders.

It should be noted that the Heritage Council set up under the Act is entrusted with investigatory powers and makes recommendations to the Minister. The Minister's powers to make interim orders may be delegated to the Chairman of the Heritage Council.

Where 'precincts' under interim orders which are land other than curtilage are concerned, the Heritage Council under S.82 can request the Director of the Department of Environment and Planning, or a local council, to make a draft environmental planning instrument. If the request is denied, the Heritage Council can, with the Minister's approval, formulate its own environmental planning instrument. This instrument is then treated as if it were made under the *Environmental Planning and Assessment Act* 1979.

There is also provision in the Act for immediate intervention to prevent demolition. Orders are made under S.136 and are effective for twenty eight days. Under Ss 118 and 119, the Heritage Council can make orders for repairs to items under the conservation instrument. A variety of offences are created by the Act in Ss 157, 160 and 161. Section 117 creates the offence of demolition by wilful neglect. There are also provisions for the resumption of land for the purposes of the Act (Ss 113 and 121(1)(a)). Sections 138–46 provide that archaeological excavators must obtain an excavation permit before an investigation takes place. Section 146 places a duty on anyone who discovers a relic to notify the council of its location, unless he has reason to believe that the council is already aware of it. The various orders are enforced through the Land and Environment Court.

In general, the Act gives scope for community participation and involvement in the preservation of the cultural heritage. Any member of the public may make submissions to an enquiry into the revocation of a permanent order. Section 153(1) also gives *any* person standing to seek remedy of a breach of the Act.

The Heritage Council is required to keep a register listing items over which there are orders or orders pending. Section 167 provides for searches of the register by members of the public and for reliance on a certificate issued by the Department of Environment and Planning.

This brief overview of the New South Wales *Heritage Act*, perhaps the most developed of the state Acts, brings out a variety of significant features:

1. There is machinery for coercive measures to protect the cultural heritage.
2. There is a body set up with wide powers of investigation and surveillance.
3. The Act has wide scope applying to the natural environment, relics and sites.
4. There is scope for public participation in survelliance of the working of the Act.
5. There is a variety of orders that can be used in different circumstances – interim orders, permanent orders, S.130 orders, S.136 orders and environmental planning instruments.
6. The Act is rationally designed to 'dovetail' with planning legislation.
7. There is control of archaeological excavation.

There are, however, still significant problems with the Act. The criterion of 'necessity' is the most obvious. There appears to be no clear meaning to be ascribed to this criterion. The orders are issued on the Minister's discretion after advice by the Heritage Council. Conservation orders under the Act are directed at sites and, in the case of relics, at the site where the relic is situated. The Act does not appear to make straightforward provision for conservation orders in respect of movable objects that are not linked with a site. The result is something considerably beyond the earlier British soft regime (though like it concentrating on buildings and sites) but far short of the French strict regime.

The relevant New South Wales Act dealing with the Aboriginal cultural heritage is the *National Parks and Wildlife Act* 1974. Although the Act was passed in 1967 amendments concerning Aboriginal cultural heritage came in 1970 and significantly in the new act of 1974. The basic scheme of additional protection involved in the 1974 Act was the specification of 'Aboriginal areas', 'places' and 'protected archaeological areas' (See Ss 62, 65 and 84). 'Aboriginal areas' are unoccupied Crown lands that are proclaimed by the Governor as such areas. S.62(4) provides that: 'Lands within an Aboriginal area shall be deemed to be dedicated for the purpose of preserving, protecting, and preventing damage to relics or to Aboriginal places therein'. An 'Aboriginal place' under S.84 is a place so declared by the Minister which in his opinion 'is or was of special significance with respect to Aboriginal culture'.

These provisions allow for protection of sites that may be of traditional importance but marked by no physical archaeological 'relic'. So they are a significant addition to the 'blanket' protection offered by the Act to all sites so marked. The Act makes it an offence to disturb or destroy such relics and so protects the sites that incorporate them. The Act also therefore provides for control of investigation, while development that impinges on sites requires consent.

A 'relic' is defined in S. 5(1) as 'any deposit, object or material evidence . . . relating to indigenous and non-European habitation of the area that comprises New South Wales, being habitation prior to and concurrent with the occupation of that area by persons of European extraction'. Sections 27 and 28 provide for the existence and functions of an Aboriginal Relics Advisory Committee (see Sullivan's discussion p. 141) to advise and report to the Minister or the Director on matters relating to relics. Section 65(1) permits the Minister to declare lands 'on which a relic or Aboriginal place is situated, to be a *protected archaeological area*'. Such lands are those other than unoccupied Crown lands. The consent of the Minister for Lands is required for Crown land and that of the owner or occupier is required for private land. The Act empowers the Director to regulate entry to and use of these areas, with the consent of owners and occupiers. The Act also creates a variety of offences relating to relics (Ss 86, 87, 90) and vests custody of relics in the Trustees of the Australian Museum.

Apart from flora and fauna reserves, the Act also provides for the proclamation of 'historic sites' (Ss 31–47). Part V of the Act provides for the development of 'plans of management' by the Director for historic sites and Aboriginal areas (not mandatory, see S.72(1)(d)). Plans of management set out the ways in which the Director proposes to deal with the site or area and the sorts of developments or activities that are proposed. They are subject to emendation or cancellation by the minister and open to comment by councils and other 'interested persons'.

The existing Commonwealth legislation on cultural heritage – itself a recent development – has been overshadowed by the dramatic implications of the Tasmanian Dams case (*The Commonwealth of Australia and Anor. v. The State of Tasmania and Others* (1982–3) 46 *Australian Law Reports* 625, (1983) 57 *Australian Law Journal Reports* 450). The Commonwealth *World Heritage Properties Conservation Act* of 1983 was designed immediately to prevent an uncooperative Tasmanian government from flooding areas of Tasmania that had earlier been nominated by the Commonwealth government, on the request of the then Tasmanian Premier, for inclusion in the World Heritage List under the UNESCO Convention for the Protection of the World Cultural and Natural Heritage. Since Commonwealth powers to legislate under the external affairs power in respect of lands in a state were still in doubt, the Act was patently drafted both to provide bases for argument on this and other issues in court, and to attach the legislation to as many Commonwealth powers as possible. The Act provided that the Governor-General could proclaim both property in any state and property under Commonwealth jurisdiction, including property in any territory (Northern Territory and Norfolk Island), or any external territory administered by the Commonwealth, to form part of the cultural or natural heritage. The definition of property included movable as well as immovable property. The Governor-General could make such a proclamation only if he were satisfied that the property or any part or feature of it was in danger of damage or destruction. In the case of property that is in a state, the Commonwealth *prima facie* could act on this issue only on the external affairs power, or a doubtful power to legislate for the good of the nation generally, where such legislation is necessary and lacking. The Act therefore distinguished such property in a state and added the following prerequisites that had to be satisfied before the Governor-General could make a proclamation in respect to property in a state (S.6(2)):

(a)   the Commonwealth has, pursuant to a request by the State, submitted to the World Heritage Committee under Article 11 of the Convention that the property is suitable for inclusion in the World Heritage List provided for in paragraph 2 of that Article, whether the request by the State was made before or after the commencement of this Act and whether or not the property was identified property at the time when the request was made;

(b)   the protection or conservation of the property by Australia is a matter of international obligation, whether by reason of the Convention or otherwise;

(c)   the protection or conservation of the property by Australia is necessary or desirable for the purpose of giving effect to a treaty (including the Convention) or for the purpose of obtaining for Australia any advantage or benefit under a treaty (including the Convention);

(d)   the protection or conservation of the property by Australia is a matter of international concern (whether or not it is also a matter of domestic concern), whether by reason that a failure by Australia to take proper measures for the protection or conservation of the property would, or would be likely to, prejudice Australia's relations with other countries or for any other reason;

(e)   the property is part of the heritage distinctive of the Australian nation –
   (i)   by reason of its aesthetic, historic, scientific or social significance; or
   (ii)   by reason of its international or national renown,
   and, by reason of the lack or inadequacy of any other available means for its protection or conservation, it is peculiarly appropriate that measures for the protection or conservation of the property be taken by the Parliament and Government of the Commonwealth as the national parliament and government of Australia.

The Act also provided that the Governor-General should have power to proclaim an Aboriginal site if he was satisfied that the site is (because of the presence of artefacts, relics or otherwise) of particular significance to the people of the Aboriginal race, if that the site, artefacts or relics are being, or are likely to be, damaged or destroyed. The section of the Act providing this is declared by the section to be necessary as special law for the people of the Aboriginal race (a specific Commonwealth power). Section 9 of the Act then provides that it is unlawful for a person, except with the consent in writing of the Minister, to do any act that damages or destroys any property that has been proclaimed. Section 9 also provides that it is unlawful for any person to carry out certain acts on proclaimed property: excavating, exploratory drilling for minerals and ancillary activities; erection of or damaging or destroying a building or substantial structure; cutting, killing or damaging any tree or trees; and constructing roads or vehicular tracks or using explosives. Ss 10 and 11 make the same activities unlawful if performed by foreign corporations incorporated in a Territory or formed within the limits of the Commonwealth in respect of which the Commonwealth has power to legislate, or in relation to Aboriginal sites, where artefacts or relics may also not be damaged or destroyed. The Act provided that acts authorized pursuant to a zoning plan in operation under the *Great Barrier Reef Marine Park Act* 1975 or pursuant to a plan of management in force under the *National Parks and Wildlife Conservation Act* 1975 could not be made unlawful under Ss 9, 10 or 11 of the *World Heritage Properties Conservation Act*.

The Act further provided that an interested person or the Attorney-General could seek an injunction from the High Court of the Federal Court to restrain persons from committing unlawful acts under Ss 9, 10 or 11. An 'interested person' is widely defined under S.14(3):

(a) a person whose use or enjoyment of any part of the property is, or is likely to be, adversely affected by the doing of the act; or

(b) an organization or association of persons, whether incorporated or not, the objects or purposes of which include, and activities of which relate to, the protection or conservation of the property or of property of a kind that includes the property.

Here, a right is given to groups and associations in S.14(3)(b). This effectively remedies the decision in *Australian Conservation Foundation v. Commonwealth of Australia*.[4] The Act provided that the Minister in giving written consent to such actions should have regard only to the protection, conservation and presentation, within the meaning of the Convention, of the property and that he should give the appropriate Minister in the Northern Territory or the Administrator of Norfolk Island, where property in their territories is involved, an opportunity to make representations. The Act recognized that affected persons might regard proclamation as amounting to acquisition as defined in the Constitution, and provided a detailed procedure for claiming that acquisition has taken place and determining compensation. A Schedule to the Act incorporated the (UNESCO) Convention for the Protection of the World Cultural and Natural Heritage.

Promptly, the validity of important sections of the Act and especially the Commonwealth's claim to be acting in pursuit of its external affairs power (S.51(xxix)) were challenged in the High Court. The fundamental and dramatic impact of the resultant High Court decision in the Dams case was to uphold, by four to three, the power of the Commonwealth to legislate under the external affairs power obligations under an international treaty or convention not entered into merely for the purpose of acquiring power to legislate, even though the matters covered would not otherwise be matters of external affairs. The court, however, struck down specific sections of the Act as going beyond Commonwealth powers, or violating the Constitution. These included those portions of Ss 9 and 11 that proclaimed specific acts to be unlawful (excavating, drilling, etc.) without requiring these acts to be in themselves destructive or damaging. These provisions appear to go beyond Australia's obligation under the convention. The court also struck down portion of the Act (Ss 8 and 11) prohibiting such acts on Aboriginal sites. It held by a majority, however, that legislation on Aboriginal sites, though directed at all comers regardless of race, was the making of special laws for a particular race. Brennan J. converted a minority of the court striking down Ss 8 and 11 of the Act in regard to Aboriginal sites into a majority, by holding those sections invalid because they amounted to acquisition of property by the Commonwealth not on just terms (S.51(xxxi)). He and hence the majority of the Court argued, however, that legislation for Aboriginal sites, even if directed at all Australians, was the making of special laws for people of a particular race, the Aborigines, and therefore within that specific Commonwealth power (S.51(xxvi)). It could be done; it had just been badly done.

The *World Heritage Properties Conservation Act* 1983 was a rushed piece of legislation by a government just come into power. It was responding to, and mobilizing, widespread public opposition to Tasmania's rejection of a national and international right to dictate provisions for conservation in Tasmania and its own refusal to put conservation uppermost. The principle that the Commonwealth has power to intervene in the states to protect cultural and natural heritage in pursuit of obligations under the UNESCO Convention to which Australia is a party is now firmly established. Sections of the Commonwealth *World Heritage Properties Conservation Act* and Regulations made under S.69 of the *National Parks and Wildlife Conservation Act* of 1975 in respect of the World Heritage (Western Tasmania's Wilderness) Regulations have been held invalid. But the Commonwealth's power to intervene in Tasmania has been upheld. The reasoning in the decision and the differences of attitude between Justices will keep lawyers busy for a long time to come, in respect of setting or extending the precise limits in borderline cases of Commonwealth power on the basis of international obligation or concern. But for those interested in the preservation of the past and in Australia's cultural heritage, as for those concerned with its natural features, a new era of systematic and thought-out Commonwealth legislation is now possible.

Notes

1   The author is grateful to Dr Gabriël Moens and Mr Roger Wilkins, then of the Department of Jurisprudence, who assisted her with research and Mr Max Bourke, then Director of the Australian Heritage Commission, who was kind enough to comment on an earlier version of this paper read at the Academy Symposium. Mr Adrian Diethelm, now working in the Department of Jurisprudence, gave me valuable help in the final version of the paper.

2   The *Australian Heritage Commission Act* 1975 established the Australian Heritage Commission. Section 7 (as amended by the *Australian Heritage Commission Amendment Act*, 1976) defines the functions of that Commission in terms of activities related to 'the national estate'. They are:

a)   to furnish advice to the Minister, either of its own motion or upon request made to it by the Minister, on matters relating to the national estate, including advice relating to action to conserve, improve and present the national estate;

b)   to encourage public interest in, and understanding of, issues relevant to the national estate;

c)   to identify places included in the national estate and to prepare a register of those places in accordance with Part IV;

d)   to furnish advice and reports in accordance with Part V;

e)   to further training and education in fields related to the conservation, improvement and presentation of the national estate;

f)   to make arrangements for the administration and control of places included in the national estate that are given or bequeathed to the Commission; and

g)   to organize and engage in research and investigation necessary for the performance of its other functions.

3   (1983) 2 *Weekly Law Reports*, 809. A Maori carving, an 'historic article' within the meaning of the *Historic Articles Act*, 1962 of New Zealand, had been unlawfully removed from New Zealand without permission. It was recognized in New Zealand when it figured in a BBC television show featuring some articles on auction at Sotheby's. In an action by the plaintiff on behalf of the Crown in the right of the Government of New Zealand claiming an injunction against the sale and an order for delivery up of the carving as having been unlawfully removed from New Zealand, a preliminary issue was whether on the facts alleged the Crown was the owner and entitled to possession, in pursuant to the *Historic Articles Act* and the *Customs Act*, 1913 and 1966, which provided for forfeiture of goods seized. The United Kingdom Court of Appeal held, reversing the trial Court, that forfeiture under S.12(2) of the *Historic Articles Act* took effect not automatically but on seizure by the Crown and that since the carving had not been forfeited under the Act, the Crown was neither the owner nor entitled to possession of the carving. As an alternative ground for decision, a majority of the Court held that the New Zealand provision constituted a penal law, and as such was not enforceable in an English Court, on

the well-established rule of private international law that the courts of the forum will not enforce foreign penal laws.

⁴ *Australian Law Reports* 28(1980), 257. In that case the Foundation was held not to have *locus standi* to sue to challenge the validity of the proposed Iwasaki agreement for a development project under the provisions of the *Environment Protection (Impact of Proposals) Act* 1974.

References

Daniel, G.E. (1975), *A Hundred and Fifty Years of Archaeology*, 2nd edn, Duckworth, London.

Klindt-Jensen O. (1975), *A History of Scandinavian Archaeology*, Thames & Hudson, London.

Korthals, Altes, A. (1974), 'Submarine antiquities and the law', *Annuaire de l'Association des auditeurs et anciens auditeurs de l'Academie de Droit Internationale de la Haye*, 44, 127ff.

Niec, H. (1976), 'Legislative models of protection of cultural property', *Hastings Law Journal* 27, 1089–122.

Palmer, N.E. (1981), 'Treasure Trove and the protection of antiquities', *Modern Law Review* 44, 178–87.

Prott, Lyndel, V. and O'Keefe, P. (1983), *Law and the Cultural Heritage*, vol. 1: *Discovery and Excavation*, Professional Books Ltd, Abingdon.

Sparrow, Charles (1982), 'Treasure Trove: a lawyers view', *Antiquity* 56, 199–201.

Williams, Sharon, A. (1978), *The International and National Protection of Movable Cultural Property: A Comparative Study*, Oceania, Dobbs Ferry.

Yales, D.E.C. (1980), 'Treasure trove – old laws and new needs', *Cambridge Law Journal* 39, 281.

8

The Custodianship of Aboriginal Sites in Southeastern Australia

Sharon Sullivan

Before the coming of Europeans, the ancestors of modern Aborigines occupied Australia for more than 40 000 years. The Australian landscape, 'virginal', 'pristine', 'untamed' to early European settlers, was in large part an artefact of human occupation. Evidence of Aboriginal occupation over this long period occurs throughout Australia, as an effect on landscape, vegetation and fauna, and in the form of Aboriginal sites – places where material evidence of Aboriginal occupation occurs, or which are sacred or significant to Aborigines, as part of their religious belief.

Aboriginal sites are numerous, diverse, and span a long period of time. In terms of the world's cultural heritage, Aboriginal sites have been judged to be much more significant than this country's remains of European settlement. The only Australian cultural sites to receive World Heritage Listing so far are Aboriginal (see Fig. 4). Their potential for research into Aboriginal and world prehistory is immense, and they have undoubted international significance.

This importance has recognized benefits for the Australian nation. Assumption of Aboriginal sites as part of the general Australian heritage assists in validating and consolidating the relatively brief European past. Australians can have a history of 40 000 years instead of 200. The Aboriginal past could be an important unifying force in an Australia which is becoming increasingly multicultural.

Sites are also of great importance to Aborigines (Fig. 11). Some are of direct religious or historic significance. The evidence about past Aboriginal occupation which they provide has a more direct effect on Aborigines than on any other group in the community and whoever controls research into such sites controls, to some extent, the Aboriginal past. Perhaps most importantly, sites have immense symbolic value to a group still struggling for legal recognition of their prior ownership of Australia, and for some form of compensation or agreement on this matter (Fig. 5). Sites are the tangible evidence of Aboriginal occupation of Australia; Aboriginal ownership of them, in cultural and moral terms, is clearly very difficult to dispute.

So the question of who should control these sites inevitably arises in any discussion about who owns the past in Australia. For historical reasons, and because of the nature of the sites and the evidence they contain, the major area of debate to date has been between archaeologists and Aborigines.

At the recent Australian Archaeological conference in Tasmania, Ros Langford, on behalf of the Tasmanian Aboriginal Centre, gave a paper which admirably summarized the Aboriginal point of view on this matter (Langford 1983). The Tasmanian Aboriginal Centre then proposed that the Australian Archaeological Association adopt a number of motions, the first of which was: 'That this conference acknowledges Aboriginal ownership of their heritage. Accordingly, this conference calls on all archaeologists to obtain permission from the Aboriginal owners prior to any research or excavation of Aboriginal sites' (Allen 1983: 7).

The resolution was adopted by the conference, and later confirmed by the Annual General Meeting. Jim Allen, in his summary of events for *Australian Archaeology* commented that some archaeologists were disturbed by this proposal because:

Philosophically they argue that the past only exists in the sense that it is created by people in the present, whether from historical documents, oral traditions or archaeological evidence. In this sense there can be many 'pasts' which depend ultimately upon the belief systems of the people who create those pasts, whether these are based on religion, logic or group-vested interests. In a practical sense this emerged in the question . . . 'How far does ownership in this case equate with censorship?' In other words [it was feared that] . . . this motion would give authority to . . . Aborigines to exclude archaeologists whose reconstructed 'pasts' do not agree with their own. (Allen 1983: 8)

This paper examines the recent history of custodianship of sites in Australia in an attempt to elucidate who have been the 'creators' of the Aboriginal past, the Aboriginal response to this, and the implications of the Tasmanian Aboriginal Centre's demands. Some of the ideas in this paper were first aired by Harry Allen at the Brisbane ANZAAS Congress in 1981, in a very stimulating and challenging paper which is presently unpublished (Allen 1981).

W.H. Stanner wrote, in the 1930s, of the Aborigines of South-eastern Australia:

About the only traces of them which would remain would be a few not-too-well preserved rock carvings and paintings, a midden or two, some scanty records, and collections in universities and museums, and a handful of inferior books. As it is, the old tribesmen of New South Wales and Victoria might as well have been shadows moving in the trees of the eighteenth century for all the imprint they have left behind . . . (Stanner 1979: 2)

Thirty years later, the 'few rock carvings' and the 'midden or two' had assumed sufficient importance to acquire legal protection, but their creators were still merely shadows in an eighteenth century landscape.

Legislation to protect Aboriginal sites was introduced in all states of Australia in the late 1960s or early 1970s. The legislation was largely a result of the lobbying of a small specialist group, encouraged by recent important advances in their discipline. The archaeologists concerned wished to protect sites from indiscriminate destruction and from unscientific, amateur, destructive research, because of their rapidly emerging scientific value, and because of their heritage value which was mainly seen in terms of the aesthetic and public value of the spectacular rock art sites. These sites were often compared in quality with, and held up as rivalling those of Europe, which were highly valued as part of the European cultural and archaeological tradition. Legislation to protect Aboriginal sites was introduced considerably before there was any effective legislation for the protection of European colonial sites, but it was not the result of any grass-roots movement in Australian society nor did it have any Aboriginal input or indeed support. In New South Wales, this was despite the fact that the committee which advised on the writing of the legislation was chaired by the eminent anthropologist A.P. Elkin.

With the exception of the Western Australian legislation the Acts of this period have many common characteristics which indicate their inspiration and aim. They refer to the items which they seek to protect as 'relics'; they lay down explicit and detailed conditions for archaeological research, especially for excavation; they set up advisory committees with exclusive or majority white membership, and with heavy archaeological input. None provides for any effective Aboriginal input, consultation or control. Ownership of sites and relics either resides with the present land owner or purchaser, or is claimed by the Crown. All Acts designate a government department, usually a museum or nature conservation service, to administer the Act. (See Edwards 1975 for details of legislation in all states and territories in the early 1970s.)

The Western Australian Aboriginal Heritage Act 1972 is a partial exception to this since it specifically provides for traditional Aboriginal use, Aboriginal custodians, and the traditional cultural use of sites and objects. This was undoubtedly because of the input of sympathetic anthropologists, working in the north of Western Australia, where the Aboriginal traditional lifestyle was still strong.

In the Northern Territory, during the 1970s, Aboriginal land rights legislation was introduced. This meant that large areas of the Northern Territory could be claimed by the traditional owners if they could prove a specifically defined and direct traditional association with the area. Sacred and significant sites within claimed areas were of crucial importance in establishing land ownership and one effect of the legislation has been to give control of such sites to successful claimants. Traditional sites not within Aboriginal land are protected by the Aboriginal Sacred Sites Authority run by a board with a majority of members being Aboriginal. Thus many Aborigines in the Northern Territory gained custodianship of sites of significance to them. However, the legislation, because of the way in which it is framed, recognizes the rights of those Aborigines least affected by European settlement – that is, those who are able to demonstrate strong and detailed traditional links with a particular site or area. The legislation excludes those Aborigines whose culture has been most severely disrupted by the European invasion, because it does not recognize custodianship of sites where traditional links have been lost, or where the evidence of continuity does not meet the rules of an exacting court.

In southeastern Australia, after 200 years of European occupation, traditional Aboriginal society had been very severely disrupted, and the connection between the present Aboriginal population and their 'relics' was believed to be almost extinct. In the 1970s in New South Wales, the National Parks and Wildlife Service, with funding from the Australian Institute of Aboriginal Studies, carried out a survey designed to locate and preserve sites of particular significance to Aborigines. Some 500 have been located and recorded to date (Creamer 1980). However, the vast majority of sites in New South Wales, Victoria, and Tasmania were unknown to Aborigines until located and recorded, and could not be shown to be of direct traditional importance to Aborigines in terms of the Northern Territory model. Hence archaeologists, and the general public, have considered that the main value of such sites is to research, or as part of the general heritage of the Australian people. At a symposium held at the Australian Institute of Aboriginal Studies in 1972 on *The Preservation of Australia's Aboriginal Heritage* the then Minister for Aboriginal Affairs outlined clearly what was considered to be the major, overriding value of such Aboriginal sites:

Having said that I see no conflict of interest between us and the Aborigines in these matters, I will go on to say that our interest in one sense may be even wider and deeper than theirs. I imagine it likely that because of the time-depth with which we are now dealing some of the earlier traces of man's occupation of Australia may be of little or no interest to living Aborigines. In many areas there are rock engravings, elaborate stone arrangements and paintings which have been accepted by recent generations of Aborigines as part of the universe shaped by their Dreamtime ancestors but which have no special significance in recent or present religious beliefs and practices. It seems possible that the engraved heads on the rocks of the Cleland Hills may be of that kind. I would think that the still older horizons of culture which have been excavated by archaeologists also fall into this class. I am in no doubt whatever about the immense significance of these discoveries to the world of learning, and we must certainly protect and preserve them as far as we can, even if some of the living Aborigines may be less concerned with them than with things of lesser antiquity but greater present or recent significance. (Edwards 1975: 3).

Until recently, this view of the prime value of the majority of Aboriginal sites in southeastern Australia – 'the immense significance . . . to the world of learning' – has prevailed (Figs 4 and 5).

In comparison with the sites of their own culture, archaeologists have been working almost in a cultural vacuum with respect to Aboriginal sites. There never has been a popular, grass-roots interest in Aboriginal sites amongst the general community, comparable to the interest in the historic sites which relate to European heritage. The reasons were outlined by Edwards.

A great deal is being achieved in the preservation of historic structures by such agencies as the National Trust of Australia, sympathetic private owners and enlightened governments. The main incentive for the preservation of the best examples is a national pride in the accomplishments of the 200 years since Captain Cook sighted Australia. These structures are equivalent to the palaces, castles and manor houses of Europe and reflect a unique colonial history.

Aboriginal monuments pose a problem of a different order as they are not fully accepted as part of Australian history and little effort has been made to ensure that surviving examples are preserved. Overseas there is an unbroken line linking present generations with populations of the recent and distant past. The great prehistoric monuments, ancient buildings, rich cave art and other relics of Europe are the product of the predecessors of existing populations. National pride ensures their preservation: cultural tourism provides an added incentive. So far there is no comparable attitude towards Aboriginal antiquities in Australia and their conservation has been relegated to low priority. (Edwards 1975: 46)

There is no doubt that Australia has Aboriginal sites of great significance at many levels – the Lake Mungo and Kakadu National

Parks were nominated for the World Heritage List at least in part because of this value. Yet Aboriginal sites have never been a popular heritage issue.

In contrast, local historical societies and branches of the National Trust have been active thoughout this century in the preservation of sites relating to European settlement and colonization, particularly those which commemorate the lives and deeds of the pioneers. The National Trust's listing procedure, which draws public attention to important historic buildings and sites, and encourages their preservation, was instituted long before there was legislation formally protecting such sites. Local historical societies have been similarly active, especially in the field of local museums and collections of local history.

In this process, Aboriginal sites and Aboriginal history have been largely ignored. Local grass-roots historians have devoted themselves to selected aspects of Aboriginal history; but their concern has been by and large, superficial. There is an interest in curios such as King Plates, and the more spectacular or unfamiliar items of material culture, and commonly, romanticized mythology about noble savages, kindly land-holders and the 'last full blood'. This interest is rarely related to the present descendants of the 'dusky tribemen'. In fact any claim for cultural continuity by Aborigines at a local level, is often met with shock and disbelief. The noble savage is indeed a figure in an eighteenth-century landscape; 'real' Aborigines are never those presently around, but those of the last generation, known to the narrators' ancestors. In some cases, there is positive opposition to (or resentment of) any attempt to document or commemorate the sites of less romantic aspects of white-black contact – such as that encountered by researchers following up a request by Aborigines for a memorial at the site of the Myall Creek massacre. With the threat of land rights claims, this incredulity, resentment and belittlement of Aboriginal claims often has an element of fear and self-interest. Recently Aboriginal sites have been destroyed in New South Wales because of this resentment and fear. A rock engraving site, nominated for the Register of the National Estate, was systematically and totally defaced soon afterwards (Holmes 1983). Similarly a carved tree was disfigured with an axe, the day following the local council's agreement that it be preserved and the area surrounding it reserved (Ahearn 1980).

There are certainly exceptions to this tendency and a growing number of them. Local historians such as Bobby Hardy (1981) with her excellent account of recent Aboriginal history in western New South Wales have done much to redress the balance, but generally it is clear that, not unnaturally, the organizations aimed at preserving the European heritage have a long history, are widespread, have strong popular support, and pay little attention to the Aboriginal heritage. So despite comparatively strong legislation to protect them, Aboriginal sites have never effectively been regarded as part of the Australian heritage. They have not been listed in any number by the National Trust, or the Australian Heritage Commission (to the commission's great regret), and they have never achieved the level of popular support which the white heritage attracts (Yenkin 1982: 101).

This is indicated by the comparatively low level of funding and management generally accorded Aboriginal sites as part of the national estate. A large proportion of funding goes to research aimed at extracting information from sites, comparatively little to conserving them. The grants distributed by the Commonwealth for the conservation of sites on the Register of the National Estate are a good indication of the priority accorded at state level. National Estate grants are given for three types of sites, those with natural values, or with cultural values, either European or Aboriginal. Between 1979 and 1982, New South Wales allocated an average 13.3 per cent of its funding to Aboriginal sites, Victoria 5.6 per cent, Queensland 11.6 per cent and South Australia 25.5 per cent. Figures for the other states and territories are available only for 1981–82. They are Western Australia 9 per cent, Tasmania 6 per cent, Northern Territory 18 per cent and Australian Capital Territory 15 per cent (figures supplied by the Australian Heritage Commission).

There are a number of reasons why there has been such a low level of funding for Aboriginal sites. The lion's share of National Estate grants goes to what is called 'the built environment' – monuments to European history. This reflects the absolute flood of applications for funding in this area, invariably received by all states. Numerous local applicants seek funding for the conservation of some piece of recent European heritage. There is no such flood of popular requests for funding for Aboriginal sites. The state authorities with statutory responsibilities certainly make numerous applications for funding; but the final division clearly reflects the popular vote.

Within such a framework of priorities, views about what is appropriate conservation work for European and Aboriginal sites also display this difference. It is considered to be acceptable (though regrettable) to cage in an Aboriginal art site or to allow unsupervised visitation to it, usually on the pretext of lack of funds. Such treatment is not allowed for the more significant European sites, even when it is clear that the world heritage value of the Aboriginal site far outweighs that of the European site.

In Elizabeth Bay House, a Sydney colonial mansion, the sumptuously restored and furnished rooms are cordoned off; visitors are ushered in and closely supervised. In Kakadu National Park, in the Northern Territory, the Aboriginal rock art listed as part of the World's Heritage is, by and large, subject to unsupervised visits and consequently to vandalism. Is it not as highly valued by the dominant society?

Clearly, though non-Aboriginal Australians assert custodianship over Aboriginal sites, they do not 'own' them in the sense of accepting and cherishing them as part of their heritage. There has been a very real and noticeable lack of such a feeling for the Aboriginal heritage in Australia in the common life and cultural pursuits of Australians. Aborigines certainly had such a feeling, but as they were not part of the mainstream of Australian culture these feelings were not accepted as legitimate, nor were they confidently articulated. This has left prehistoric archaeologists to operate in a vacuum which at once privileges and disadvantages both themselves and their subject.

Prehistoric archaeologists are privileged because legislation to protect Aboriginal sites has been written more or less for their benefit, and to their specifications; a large percentage of money devoted to sites has gone to archaeological research; the archaeological view of the Aboriginal past has been that accepted in official circles and by the general public. There have been no serious competing popular interests in Aboriginal sites researched by archaeologists, or in their theories, or about financial priorities for conservation or site management. The main value of Aboriginal sites was judged to be their research value, and this was reflected in the way they were dealt with. This can be readily perceived by contrasting the situation for historical archaeologists. The popular movement for historic conservation, spearheaded by the National Trust, has been in the direction of conservation and restoration of historic buildings. Archaeologists have had to argue the value of their profession for heritage conservation, and to lobby strongly for consideration of archaeological matters. For instance there is no archaeologist on the Heritage Council of New South Wales, though architects and historians are represented. It has been necessary to justify and popularize archaeology and archaeological sites. Certainly one reason for this difference has been that archaeology is more peripheral to the study of historic sites than to prehistoric sites; but another important reason is that there is a constant popular interest in and pressure on the European Heritage movement which directs priorities into other areas than archaeology. In comparison, prehistoric archaeologists have not had this kind of competition.

However, there have also been disadvantages in this situation, and some unfortunate results. Prehistoric archaeology is often seen as sterile and apparently irrelevant by the public. It does not have the dynamic and creative tension which results from ongoing popular interest and popular input. In the European historic field, arguments often rage between archaeologists, local historians, architects, the National Trust and the state authority, about the primary significance of a site. Anne Bickford has described such a conflict in the interpretation of Elizabeth Farm, Parramatta (Bickford 1981). Often archaeology has had to take second place to other heritage values: archaeological material has sometimes been sacrificed to more popular values, because the general heritage movement does not rate archaeological, or research value as highly as other concerns. On the other hand, the sites themselves have been highly esteemed by the community, because of their rich and multifaceted symbolic value.

Until recently, there was no such dispute about prehistoric sites in Australia. Their overriding value was as resources for research. Thus they were assessed, their importance gauged, and priorities for conservation assigned. For this very reason they had a generally low priority for the community.

I have discussed elsewhere the very real problems for Aborigines in this particular use of their heritage and its consequent 'creation' of their past, to use Jim Allen's term (Sullivan 1983). Basically, the problems are those common to any indigenous group, whose past is studied by a dominant culture which tends to provide a self-serving or ethnocentric interpretation of the evidence and, even with the best intentions in the world, often unconsciously harms or insults the studied group. The problems have been admirably discussed by Trigger, in the American context (Trigger 1980).

Aborigines, like American Indians, have had a bad press from anthropologists and archaeologists in the past. Mulvaney (1958–59) has outlined nineteenth-century attitudes, which sanctioned dispossession of Aborigines on the scientific grounds that they were sub-human, a lower link in the evolutionary chain, destined to be displaced by a higher order. A.P. Elkin, in 1924, referred to the Australian Aborigines thus: 'In England they became extinct, but in the Southern Continent they lived on till now living fossils of a former stage in the evolution of modern man' (quoted in Goodall 1982).

Though prehistorians have long since developed a more sophisticated picture of Aboriginal society, this early view still lingers in the public consciousness. Archaeologists, in defence of their work, have pointed out that recent research – which illustrates the long Aboriginal occupation of Australia, and the richness, diversity and adaptability of Aboriginal culture – has had a positive effect on the general public's view of Aboriginal society, and has been used by Aborigines in arguments justifying land rights. This is true, and it seems to me that archaeology has a lot to offer Aboriginal society in the long run. However, in the present climate, these arguments cut little ice with Aborigines. According to their traditional beliefs, they have always lived in Australia, so the revelation that 'science' proves they have been here 40 000 years is hardly a surprise. Moreover, it can be argued that new positive evidence about the Aboriginal past provided by archaeologists is only necessary to dispel the public's misconceptions which are based in part on early anthropological theory, such as that cited above.

Trigger (1980) and Miller (1980) have both discussed the problems for indigenous people of a positivist approach to prehistory which eschews culture history. In Australia, Aborigines are aware that a lot of research into Aboriginal culture has not elucidated that culture but, because it is deemed particularly suitable for this role, is in fact being used by Europeans to learn more about their own culture, and to attempt to produce universally valid generalizations about human society. Hence for Aborigines much prehistory is, at best, irrelevant. Of greater concern is the fact that it is still easy for those who wish to do so to mis-use statements of conjecture or hypothesis, put forward by archaeologists explaining a theory or pursuing an academic argument.

In 1977 Jones argued that the Aboriginal population of Tasmania was perhaps doomed to extinction by the isolation as rising sea levels cut them off from the mainland 6000 years ago.

Let us end with Tasmania and consider the trauma which the severance of the Bassian bridge delivered to the society isolated there. Like a blow above the heart, it took a long time to take effect, but slowly but surely there was a simplification in the tool kit, a diminution in the range of foods eaten, perhaps a squeezing of intellectuality. The world's longest isolation, the world's simplest technology. Were 4000 people enough to propel forever the cultural inheritance of Late Pleistocene Australia? Even if Abel Tasman had not sailed the winds of the Roaring Forties in 1642, were they in fact doomed – doomed to a slow strangulation of the mind? (Jones 1977: 203–4)

This conjecture, later put more simply for the general public in a sympathetic film about the Tasmanian Aborigines, *The Last Tasmanian*, has provided well-used ammunition for those opposed to rights for Tasmanian Aborigines. In Victoria, an assessment of the archaeological value of sites was used as the main measure of their significance and as a weapon to allow a major development, against Aboriginal wishes. The problem is not that such findings or theories are put forward; it is rather that they have, until recently, automatically been validated by our society. Aborigines have had no effective input into this process, and no effective way of influencing the outcome. Yet they are the people whose lives are actually affected by the way society receives these findings. Research into sites has also often been without consultation with Aborigines, and has sometimes been offensive to them. This is particularly the case where skeletal material is involved. Though it is now common for state authorities to request consultation with Aborigines prior to research work, and for archaeologists to carry this out, it is still not mandatory.

Archaeologists are the group in the community attacked most often by Aborigines over these and similar matters relating to Aboriginal sites. This is because both Aborigines and archaeologists have a deep interest in Aboriginal sites; and because to date archaeologists have effectively held the custodianship of sites – have lobbied for the legislation, carried out research, interpreted the Aboriginal past for the general public, and have tried to incorporate Aboriginal sites as part of the nation's heritage.

Perhaps most important for Aborigines is the question of appropriateness. It does not seem *appropriate* to Aborigines that the main value accorded their sites is their research potential, because all sites in southeastern Australia have other values for Aborigines.

For Aborigines, sites have strong symbolic or religious value. Some sites are specifically sacred or significant, but all sites are, to many Aborigines, tangible proof of their ancestors' life in Australia from what is, to them, literally time immemorial. The Aboriginal community regards all Aboriginal sites as 'sacred' sites in this sense, and uses this term increasingly in southeastern Australia to describe all Aboriginal sites.

Sites provide evidence of prior occupation of the whole of Australia by Aborigines, and are a basis for land rights claims. There has never been any agreement or treaty with Aborigines to acknowledge this prior ownership, and from the Aboriginal point of view this occupation is illegal. The issue of custodianship of sites is, for this reason, inextricably bound up with the issue of land rights. Assertion of custodianship of sites is for Aborigines at least a symbolic assertion of their ownership of Australia.

In addition Aborigines have a deep personal attachment to sites and areas which commemorate their recent history. The injustices of the last 200 years are remembered with strong and bitter emotion, and the sites of these events are redolent of it. In particular the stolen refuges – the mission stations first given, and then retaken, by whites – are remembered as havens and their loss is bitterly regretted.

Such significance of sites for Aborigines has been largely dis-
regarded by the general public until now. Archaeologists have
largely controlled sites, and have thus incurred a major share of
Aboriginal attention and disapproval. For good or ill, archaeologists have wielded great power. Sandra Onus of the Gundich
Mara tribe, recently summed up a common Aboriginal attitude
when she said 'archaeologists freak the people out' (Anne Bickford,
pers. comm.).

Now, relatively quickly, the balance of power shows signs of
changing in Australia. Aborigines are moving from a position of
abject powerlessness in the community to a position where they
feel the power and the ability to express their concern about their
own heritage as white Australians have done about theirs. Aborigines are moving into the mainstream of Australian culture, and
their concerns are increasingly clearly articulated and accepted by
others in Australian society.

Recently the Tasmanian Aboriginal Centre publicly and effectively moved to reclaim Aboriginal skeletal material illegally dug
up from a Christian cemetery and lodged with the Tasmanian
Museum. The first Aboriginal Principal of the Australian Institute
of Aboriginal Studies, Eric Willmot, was asked by a reporter why,
at this time, the claim was made. He replied: 'It's a growing feeling
of normalness and powerfulness as if they were normal members
of the Tasmanian society that has made them now make this claim'
(ABC programme *Monitor*, 29 November 1982).

This feeling of 'normalness' and 'powerfulness' is making an impact on the general Australian community which is gradually coming to recognize the validity of Aboriginal claims to land rights, and
to their heritage. There seems little doubt that the present leaders
of this country believe that Aborigines should be given land rights,
and a large say in the custodianship of Aboriginal sites – control
at policy level, of site management, research, and interpretation.
The Federal government has announced its intention of introducing uniform land rights and Aboriginal heritage legislation throughout Australia. In New South Wales, the Parliamentary Select
Committee report, adopted in principle by the New South Wales
government, recommended the implementation of land rights, and
the setting up of an Aboriginal Heritage Commission, run by
Aborigines, to manage Aboriginal sites in New South Wales, in
association with local Aboriginal land councils (Parliament of New
South Wales, 1980). In Victoria, South Australia and Western
Australia similar enquiries or proposed legislative amendments are
under way.

On a day-to-day basis, most Europeans of goodwill accept it as
natural that the group primarily involved in Aboriginal history

should be Aboriginal. Increasingly, government authorities and local shire councils in southeastern Australia are independently seeking local Aboriginal advice and assistance in site management. This year in New South Wales various local councils are applying for National Estate grants to have Aboriginal heritage studies conducted for their areas, with the intention of making the money available to local Aboriginal sites committees, which will, in turn, employ the archaeological expertise they require.

Ten years ago, teachers and others in the community wanting information or lectures on the Aboriginal past would turn to archaeologists. Now they seek out the Aboriginal community, or approach the state authority with a request for an Aboriginal speaker. Archaeologists are no longer, in the public mind, the principal experts on the Aboriginal past. Eric Willmot succinctly summarizes current liberal thinking on the matter:

The future is this: that Australia's human past is an Aboriginal past: and you cannot expect any kind of an authority to deal with human finds of the distant past to be of any use whatsoever until: one, it really has some power, that it can tell authority what it can and can't do; two, that it, of course, has a predominance of people whose fundamental position in the human race is being questioned one way and another by the finds and investigation. (ABC programme *Monitor*, 29 November 1982)

There is considerable evidence that increasing Aboriginal involvement and control will have very exciting and beneficial results for Aborigines, for Aboriginal studies, and for the general community. Evidence to date indicates that Aborigines are more concerned about site conservation than the general white community, and have a grass-roots movement which would be a strong basis for any Aboriginal Heritage Commission, and provide more political clout than is presently being exercised in favour of proper funding for Aboriginal site conservation.

Aboriginal communities throughout southeastern Australia have begun to take a much deeper interest in their heritage than was ever taken by local white historians. Aborigines have set up local sites or heritage groups in many areas, and are enthusiastically recording history and sites, and seeking funding and training in this area. Applications to the Australian Institute of Aboriginal Studies for local Aboriginal community groups for history and site recording programmes have increased greatly over the past five years, necessitating the creation of an Aboriginal History Committee. Demand now far outstrips supply. Even where only very limited funding is available for Aboriginal development in general, a high priority is given to this work by local Aboriginal communities. Traditional sacred and significant sites are probably most important to

Aborigines. However, all local Aboriginal sites are of particular interest to the local Aboriginal community. All aspects of the heritage are valued; the concern is for the conservation of all types of sites.

For three years, the New South Wales National Parks and Wildlife Service has had an Interim Aboriginal Sites Committee, made up of archaeologists and Aborigines from throughout the state to advise the Minister and the Director on all aspects of Aboriginal site management (Figs 10 and 11). The archaeologists tend to place the highest value on sites with research potential, and to concern themselves with the conservation of a representative sample of such sites. This is, in part, because the archaeologists themselves have realized that their role is, properly, a limited one. Aborigines on the committee have shown a much broader and deeper interest. This concern reflects that of the Aboriginal community. The idea of conservation of a sample of sites does not satisfy the Aboriginal concern for their heritage. In addition sites with little or no current research value such as recent historical sites, scarred and carved trees, and stone arrangements, are valued highly by the Aboriginal members, as one would expect, and are conserved on the basis of their general symbolic and heritage value. A new set of priorities on site conservation has emerged (Sullivan, 1983a).

The Aboriginal members of the committee also demand evidence of local Aboriginal involvement and consultation on any decisions relating to sites. Aborigines consider that the local Land Council or local community should be the final arbitrators of site management. The National Parks and Wildlife Service has been for three years holding field workshops for Aboriginal communities on the recognition, recording, assessment and management of local sites. The demand for such workshops is overwhelming, and the eagerness of the entire Aboriginal community to learn more about the management of their heritage represents a very powerful movement.

The National Parks and Wildlife Service is now almost daily alerted to the possible destruction of sites by Aboriginal communities, displaying an interest in their own heritage which simply is not apparent in the local white community. Recently for example, the NPWS was contacted by the Western Aboriginal Lands Council concerning the actions of a major petroleum exploration company, which was operating in the area without having conducted any preliminary archaeological surveys or carried out any consultation with local Aboriginal people. The council was most concerned that archaeological sites (exposed scatters of stone artefacts and hearths) were being destroyed by the bulldozers' activity, though there were no known traditional sacred or significant sites in the area. The council subsequently held a community meeting on site, inspected the damage, opened negotiations with the company, and arranged for the employment of an archaeologist to carry out further surveys, before work proceeded. In my experience this level of care for relatively unspectacular prehistoric sites is almost unknown in the general white community, though such sites have been and are of interest to archaeologists, from a different perspective.

This survey utilized archaeological expertise to locate sites previously unknown to Aborigines, and illustrates the fact that Aborigines value and utilize archaeological skills. The emphasis however, was on conservation rather than research, reflecting the symbolic and emotional value of the sites to the local people. Sites were not assessed or sampled in detail, and certainly not salvaged; rather the exploration team was diverted away from sensitive areas. This total diversion may not have been justifiable, by white archaeologists and bureaucrats, on archaeological grounds, but the general importance of the sites to the local Aboriginal community was a more effective and powerful argument.

The assertion of control by Aborigines (Fig. 5) and legislative moves to support this, is of concern to many archaeologists. Certainly, in view of the position which archaeologists have occupied *vis à vis* Aboriginal sites, it is understandable that such change may seem threatening. Archaeologists fear exclusion by Aborigines, lack of research opportunity, a change in priorities which will downgrade the importance of prehistoric sites and their management, and as mentioned by Allen (1983) censorship of unacceptable theories about the Aboriginal past.

It is true that for the reasons outlined above, many Aborigines are suspicious of archaeologists and their work, and oppose it on principle. A lot of this opposition arises from resentment and frustration over lack of any power or control of an area vital to Aboriginal identity and self-determination; this also accounts in some measure for the sometimes exaggerated and poorly-backed Aboriginal claims for special extensive knowledge, skill and expertise concerning sites. When Aborigines have real power this situation should change, especially if archaeologists do not withdraw their skills. A more equal partnership between Aborigines and archaeologists and more room for a frank exchange of views, because of this equality may emerge. If Aborigines have custodianship of sites, then the responsibility for site conservation and management will rest clearly with them. Archaeologists will be a group with particular interests and skills who will be able to put their case and offer their assistance as equals.

The Aboriginal heritage movement should acquire a whole new

dimension. Priorities for funding and conservation can be expected to change, with Aborigines, like other Australians, showing a special interest in recent history, and in particular in contact sites – mission stations and massacre sites, for instance. Evidence to date, however, indicates that Aborigines will continue to be concerned about prehistoric sites, and to request (as they now do) that archaeologists carry out research into such sites.

Recently, on the initiative of the local Aboriginal community, the Victoria Archaeological Survey provided a consultant, Sandra Bowdler, to excavate and remove prehistoric burials near the Murray River which were threatened by water erosion. The excavation was carried out with Aboriginal assistance and its extent and conduct was the result of close and continuous consultation with the Aboriginal community, which was, to all intent and purposes, the employer. The excavation generated a great deal of Aboriginal interest; there was considerable debate about the extent of the excavation, the nature of the evidence revealed, and the correct final resolution of the problem. The investigation showed that the site was an extensive burial ground; that it had been used over a long period, and that earlier burials had been disturbed to make way for later ones. This was interpreted by the Aboriginal community as evidence of a massacre by Europeans and their subsequent burial of the victims, since it was said that Aborigines would not disturb the earlier dead in this way. There was a lot of debate with the archaeologist on this point. When it became apparent that the site was a major burial ground, the community called a halt to the work, and requested that soil conservation experts attempt to save the whole site. This was done and a stabilization and monitoring programme has now been carried out by the community. The skeletal material was excavated and documented in the field prior to reburial. Archaeology, carried out at the request of the community, established the significance of the site and supplied information and a time scale for the local people; within this context debates about interpretation and decisions about future management were possible. Since neither was imposed by the archaeologist her own interpretation of the site was not offensive or objectionable. Considerable scientific information was derived from the site, and it was conserved as part of the Aboriginal heritage, and available for future research, should the community wish it (Bowdler 1983, 1983a). This sort of cooperative venture will, I hope, be the pattern for future archaeological work in Australia. It rests on recognition of Aboriginal ownership of the Aboriginal heritage and of the fact that in southeastern Australia all Aboriginal sites have significance to Aborigines. The distinctions between 'sacred', 'significant' and 'prehistoric' sites are no longer applicable or relevant in southeastern Australia, and will not hold.

Bowdler discussed the possibilities for an intellectual relationship between archaeologists and Aborigines in more general terms in a keynote address at the Pan Pacific Science Congress in Dunedin (Bowdler 1983b). She urged a mature, integrated study which connects the past with the present, and helps to explain it, uses ethnography creatively for this purpose, and consequently has meaning and importance to Aborigines today. Prehistoric archaeologists will have to give consideration to such matters, if they wish to justify their research in the present context, and to demonstrate its relevance to a new set of consumers. This will undoubtedly create problems of adjustment for both groups, but since archaeologists and Aborigines share a deep interest in Aboriginal sites, it seems to me that this will be achieved with good will. In the process, prehistoric archaeology in Australia should become more dynamic, more exciting and challenging and more a part of the Australian cultural mainstream.

* I would like to thank Sandra Bowdler and Isabel McBryde for their helpful comments on this paper.

References

Ahern, L. (1980), Report to the National Parks and Wildlife Service. NPWS.A. 1738.

Allen, H. (1981), Indigenous Involvement in the Discipline of Archaeology, typescript of paper delivered at 51st ANZAAS Congress, Brisbane, 1981.

Allen, J. (1983), 'Aborigines and archaeologists in Tasmania, 1983', *Australian Archaeology* 16, 7–10.

Australian Heritage Commission (1980), Nomination of the Willandra Lakes region for inclusion in the World Heritage List, Australian Heritage Commission, Canberra.

Bickford, A., (1981), 'The patina of nostalgia', *Australian Archaeology*, 13, 1–7.

Bowdler, S. (1983), 'Archaeological Investigation of a Threatened Aboriginal Burial Site near Robinvale, on the Murray River, Victoria', report to the Victoria Archaeological Survey.

—— (1983a), An Archaeological Investigation of a Threatened Aboriginal Burial Site near Robinvale, on the Murray River, Victoria, report to the Murray Valley Aboriginal Co-operative, Robinvale.

—— (1983b), Aborigines and Archaeologists: Fear and Loathing or

Mutual Benefit', paper given at the XV Pan Pacific Science Congress, Dunedin, New Zealand, February 1983.

Creamer, H. (1980), 'The Aboriginal Heritage in New South Wales', in Haig, C. and Goldstein, W. (eds), *The Aborigines of New South Wales*, National Parks and Wildlife Service, Sydney, 88–93.

Edwards, R. (ed.) (1975), *The Preservation of Australia's Aboriginal Heritage*, Australian Institute of Aboriginal Studies, Canberra.

Goodall, H. (1982), An Intelligent Parasite: A.P. Elkin and White Perceptions of the History of Aboriginal People in New South Wales, typescript of paper given at the History '82 Conference, August 1982.

Hardy, Bobbie (1981), *Lament for the Barkindji*, Alpha Books, Sydney.

Holmes, R. (1983), Vandalism of Aboriginal Engravings, report to the National Parks and Wildlife Service, Western Region, 426.

Jones, R. (1977), 'The Tasmanian Paradox', in Wright, R.V.S. (ed.), *Stone Tools as Cultural Markers*, Australian Institute of Aboriginal Studies, Canberra, 189–204.

Langford, R.J. (1983), 'Our heritage, your playground', *Australian Archaeology* 16, 1–6.

Miller, D. (1980), 'Archaeology and development', *Current Anthropology* 21(6), 709–15.

Mulvaney, D.J. (1958–9), 'The Australian Aborigines 1606–1929: Opinion and fieldwork', *Historical Studies, Australia and New Zealand* 8, 131–51, 297–314.

Parliament of New South Wales (1980), *Aboriginal Land Rights and Sacred and Significant Sites*, first report from the Select Committee of the legislative Assembly upon Aborigines, Part 1 (Report and Minutes of Proceedings), New South Wales Government Printer, Sydney.

Stanner, W.E.H. (1979), *White Man Got No Dreaming: Essays 1935–1973*, Australian National University Press, Canberra.

Sullivan, S. (1983), 'Aboriginal sites and ICOMOS guidelines', *Historic Environment* 3(1), 14–33.

—— (1983a), 'The New South Wales Interim Aboriginal Sites Committee', in M. Smith (ed.), *Archaeology at ANZAAS 1983*, Western Australian Museum, Perth, 322–28.

Trigger, B.G. (1980), 'Archaeology and the image of the American Indian', *American Antiquity* 45(4), 662–76.

Yenkin, D. (1982), *The National Estate in 1981*, Australian Government Publishing Service, Canberra.

9

Byzantium

The Transmission of a Heritage

Elizabeth Jeffreys

I would like to start by reminding you that Byzantium was the city that was re-founded by Constantine the Great in 330 and renamed Constantinople the New Rome, to serve as the administrative and cultural centre of the East Roman Empire. It continued to play this role until captured by the Turks in 1453. The inhabitants of the Byzantine Empire, whose borders fluctuated over the centuries, were a mixed conglomeration of Syrians, Armenians, Georgians, Slavs, Arabs and Copts: I shall return to the question of Greeks in a moment. Except perhaps in the last decades of its existence when reduced to little more than the city itself, Byzantium was never a nation-state whose territorial, linguistic and racial borders all coincided. The disparate groups subject to its one central ruler and dispenser of authority received their unity from their common heritage and from a long-lasting awareness of that heritage, despite strong local centrifugal tendencies (Mango 1980). Byzantium is thus a particularly appropriate subject for this symposium.

There were three strands to the heritage that Byzantium received from the ancient world: the Roman, the Greek and the Christian. To put it briefly, the law, institutions and administrative system of the Empire were Roman; the language, together with the literary and philosophical culture, was Greek, while to this was added the beliefs and rituals of Christianity, in the forms sanctioned by the Orthodox church. The interaction of these elements is reflected throughout the literary and cultural life of the Byzantine Empire.

Of the three strands the most deeply embedded were the Roman and the Christian. Until the very last days of Constantinople the emperor remained *autokrator tōn Romaiōn* (the emperor of the Romans) with the Roman legal justification for his position that had been formulated in the Justinianic code still unchallenged (Ostrogorsky 1968: 27–33; Ahrweiler 1975; Beck 1978). The inhabitants of the Empire never thought of themselves as other than Roman. The use of the term 'Byzantine' to refer to the whole state is a post-Renaissance and West European practice whose only justification lies now in its familiarity and a certain conciseness: for the alternatives involve circumlocutions like East Roman Empire or Late Roman Empire (Browning 1980: 8). In the contemporary sources *i Byzantii* refers only to the inhabitants of that city, an expression equivalent to, say, the Ephesians. The only possible alternative description for an inhabitant of the empire as a whole, as distinct from an inhabitant of a particular region, was 'Christian', even if this produced odd collocations – as when the officers of Romanos Lekapenos swore to defend the Christians (that is, their fellow-citizens) to the death against the Slavs, who by this time were also (nominally at least) Christian (Mango 1980: 31). This gives an added urgency to the fierce struggles in the Church councils to define orthodox belief against heretical views, when orthodoxy had some of the connotations which nationalism has for us today.

It was a tight hold on these past traditions, on the name of Rome and on the universal Christian Church, as well as the existence of a well-established bureaucracy which gave the empire much of its ability to endure over the centuries. I am of course passing over economic and military factors with cavalier disregard.

What I want to focus on today is the Greek element, the third and least dominant part of this Byzantine heritage. First we must be aware that the term 'Greek' has almost no racial meaning. The emperor was never ruler of the Greeks (*Ellines*) and Western diplomats who referred to him as Emperor of the Greeks (*Greci*) were usually trying to cut him down to size and were regarded with deep disfavour. Inhabitants of Greece itself used regional names to describe themselves: they were Thracians or Peloponnesians for example. If a more general term was required they were *Helladiki*, inhabitants of the theme (administrative district) of Hellas (Charanis 1978: 87–101). For most of the Byzantine centuries *Ellin*, Greek, carried the overtone of 'pagan',one who was involved – too involved probably – with Hellenic learning. Not until the twelfth century, under the Comnenian dynasty when the empire's territories had shrunk and the Crusading armies had harshly brought Western attitudes into Constantinople, do we find the first signs that *Ellin*, Greek, was emerging as an expression of national affiliation (Runciman 1970: 19–23; Nicol 1969: 23–5). We shall return to this.

Nevertheless one could say that the Greek language provided one of the vital cohesive elements in the Byzantine state. There were many regional languages – Syriac, Coptic, Armenian, Laz,

Georgian; some of these had writing systems and a literature of their own (Armenian, for example); some, like Laz, remained at the level of an unwritten, regional language. None was used for administrative purposes: this role was reserved for Greek in the East and for Latin in the West. With the division of the empire on the death of Theodosius I in 395 and the erosion of contact between the two halves, Latin slipped out of sight, as it were, in Constantinople. The last gasp comes in the reign of Justinian and his immediate successor when we find the last administrative documents to be issued in the two languages and the last Latin writers to operate in the Eastern capital: the chronicler Marcellinus Comes, the grammarian Priscian and the poet Corippus (Mango 1980: 16). Thereafter Greek became the sole medium for administration and for communication, for all educated persons throughout the East Mediterranean, a tendency that had existed since the time of Alexander the Great.

The Greek heritage has many facets. I shall be confining my comments to its literary and linguistic aspects, and not the philosophical or artistic – profitable and revealing though it would be to examine these. I have in mind the literary works written in Greek that continued to be read and studied, works of writers such as Homer, Euripides, or Thucydides – from the classical period of Greece, to use modern terminology. These set the standard for literary composition and linguistic usage – in structure, forms and style – that was aspired to by literary practitioners. In the context of this symposium I want to ask who owned this Greek literary heritage, how was this ownership achieved and what were its implications, and can we distinguish more than one method of access to it?

In looking for the answers to these questions we need to be aware first of the ways in which the Greek language had developed since the fifth century BC. The Attic dialect, which had been used by Thucydides and Plato, became the accepted medium for prose composition for the next generation, despite the existence of regional dialects which continued to be felt appropriate to certain genres; pastoral verse, for example, conventionally had a Doric tinge. Attic usage became the basis for the *koine dialektos*, the *koine* as it was more generally known, that was spread round the East Mediterranean in the wake of the conquests of Alexander the Great. The *koine* evolved away from some of the grammatical and syntactical complexities of earlier Greek, as can be observed in the writings of Polybius or Diodorus Siculus. That this trend reflected developments in the spoken language is confirmed by the nonliterary papyri, where even greater simplification exists. These documents on papyrus cover a wide range of material written at all levels of educational attainment, and amongst the most revealing of changes in the spoken language are letters by the barely literate. From the first century AD the language of the New Testament demonstrates another type of linguistic change, the effect on Greek of a mixed community of Greek and non-Greek speakers – in this case Semitic speakers, but the situation can be paralleled in other areas. This constant evolution in the acceptable forms of Greek set up the so-called Atticist reaction, an attempt to return to the syntax and style of, at the very least, the early *koine* of the third century BC, or preferably to the style of earlier writers still. We can observe the efforts of grammarians like Phrynichos to correct the neologisms of current speech (Browning 1969: 26–58).

In other words there existed a dichotomy between the spoken language of everyday and the written form, and to a lesser but still appreciable extent between the contemporary written form and their models from earlier centuries. This is relevant to our present argument in that this diglossy, which is present in every language to some extent, continued into the Byzantine period, and became even more marked over the centuries. One can talk of a Byzantine linguistic censorship which prevented the spoken forms of the language appearing on paper. But we can be sure that, however constant the written forms might appear to be, the spoken language did evolve significantly, in pronunciation, morphology and syntax. We can see this from the last years of Byzantium when eventually a version of the spoken language was written down, as well as from the odd scraps which occasionally emerge earlier in formal texts – snatches of vernacular vocabulary quoted by scandalized conventional writers, or handy travellers' hints, for example (Jeffreys 1973: 172). The dichotomy meant that a tremendous emphasis came to be put on the purely linguistic aspects of education. Correct orthography and grammar had to be learnt almost, though not quite, as a foreign language. I will comment in passing that though Greek developed levels of language and dialect forms these never ceased to be recognised as varieties of Greek, unlike the case of Latin and the development of the Romance languages.

Now, how widespread was literacy amongst the Byzantines? In other words, how broad was the base for ownership of the classical Greek past? This is regrettably a question that, however illuminating its answers might be to our understanding of Byzantine culture, has yet to be studied in the detail it deserves. Robert Browning, as far as I know the only person to tackle this problem, has made some preliminary observations and concluded that at most periods one can argue for the existence of a fairly widespread minimal literacy (Browning 1978*a*). The evidence comes, for example, from the tenth century onwards from the all-too-rare surviving archival documents; these survive particularly in the monasteries on Mt Athos and preserve autograph signatures of abbots, monks and local land-owners. For the earlier period evidence comes from the largely casual references, for the most part in saints' lives, to the role of books and writing in everyday life. The weightiest argument at all stages derives from one of the most enduring legacies of the Roman state, the centralized bureaucracy which saw to the collection of tax-revenues, custom dues and so on (Ahrweiler 1960; Weiss 1973). Our evidence for this civil service varies in quantity and detail. For example, for the sixth century, we have the writings of John Lydus; for the tenth, the Constantinoplitan Book of the Eparch; for the eleventh, Kekaumenos' cynical comments on how to deal with petty officials. Most telling of all perhaps are the abundant lead seals used to secure documents and valuables of all shapes and sizes. The seals identify the name, rank and usually the function of the individual who affixed them. There would have been a constant demand for moderately literate officials to carry out these duties. Most conspicuous are the top functionaries, both lay and ecclesiastic, who head the imperial or patriarchal chancelleries – men like Photios in the ninth century, Psellos in the eleventh, Metochites in the fourteenth. We know from their writings produced at other phases of their careers that these were totally literate and widely read men, in full ownership of the Greek literary heritage.

If we move to the next stage of the question, which is, 'How widely available was this education?', we find once more that the evidence is tantalizingly scrappy. Much of the basic research still needs to be done, though the collection of names of teachers and terms for the profession will become much easier when the next volume of the *Prosopography of the Later Roman Empire* appears, and better still when the project is taken through to 1261. There would appear to have been many *grammatiki*, elementary schoolmasters, providing instruction in the rudiments of reading and correct orthography. Perhaps a *grammatikos* was to be found in every village of moderate size. For slightly more advanced work, shall we say at secondary school level, evidence is very scanty indeed. An anonymous tenth-century *grammatikos* in Constantinople seems to have had pupils ranging in age from six to fifteen. It is however plain that after the closure of the law school in Beyrout (Beirut) in the sixth century, advanced (that is, tertiary) studies were available only in Constantinople. But even here the official institutions disappeared at times and the number of teachers functioning in each generation, whether inside or outside an official framework, was very small. The question of what was taught at each stage is still a matter for debate. It would appear though that, after the basic elements of written language had been learnt, the main skill taught was rhetoric: that is, at its most basic, correct syntax, and at a more elevated level, prose composition. Our witnesses are lists of grammatical hints, outlines of brief essays and rhetorical handbooks, some anonymous, some with authors' names attached. Content seems always to have been subordinate to form (Lemerle 1971: 242–266; Speck 1974).

One finds examples, again most often in saints' lives, of bright lads from villages or country districts who are sent to finish their studies in the great city of Constantinople. But by and large one must assume that those best able to take advantage of educational opportunities were comfortably-off families in Constantinople itself. However both the anonymous tenth-century schoolmaster and Tzetzes in the twelfth century complain about fees being paid late or not at all, or in kind and not cash – which might or might not tell us something about the financial resources of their pupils' parents. It was certainly recognized that material advantages could follow a sound education, even if they were not always achieved. The most eloquent witness to this is Ptochoprodromos in the twelfth century, who complains bitterly that the rewards for his years of study are meagre compared to those of an uneducated tradesman (Browning 1954; Jeffreys 1974: 150).

Now in terms of the symposium theme the most highly literate, who had gone through all the stages of the educational process and who were capable of filling the senior posts in the administrative hierarchy, were those who had fullest access to the Greek literary heritage and who owned it to the fullest extent. They demonstrated their ownership in a comprehensive imitation, *mimesis*, of the literary genres, rhetorical structures, vocabulary and imagery used by the classical Greek writers (Hunger 1969–70). To take examples more or less at random, ownership is demonstrated in the Homeric tags in Paul the Silentiary's hexameter description of St Sophia and its dedication in the reign of Justinian, or in Tzetzes' twelfth-century experiments with the hexameter; in the reflections of Achilles Tatius in Makrembolitis' romance in the twelfth century; in the quotations from Thucydides made by Agathias in the sixth century or Kantakouzenos in the fourteenth (Hunger 1976; Cameron 1964; Alexioo 1977). The allusions were intended to add piquancy to the composition and assumed that the reader would both recognize and savour the quotation. On occasions this appears to have been done to excess and we find works consisting of nothing but a mosaic of quotations – like the *Christus Patiens* made up of lines from Euripides. I suspect in fact that the quotation habit was even more widespread than is generally thought.

However, we must pause and tell ourselves to beware of taking a spectacular part as being truly representative of the whole, a trap always easy to fall into when examining Byzantine society and its artefacts. Some of the art objects are so supremely spectacular – the mosaics and the illuminated manuscripts, for example – that one overlooks the commonplace – the dull grey pilgrim flasks and the tatty little seals. Or in the case of the literature, our attention is caught by the highly wrought classicizing products of a Photios or a Psellos or an Anna Comnene, which, as most Byzantinists begin their training as classicists, strike a familiar and reassuring note.

Highly literate groups of writers, the products of the advanced schools of Constantinople, are apparent in every Byzantine century except the mid-seventh to mid-eighth. Yet they were never, it would seem, at any stage numerically large. Attempts have been made to quantify their numbers, basing calculations on works surviving from a given period and the contemporaries referred to in those works. Figures have been published for the tenth and the fourteenth centuries, both suggesting that at no stage were there more than two or three hundred representatives of this highly literate group functioning in Constantinople, and travelling to provincial centres only when compelled to by unavoidable administrative duties (Lemerle 1971: 255–257; Ševčenko 1974). Unpublished figures for the twelfth century confirm this picture. In the twelfth and fourteenth centuries one can be reasonably sure of one's ground. It would seem that a very large proportion of what was 'published', so to speak, then has survived and personal contacts between these writers, as shown by their correspondence, mean that comparatively few names slip through our nets.

There are other elements in Byzantine literature that are far more representative of the interests and values of the society as a whole, however one may choose one's criteria. Perhaps the number of surviving manuscript copies is one valid bench-mark. The classicizing writers, say of history, on the whole survive somewhat precariously in two or three, sometimes only one copy until West European interest was aroused in the sixteenth century. By contrast, biblical commentaries (whether by the Cappodocian Fathers or later theologians), collections of sermons, sayings of the Fathers, saints' lives, hymns, all had an extensive readership to judge from the number of copies that survive.[1]

We must remember that the Byzantine attitude to the ownership of the classical Greek heritage was always ambivalent. While the acquisition of the linguistic part of classical learning and culture was almost always the prerequisite for social and career advancement (in civil life at least), too close a study of the inner meaning was distrusted, particularly if it brought a sympathy which might undermine Christian faith. The attitude of St Basil's *Advice to Young Men* remained typical: Take what is useful and ignore the rest; read the Holy Scriptures for a guide to a moral life but look to the outside learning (that is, to the literature of classical Greece), only for guidance in elegant writing. This is the principle behind Photios' judgments on the pagan authors he discusses in his *Bibliotheca*; for example, he comments on the romance of Achilles Tatius that the style is good but the content is disgraceful. The same attitude reappears in the monk Iakovos' quotations from St Basil in the letters he addressed in the twelfth century to his spiritual daughter, the Sevastokratorissa Eirene, who was being tempted to delve too deeply into Homer and the philosophers. Those who did succumb to this temptation – like John Italos in the eleventh century or Gemistos Plethon in the fifteenth – paid the penalty for their over-enthusiasm with imprisonment or exile or worse (Boulenger 1965; Henry 1960; Clucas 1981; Masai 1956).

Although the spoken language was not allowed written expression, nevertheless there existed levels of language and style beneath the highly literate classicizing mode and which were more immediately accessible and comprehensible both for author and reader. From the tenth century, for example, we have the apologies of Constantine Porphyrogennetos in his *De Administrando Imperio* for not having corrected the vocabulary and syntax of the administrative documents he had incorporated. We can see what might have happened to the documents if we look at Symeon Metaphrastes' revision of the corpus of Saints' Lives in the Menologion. He has imposed a bland homogeneity of 'middle-brow' language onto the uneven originals, as one can see in the comparatively rare instances where we do also have the pre-Metaphrastean Life. In the twelfth century John Tzetzes suffers acutely from the criticism he has received for having used the vernacular word for moth (Jeffreys 1974). We can see in a practical way how Byzantines approached language from the grammars, aides for memorizing vocabulary and gender (sometimes in verse) and specimen compositions of the sort that I mentioned earlier. But study of Byzantine levels of style is yet another topic that still has to be given the attention it deserves, though Ihor Ševčenko has recently contributed a pioneering survey (1981). The edition of the paraphrase of Anna Comnene's *Alexiad* is also a most welcome step in this direction. Here we can observe how the more recondite vocabulary and syntax is stripped from a high-level text in a way that is most revealing both of the expectations of a less erudite audience and of the fact that such an audience exists (Hunger 1981).

Now the reading material available to this wider group would have been largely religious in tone, as one might expect from the number and distribution of manuscript copies. This is confirmed by, for example, the will of Eustathios Boilas, a landowner in Armenia, who in 1059 bequeathed his personal library to the monastery he had founded. The books he had owned were almost entirely theological, hagiographical or liturgical but they did also include a copy of Achilles Tatius' romance and two chronicles (Vryonis 1957: 269). A similar picture emerges from Kekaumenos' *Strategikon*. Kekaumenos was a practical soldier who had a respect for book-learning and those who purveyed it though considered it not entirely relevant to his life on the frontiers of the empire. He recommended the Bible above everything else, and then close and persistent perusal of a few books, with the encouraging comment that you should not be put off if you did not understand everything first time through (Wassiliewsky and Jernstedt 1965 (1896): 9,47). Writers like Kekaumenos, though their language is certainly Greek, would be excluded from the caste of high civil servants whose distinction was owed to their possession of the ancient Greek heritage.

Now can we make any estimate of what view the large non-specialist group of both authors and audience might have had of the past? For this we can turn to the chronicles, surveys of world history from the Creation till the compiler's own day. They were written at the lower end of the stylistic spectrum and are perhaps the most widely copied non-theological material to have survived. As I have just mentioned, Boilas' library contained two chronicles, though unfortunately they cannot be identified. The chroniclers are dominated no less than the classicizing writers by the Byzantine inheritance from the past. But for them the connection is with Rome and Christianity and not with ancient Greece.

The writing of histories is probably the literary genre for which Byzantium is most distinguished; it also exemplifies our theme neatly. For most of the period there are two types of historical writing being produced at approximately the same time. There is a high-level classicizing type of history dealing with events of the recent past and written with an eye on the vocabulary and structures of Herodotus, Thucydides or Xenophon. Contrasting with this are the world chronicles. Thus, for example, in the sixth century we find Procopius on Justinian's wars and Agathias on Justin II, writing at a high level, and parallel with these but at a totally different linguistic pitch there is the chronicle of Malalas. In the next century there is Theophylact Simocatta's recondite version of the deeds of the Emperor Maurice and at the same time the Chronicon Paschale's updating of the world chronicle as far as Heraclius. In the eleventh century there is Psellos' *Chronographia*, which is a misleading title in this context for it deals with the reigns of fourteen emperors and is, linguistically at least, high-level history; at the same time there develops a tangled mass of chronicles which no-one has yet satisfactorily disentangled or edited. In the twelfth century the histories of Nikephoros Bryennios and Anna Comnene have parallels in the chronicles of Kedrenos or Zonaras or Manasses (Hunger 1978; Scott 1981).

As a general rule the historians, even if attempting to write a sequel to a predecessor's work, cover events of the recent past only, after duly explaining the unique importance of their topic or hero. The chroniclers on the other hand reproduce much of their predecessors' contents before moving on to a new contribution in the final segment. At the head of the chronicle tradition as we know it stands the chronicle of John Malalas, and it is largely his interpretation of ancient history which moulded the viewpoint of the later chroniclers and thus eventually of the 'average' Byzantine.

We cannot place Malalas precisely, or rather, though it is plain from his chronicle that he came from Antioch and put his material together in the middle of the sixth century, we do not know who his friends and family were, nor what his career was (as we do for Agathias and Procopius, for instance). A case has been made that he was the Patriarch John Scholasticus (died 574), but the arguments are not convincing. Malalas remains something of an enigma. He is by no means the first to have written a Christian world chronicle. That honour goes to Sextus Julius Africanus (160–240) and to Eusebius (260–340), on both of whom he drew extensively. He is however the first whose work has survived in anything like a complete state, though even so there are problems about the condition of the text as we have it today. Malalas cites his sources copiously, but his references are frequently inaccurate and misleading, and he would seem to have known many of them only at second-hand. Nevertheless we must accept that, derivative though he may have been, a distinctive pattern emerges from the events narrated and we must admit that Malalas has manipulated his material in accordance with his own preoccupations. Like Africanus and Eusebius, Malalas is attempting to reconcile a Christian with a Graeco-Roman chronology, or rather, to impose a Christian perception of time onto the past as recorded by the Graeco-Roman historians. His chronological framework pivots on Christ's Incarnation, which is fixed in terms of years calculated from Adam, that is from the creation of the first man. Malalas is trying to use a milleniarist calculation based on Psalm 90:4, in which it is stated that a thousand years are but a day in the sight of the Lord. Applying this to the days of Creation, the world will come to an end in the year 6000 when the Lord rests from his labours. Regrettably Malalas' sources at this point, Clement and Theophilos, disagree as to whether the Incarnation should be calculated for the year 5500 or 6000 and there are two passages of honest puzzlement where Malalas attempts to reconcile his conflicting authorities. Our efforts at interpretation however are not helped by severe corruption of the text. This is the sort of problem being attacked by the Australian Malalas project. Throughout the first part of the chronicle, up to Christ's Incarnation in the forty-second year of Augustus' reign, dates from Graeco-Roman history are correlated with years reckoned from Adam (Dindorf 1831; Schenk von Stauffenberg 1931; Hunger 1978, I: 319–26).

On to this underlying chronological framework Malalas has added a selection of narratives which, on first acquaintance, appear bizarre. They however fit into the pattern of reconciling Christian and Graeco-Roman traditions, though one other important factor has influenced Malalas and that is his deep interest in Antioch and its own local history. So we find that Malalas relates many of the pagan literary myths – the story of Bellerophon, Meleager, Dirke and Oidipous, for example. But he gives a rationalistic version of the supernatural elements, many of which he does not mention specifically but of which he seems to assume his audience is aware. The source of these versions he names as Palaiphatos, whose *Peri apiston* ('On the Unbelievable') does in fact survive, though there are some discrepancies between the interpretation Malalas ascribes to Palaiphatos and the book that goes under his name (Hörling 1980; Reinert 1981).

Apart from the overall rationalistic interpretation that Malalas gives, one can observe some principles in his choice of pagan myth. There is very often a connection with Antiochene history, either with the city as a whole as is the case with the story of Io which provides a foundation legend for Antioch, or with particular buildings, for example in the case of the Dirke story which seems to be given disproportionate prominence in the early books but which falls into place as a background for a shrine that was re-dedicated later. Or the stories have a prominent role in literary culture. The emphasis placed on material drawn from plays by Euripides reflects possibly the use made of them as educational textbooks but also the role they played in performances of mime in sixth-century Antioch. Even Malalas at his almost wholly vernacular language level is not free from a learned desire to show his command of the Hellenic past. Or there is a connection with the mystery religions, which seem to have had an especial fascination for Malalas. This accounts for the prominence given to Orpheus and Hermes. There are two further elements which motivate the inclusion of narratives. One is an interest in Persia, which seems partly to arise out of the Old Testament and partly out of local preoccupations since Antioch was captured by the Persians during Malalas' lifetime. The other interest that Malalas demonstrates is in civic rituals[2]: why do the magistrates wear official robes, why is the plural used in imperial rescripts, why are imperial portraits placed beside the magistrates on official occasions, what were the origins of the Festival of the Brumalia and of the rival parties in the Hippodrome? All these concern aspects of the Roman life of Antioch (Fishman-Duker 1977; Jeffreys 1979).

This is the narrative of, as it were, 'ancient history' on which Malalas builds his history of late Roman and early Byzantine times. It is a highly idiosyncratic choice of material beneath which one is justified in seeing an individual with his own perspective on events, regardless of the mixed nature of his sources. However Malalas' interpretation of the past, once made, stuck fast in the chronicle tradition. Much of his chronicle, particularly from the first ten books, as far as the life of Christ and the early principate, is repeated almost verbatim over the succeeding centuries. Parts are left out and sections on the Old Testament are expanded but the balance of emphasis and the relative importance assigned to the elements that make up the whole is not changed.

Now, given that Malalas is writing in Greek and using Greek literary sources whose authors he names, what sort of shape does he give to the Greek past? Here we come up against another set of the prejudices that make up Malalas' character. He is immovably a citizen of an empire, the Roman Empire, which is presided over by a single authority, the emperor. Malalas, like his chronological sources, can function only in terms of kings and kingdoms, or emperors and empires – which can be conveniently listed out in tables (Gelzer 1885; Mosshammer 1979). Thus Athens is comprehensible only in the context of a list of kings, including some doubtful names like King Aischylos. The same holds for Sparta, Corinth or Argos. Once the king lists cease, the life of these communities for Malalas comes to an end, despite the fact that he notes at intervals, normally at grossly inappropriate moments, classical Greek poets, tragedians, philosophers, sculptors or historians. There is no narrative to supplement these bare lists and no chronological information about Greek communities from the time when they ceased to be ruled by kings until the rise of the Macedonian kingdom and the career of Alexander. A similar sequence can be observed in the presentation of Roman history, where there is a void between the expulsion of Tarquinius Superbus and the appearance of Julius Caesar, bridged by a quick reference to the number of consuls and a couple of stories on the Gallic invasions. Thus for practical purposes Malalas' view of ancient history omits classical Greece and the Roman Republic.[3]

There is no historical setting into which Malalas' Greek literary heritage can be fitted. That heritage, the source of literary authority and public power for his learned contemporaries, appears to derive from a historical vacuum. I have said already that Malalas' interpretation can be found in all subsequent chronicles. Perhaps the vital factor in the acceptance of this stand-point is not so much its intrinsic attractiveness, though there must be an element of that, as the ease with which he could be understood. Malalas is almost the only writer to ignore the linguistic censorship imposed by Byzantine education, and he wrote almost as he spoke. He is the best example for the historian of the spoken language within nearly a thousand years of obscurity (Psaltis 1913; Weierholt 1963; Helms 1971–1972).

Linguistic matters apart, this then is the perspective on the past that was available to the Byzantine who was literate but not part of the small literary elite. It was an 'alternative' Christian and Roman view which contrasted with that found in the historians read by the élite and imitated by them in their own works.

Of the two main elements in the chronicle tradition the Christian never needed emphasis in Byzantium. Half a millennium after the loss of full sovereignty over Rome, the Romanness of the Byzantine heritage became increasingly a matter of tradition rather than fact. It says much for the power of the past in Byzantine society and the conservative force of its traditions that it was not felt necessary to defend Byzantium's claims to the heritage of Rome before the twelfth century.

This was a period when many of the assumptions of the Byzantine thought world began to be challenged. Byzantine society began to open up culturally, partly under the shock of the massive defeat by the Turks at Manzikert in 1071, partly in response to the pan-European dynamism of the time. One change was in the highest levels of literary patronage. There appeared in positions of influence a number of people who did not accept the relevance of power derived from ownership of the language of ancient Greece. These were magnates from Anatolia, like the new ruling dynasty of the Comneni, or Norman adventurers who married into that family and so into the imperial heirarchy, like the Caesar Roger. In the context of language we find the first attempts since Malalas to write in the spoken Greek language and to reject the literary models from ancient Greece. Writers like Ptochoprodromos or

Glykas experiment with vernacular vocabulary and morphology in satirical poems (Chalandon 1900–1912 [1971]; Beck 1975: 99–114).

The strands come together in the chronicle of Constantine Manasses who, himself a bishop and a member of the literary élite, wrote a chronicle in the tradition that derived from Malalas. Manasses' chronicle is a world history, beginning from the Creation and pivoting on Christ's Incarnation, though the milleniarist details have long since been omitted from the tradition. There is an emphasis on the Assyrian empire of Old Testament times and on the Greek empire of Alexander the Great, but – as always in such chronicles – there is no mention of the Greek city states. Despite the simple verse form and the straight-forward syntax that he uses, Manasses demonstrates his membership of the literary élite – and his ownership of the Greek heritage – by introducing into his composition decorative phrases from Sophocles and Homer, amongst others, and larger quotations from Herodotus.[4]

But, for Manasses, Herodotus' connection with Byzantine prehistory comes through Persia and not Greece, as a textbook of useful details on the history of the Persian empire. Herodotus' ancient Greek phrases will also have had a positive effect in emphasizing Manasses' learning. It is interesting that this authentification from the past can merge at the same moment into an historical identification with the Persian empire, Greece's enemy.

Manasses' chronicle was a commission, not entirely a welcome one, from the Sevastokratorissa Eirene, whom we have met briefly earlier as the spiritual daughter of the plagiarizing monk Iakovos. Eirene was the widowed sister-in-law of the Emperor Manuel. She was almost certainly a Western bride, probably an Italian, that is, she was one of the powerful figures to whom the authority of the ancient Greek past meant relatively little. She seems to have requested the simple verse forms to guarantee comprehensibility and the purpose of the chronicle is to inform her of Byzantine, or rather Roman, history. What we find is that Constantinople's claims to be the New Rome, the new and vigorous Rome stronger and mightier than the Old Rome, are given great prominence, especially in the paean of praise to the Emperor Manuel.[5]

Manasses' claims for Constantinople as the New Rome are not a personal quirk. They can be paralleled in the ceremonial verse produced in abundance at Manuel's court in the late 1140s to counteract the arrogance of the leaders of the Second Crusade. Similar attitudes emerge in diplomatic exchanges with the German imperial chancellery (Lamma 1955). In effect Manasses and the Byzantine court have responded to a challenge from the West to Constantinople's assumption of ownership of the past by restating that ownership more firmly, even if in material terms rather unrealistically (Hörandner 1974).

There was a sequel. The simple form and firm imperial ideology of Manasses' chronicle struck a responsive note. There are over seventy manuscripts still surviving and plainly many more have been lost. The chronicle is quoted in the vernacular verse literature of the fourteenth century, which otherwise shows little acquaintance with high-level material. Together with the version of Malalas incorporated in Dorotheos of Monemvasia's historical compendium in the sixteenth century, it continued to mould Greek attitudes to the past until the eighteenth century. More importantly, the Slavic translation of Manasses made in the fourteenth century, with its enhanced emphasis on the Roman element in Constantinople's traditions, became a significant part of the national image of the Slavic peoples and especially the Russian empire. It fed the concept that Moscow was the heir to Constantinople's empire and thus that Moscow was the Third Rome (Schaeder 1957: 12–25; Obolensky 1971: 245–6, 414).

To sum up: I have focussed on the Greek element in the Byzantine heritage from the past, which is represented by the literature read and imitated by a highly literate élite. Ostensibly this élite, with their accurate linguistic usages, owned the Greek past most completely and used their ownership to enter upon positions of power over their peers. However, the view of the past that had the widest circulation and finally prevailed was one which bore little relation to that contained in the texts read by that élite. It was a view which claimed continuing Byzantine ownership of the medieval universals, Rome and Christianity.

Notes

1   For lists of manuscripts of historians, see G. Moravcsik, *Byzantinoturcica* I, (2nd edn, Berlin, 1958), under each author; for general discussions, see the papers by N.G. Wilson and J. Irigoin (1975), in *Byzantine Books and Bookmen*, Washington, D.C., and by E. Gamillscheg, G. Cavallo, B. Fonkic and S. Dufrenne (1981) in 'Buch und Gesellschaft in Byzanz', *Jahrbuch der Österreichischen Byzantinistik* 31.2, 282–470.
2   Io: Malalas pp. 28–30 (all references are to pages of Dindorf's 1831 edition); Dirke: pp. 45–49; Euripides: pp. 34, 43, 53, 72, 84, 86, 88, 117, 119, 137, 166, 359; Orpheus: pp. 72–6; Persia: pp. 26, 37, 194, 270, 310; Assyria: pp. 150–8; Civic rituals: pp. 33, 173, 179, 183.

3 King lists: Athens, pp. 70, 72; Sparta, p. 90; Corinth, p. 90; Argos, pp. 68, 83, 85. Lists of famous men: pp. 72, 161, 169. Roman history: Aeneas, p. 162; Romulus, p. 171; Tarquinius, p. 180; Gallic invasions, p. 183; Consuls, p. 187; Julius Caesar, p. 214. [Page references to those of Dindorf's 1831 edition.]

4 Edition: I. Bekker (1837); for bibliography, see H. Hunger (1978, I: 419–22); on quotations, see E.M. Jeffreys (1979: 209–14).

5 Manasses, lines 2348–55, 2546–55, and see F. Dölger (1964), 'Rom in der Gedanken welt der Byzantiner', in *Byzanz und die europäische Staatenwelt*, Darmstadt, 70–115. On Eirene, see E.M. Jeffreys (1980).

References

Ahrweiler, H. (1960), 'Recherches sur l'administration de l'empire byzantin au IXᵉ–XIᵉ siècles', *Bulletin de correspondence hellénique* 84, 1–111.

—— (1975), *L'idéologie politique de l'empire byzantin*, Presses Universitaires de France, Paris.

Alexiou, M. (1977), 'A critical reappraisal of Eustathius Makrembolitis' *Hysmine and Hysminias*', *Byzantine and Modern Greek Studies* 3, 23–44.

Beck, H.-G. (1975), *Geschichte der byzantinischen Volksliteratur*, C.H. Beck'sche Verlagsbuchhandlung, München.

—— (1978), *Das byzantinishe Jahrtausend*, C.H. Beck, München.

Bekker, I. (ed.) (1837), *Constantini Manassis Breviarum Historiae Metricum*, Corpus scriptorum historiae byzantinae, E. Weber, Bonn.

Boulenger, F. (ed.) (1965), *Saint Basile: Aux jeunes gens sur la manière de tirer profit des lettres helléniques*, Les Belles Lettres, Paris.

Browning, R. (1954), 'The correspondence of a tenth-century Byzantine scholar', *Byzantion*, 24, 397–452.

—— (1969), *Medieval and Modern Greek*, Hutchinson University Library, London (2nd edn, Cambridge University Press, Cambridge, 1983).

—— (1978a), 'Literacy in the Byzantine world', *Byzantine and Modern The 'Past' in Medieval and Modern Greek Culture (Byzantina kai Metabyzantina 1)*, Undena Publications, Malibu, 103–33.

—— (1978), 'Literacy in the Byzantine world', *Byzantine and Modern Greek Studies*, 4, 39–54.

—— (1980), *The Byzantine Empire*, Weidenfeld & Nicolson, London.

Cameron, A. (1964), 'Herodotus and Thucydides in Agathias', *Byzantinische Zeitschrift* 57, 33–52.

Chalandon, F. (1900–1912), *Les Comnène*, (2 vols, A. Picard, Paris, 1900–12) (reprinted B. Franklin, New York, 1971).

Charanis, P. (1978), 'The formation of the Greek people', in Vryonis, S. (ed), *The 'Past' in Medieval and Modern Greek Culture (Byzantina kai Metabyzantina 1)*, Undena Publications, Malibu, 87–101.

Clucas, L. (1981), *The trial of John Italos and the crisis of intellectual val-*

ues in Byzantium in the eleventh century, Institut für Byzantinistik und neugriechische Philologie, Universität München.

Dindorf, L. (ed.) (1831), *Ioannis Malalae Chronographia*, Corpus scriptorum historiae byzantinae, E. Weber, Bonn.

Fishman-Duker, R. (1977), 'The second temple period in Byzantine chronicles', *Byzantion* 47, 126–56.

Gelzer, H. (1885), *Sextus Julius Africanus und die byzantinische Chronographie*, Leipzig, 1885 (Reprinted B. Franklin, New York, n.d.).

Helms, P. (1971–2), 'Syntaktische Untersuchungen zu Joannes Malalas und Georgios Phrantzes', *Helikon* 11–12, 309–88.

Henry, R. (ed.) (1960), *Photius: bibliothèque*, vol. 2, Les Belles Lettres, Paris, Codex 87.

Hörandner, W. (1974), *Theodoros Prodromos: Historische Gedichte*, Verlag der Österreichischen Akademie der Wissenschaften, Wien.

Hörling, E. (1980), *Mythos und Pistis: zur Deutung heidnischer Mythen in der christlichen Weltchronik des Johannes Malalas*, Lund.

Hunger, H. (1969–1970), 'On the imitation (*mimesis*) of antiquity in Byzantine literature', *Dumbarton Oaks Papers* 23–24, 15–38.

—— (1976), 'Thucydides bei Johannes Kantakuzenos. Beobachtungen zur Mimesis', *Jahrbuch der Österreichischen Byzantinistik*, 29, 181–93.

—— (1978), *Die hochsprachliche profane Literatur der Byzantiner*, 2 vols, C.H. Beck'sche Verlag, Wien.

—— (1981), *Anonyme Metaphrase zu Anna Komnene, Alexias XI-XIII*, Verlag der Österreichischen Akademie der Wissenschaften, Wien.

Irigoin, J. (1975), 'Centres de copie et bibliothèques', in *Byzantine Books and Bookmen*, Dumbarton Oaks, Washington D.C., 17–27.

Jeffreys, E.M. (1979), 'The attitude of Byzantine chroniclers to ancient history', *Byzantion* 49, 199–238.

—— (1980), 'The Comnenian background to the *romans d'antiquité*', *Byzantion*, 50, 474–481.

Jeffreys, M.J. (1973), 'The literary emergence of vernacular Greek', *Mosaic* (Manitoba) 8.4, 171–93.

—— (1974), 'The nature and origins of the political verse', *Dumbarton Oaks Papers* 28, 141–95.

Lamma, P. (1955), *Comneni e Staufer*, 2 vols, Istituto storico italiano per il Medio Evo, Rome.

Lemerle, P. (1971), *Le premier humanisme byzantin*, Presses Universitaires de France, Paris.

Mango, C.A. (1980), *Byzantium: the Empire of New Rome*, Weidenfeld & Nicolson, London.

Masai, F. (1956), *Pléthon et le platonisme de Mistra*, Les Belles Lettres, Paris.

Moravcsik, G. (1958), *Byzantinoturcica 1*, 2nd edn, Akademie-Verlag, Berlin.

Mosshammer, A.A. (1979), *The chronicle of Eusebius and the Greek Chronographic Tradition*, Bucknell University Press, Lewisburg.

Nicol, D.M. (1969), 'The Byzantine church and Hellenic learning in the fourteenth century', in Cuming, G.J. (ed.), *Studies in Church History*, vol. 5, E.J. Brill, Leiden, 23–57.

Obolensky, D. (1968), *The Byzantine Commonwealth*, Weidenfeld & Nicolson, London.

Ostrogorsky, G. (1968), *History of the Byzantine State* (trans. J. Hussey), Blackwell, Oxford.

Psaltis, S.B. (1913), *Grammatik der byzantinischen Chroniken*, Berlin (Reprinted Vanderhoeck and Ruprecht, Göttingen, 1974).

Reinert, S. (1981), *Greek Myth in Johannes Malalas' Account of Ancient History before the Trojan War*, Ph.D. dissertation, University of California, Los Angeles.

Runciman, S. (1970), *The Last Byzantine Renaissance*, Cambridge University Press, Cambridge.

ᶜ⁻haeder, H. (1957), *Moskau das dritte Rom: Studien zur Geschichte der politischen Theorie in der slavischen Welt*, 2nd edn, Darmstadt.

Schenk von Stauffenberg, A. (1931), *Die römische Kaisergeschichte bei Malalas, Griechischer Text der Bücher IX-XII und Untersuchungen*, Kohlhammer, Stuttgart.

Scott, R. (1981), 'The classical tradition in Byzantine historiography', in Mullett, M. and Scott, R. (eds) *Byzantium and the Classical Tradition*, Centre for Byzantine Studies, University of Birmingham, 61–74.

Ševčenko, I. (1974), 'Society and intellectual life in the fourteenth century', *Actes du XIVᵉ Congrès International des études Byzantines*, Bucarest, 1971, vol. I, Bucarest, 69–92.

—— (1981), 'Levels of style in Byzantine literature', *Jahrbuch der Österreichischen Byzantinistik* 31.1, 289–312.

Speck, P. (1974), *Die kaiserliche Universität von Konstantinopel*, Munich.

Vryonis, S. (1957), 'The will of a provincial magistrate, Eustathius Boilas (1059)', *Dumbarton Oaks Papers* 11, 263–77.

Wassiliewsky, B. and Jernstedt, V. (eds) (1896), *Cecaumeni strategicon*, St Petersburg (Reprinted A.M. Hakkert, Amsterdam, 1965).

Weierholt, K. (1963), *Studien im sprachgebrauch des Malalas*, Universitetsforlaget, Oslo.

Weiss, G. (1973), *Oströmische Beamte im Spiegel der Schriften des Michael Psellos*, Institut für Byzantinistik und neugriechische Philologie, Universität München.

Wilson, N.G. (1975), 'Books and readers in Byzantium', in *Byzantine Books and Bookmen*, Dumbarton Oaks, Washington D.C., 1–15.

10
Loving the Ancient in China

Wang Gungwu

This essay is not about the ownership of all aspects of the past. It leaves out physical objects and focusses on ideas and values embodied in literate artefacts. In this context, ownership is not about exclusive possession, but about a shared heritage. It is about the right to select the past for all to use, about who determines what ideas about the past should be preserved. Also, unlike some of the other peoples dealt with in this volume, the Chinese had never been colonized by culturally dominant foreigners. Their past is not that of a minority, but that of the majority. It is China's own past and it was a powerful unifying past for over two thousand years. Although the Chinese thought it was a superior past, they claimed it only for themselves and never claimed to speak for mankind.

Let me begin with some of my own observations about the traditional Chinese view of the past. First, I find that it assumes that most of the past was unknown and not worth knowing. There was no point in knowing the past for its own sake and therefore no point in seeking to own all of it. What could be known were those parts that had been highlighted for us and done so for a purpose. If the purpose was high-minded enough, it might persuade people that the past so selected had something to teach us. This kind of past would be worth owning and was therefore preserved in the classics, in works of history and other kinds of documents. If the purpose was obviously manipulative, then those who used the past would try to use it to control people and thus used the past to own the present. This, however, could only have been temporary; if it had nothing to teach, it would not last.

Second, the Chinese had different views of the recent past and the ancient past. The recent past was simply too much, too fragmented, too specialized and mostly highly technical. Also, it was usually in government hands or state-controlled archives and accessible only to a very few. For officials and scholars, it might have been necessary and valuable for practical politics and effective government but useless for teaching about civilization and moral lessons. The ancient past, on the other hand, survived in a limited number of texts and these had been selected over time for the lessons they taught. The documents being limited, almost everyone who was literate could know it, control it, and even claim to own it. Having been tested out over the centuries and found to be valid for all times, they in fact provided the principles for determining how to deal with the recent past. Furthermore, the ancient past was not a threat to anyone. You could immerse yourself in it safely, escape into it, draw grand lessons from it, and everyone could conduct social discourse based on a common knowledge of that ancient past. With this in mind, it is understandable why the Chinese believed it was natural to think that the ancient past was more worth knowing, more attractive, even more loveable than the recent past.

It would be hard to find a people more obviously concerned about their past than the Chinese. But the Chinese have never asked the question, 'Who owns the past?'. They would not have seen the need to. At one level, they would have said that their ancestors owned the past. At another, they would first think of the Confucian scholars who read all the ancient classics and wrote all the history, and then perhaps the emperor and his court who saw themselves as guardians of all that was ancient and who used the past to legitimize themselves. In any case, there would be the reasonable assumption that the past which had moulded the Chinese people continuously for so long must belong to the Chinese in some way. In what way would depend on what people wanted to know and whether the Chinese believed there was anything to learn from it.

I shall not try to cover the many aspects of this question here, especially not the deeper, more subtle and more interesting issues of how the ancestors owned the past. Instead, I shall focus on the Confucian scholars and their involvement with imperial power. Let me begin with Confucius – from whom my title 'Loving the Ancient' comes – with two texts from *Confucian Analects*. The first says: Confucius said, 'I transmit but do not create. I believe in and love the ancient.' The second text says: Confucius said, 'I am not one who was born with knowledge; I love the ancient and earnestly seek it.'[1] There are four points to these two texts: loving the ancient; believing in it; transmitting and not creating; seeking knowledge or learning from the past. All four have played a part in making the Chinese after the Han dynasty deeply conscious of their ancient past. That past is vital knowledge. Seeking and acquiring knowledge of that past seems to have been the closest thing to owing it. At least that seems to have been the underlying idea that makes 'loving the ancient' a powerful influence in Chinese history.

This is a vast subject and it would be foolish to try to cover much of it here. What this paper will do is to examine the phrase in the context of two critical periods in Chinese history and see how some Chinese used or responded to the past during those periods, how they turned to the ancient past at times of crisis. The first concerns the critical century after AD 960 (the Northern Sung) and the second is our century, from the 1880s to the present. By 'ancient' the Chinese in these two periods meant before the unification of China, before the second century BC. For Confucius and his contemporaries, of course, it would have been even earlier than that, not only the periods of the Shang and the Western Chou dynasty, but also various reigns of legendary sage-kings. But for the two periods covered in this paper, 'ancient' would include the times of Confucius down to the end of the Warring States period just before the Ch'in unification in 222 BC. Also, it needs to be noted that Confucius' love of the ancient was not shared by other philosophers. Most of the Warring States philosophers who mentioned the 'ancient' at all did so merely to admit the usefulness of knowing it, but often also to underline its inadequacy for dealing with present problems. Many were keen to change the past rather than love it (Lo Ken-tse 1937). A common idea was simply that it was good and necessary to know the past in order to understand the present. Philosophers like Chuang Tzu and Hsun Tzu were critical of those who constantly referred to the ancient. 'To admire antiquity and despise the present' – this is the fashion of scholars said Chuang Tzu (Burton Watson 1968: 300) – while Hsun Tzu was even more contemptuous of such scholars 'calling on ancient kings to deceive the stupid in order to make a living' (Hsun Tzu 8: Ju-hsiao). Yet Lao Tzu said, 'hold fast to the way of antiquity, in order to keep in control of the realm today' (Lau 1963: 70).

After Confucianism became the dominant school during the Western and Eastern Han dynasties (first century BC to third century AD), 'loving the ancient' had come to be equated with 'love of learning'.[2] The 'ancient' had become so important that it became common to say that it was crucial to study the ancient if anything were to succeed and even that it was necessary to study the ancient before one went to serve the imperial government. Both refer to frequent quotations from the *Book of History* (Legge 1960, III: 260, 531). Indeed, by the Eastern Han, studying the ancient was the road to wealth, status and influence, as summarized in the notorious remark by Huan Jung: 'All these present rewards I owe to the close study of the ancient' (*Hou Han Shu* [Chung-hua edition]

37, 1251). There were, of course, sceptics as can be seen in the debates during the first century contained in the *Debates on Salt and Iron*, best summarized in the phrase 'believing that which is past when it is contrary to the present; following the ancient when it does not fit present needs' (Huan K'uan 1958: 71). But these doubts disappeared when Han Confucianism became dominant. The study of the ancient had by the end of Han become too profitable.

The fall of the Han, the civil war that followed and the conquest of North China by various non-Chinese tribes changed all that. After the third century, for more than 700 years, 'loving the ancient' faded away to become a minority faith that had little influence on state and society. There was no shortage of historians who acknowledged continuities with the ancient, but they were mainly preoccupied with the technical problems of recording the recent past.[3] There were some exceptions, especially during the T'ang dynasty (618–906), but I shall pass over them quickly to talk about the first of the two critical periods covered in this paper. I do need to mention, however, the revival of interest in the ancient after the disastrous civil wars following upon the An Lu-shan rebellion in the middle of the eighth century. Out of the chaos and the uncertain recovery, a few men, notably Han Yü, turned away from Buddhism and re-read the Confucian classics with new eyes (Pulleyblank 1960: 110–3). In particular, he and his followers during the ninth century rejected the literary flourishes in the writings of their day and sought the simple, clear and direct style of the ancient. Most important of all was a growing reaction against a rigid and barren orthodoxy that seemed to have lost its sense of moral direction. The time seemed to be ripe for a new look at the ancient past, but it still took a long time for that past to be loved again.

The T'ang dynasty collapsed at the end of the ninth century and the old empire was fragmented for nearly a hundred years. This was a major turning-point in Chinese history. The great aristocratic clans were destroyed and nearly a century of civil war brought forth a different set of élites. By the middle of the tenth century, a few active scholars were struggling to restore T'ang institutions, efforts were made to have the classics printed and archives were collected and recent history was once again compiled. But it was not an age for scholars and literary men. Military, managerial and financial skills were much more in demand and a little literacy went a long way. All the same, there were the few who studied the classics in some form, passed the examinations and held high official positions in order to maintain T'ang ceremonial, legal and administrative institutions. During the reign of the second and third emperors of the Sung dynasty (end of the tenth century) the emperors encouraged higher standards at the examinations and employed senior officials to take on scholarly work, including the compilation of several encyclopaedias which preserved the texts of a large number of earlier writings and certainly gave the impression that the state owned the past in some clearly tangible ways (Kracke 1953: 18–21).

Much of this, however, was work on literary remains and surviving documents. They were useful but in themselves contributed little towards the deeper understanding of Chinese civilization that some scholars were demanding. It was not until another three or four decades later that scholars began to challenge the conventional ideas embodied in the large encyclopaedias. Then suddenly a burst of activity occurred and the generation born at the turn of the eleventh century re-interpreted the major classics and laid the foundations for the Neo-Confucianism that was to dominate China for nearly 900 years. How the debates were conducted, how scholarship spilled over into politics and fierce purges and how the great synthesis under Chu Hsi was achieved are stories that have often been told and I shall not repeat them here. What I shall suggest is that, before the new ideas could produce fresh insights about the nature of ethics, the origins of good, the place of man in the universe, there was a crucial thread which made them possible. This was the thread taking the Chinese back to the ancient past and studying it with loving care. The climax of this new emphasis on the ancient was the work of Ou-yang Hsiu (1007–72), especially his contributions towards the writing of the New History or the re-writing of the *History of the T'ang* and the *History of the Five Dynasties* (Liu 1967: 100–13).

The key to this return to the ancient lies in that work of history, the Tso Commentary to the *Spring and Autumn Annals* and the encouragement it gave to follow up and study Ssu-ma Ch'ien's *Shih Chi* and Pan Ku's *Han Shu*.[4]

A good example is a famous essay by Liu Pen (fl. 820–35) early in the ninth century. It is no accident that this essay was written within a few years of Han Yü's famous appeal to the ancient traditions in order to attack the foreign origins, and recent arrival, of Buddhism. Liu Pen wrote an elaborate criticism of the eunuch-dominated T'ang court. This was in 828. It became such a striking document of protest that both the *Old T'ang History* completed in 945 and the *New T'ang History* thoroughly revised and expanded in 1058 included the text in full (*Chiu Tang Shu*, 190C, 5064–77; *Hsin T'ang Shu*, 178, 5293–307). The revised version had been done by Ou-Yang Hsiu and his colleagues largely because a new view of the use of history had come to the fore. But despite the 'revisionism', Liu Pen's critique was given the same prominence in the *New History*. What was specially notable was Liu Pen's eleven specific uses of the Tso Commentary (hereafter, the *Annals*) to make his political points. The document is too long to quote here, nor is it a profound one. The Confucian ideas in it were conventional and the exhortations to learn from the ancient sage-rulers were obvious. I shall not go into how Liu Pen criticized the T'ang court but give two simple examples of how the *Annals* was supposedly used by Confucius to show approval or disapproval: For the nineteenth year of Duke Hsi, it is recorded that (the state of) 'Liang perished' and no reference was made to the fact that the Ch'in state had conquered it. This was thought to have been Confucius' way of saying that Liang had destroyed itself because its ruler was unwilling to listen to good advice and drove his people to abandon him. By the simple word 'perished', Confucius showed how much he disapproved of Liang (*Chiu.* 5071; *Hsin* 5299–300, Legge 1960, V: 175–7). Also, another example: during the time of Duke Hsi, Confucius was said to have mentioned 'No rain' three times in six months, in order to show that the ruler cared for his people and there was no disaster. For the time of Duke Wen, however, Confucius mentioned 'No rain' only once in a three-year period and this was to show that he thought the ruler did not care for his people and the drought led to disaster (*Chiu* 5073; *Hsin* 5302; Legge 1960, V: 135–8 and 321–4). You have to be well-versed in the *Annals* to understand what Liu Pen meant by using such examples.

The significance of these eleven specific quotations from the *Annals* lies in the admiration Liu Pen's document aroused in the ninth century. It remained admired in the tenth century, when the first *T'ang History* was compiled and was still admired in the eleventh century when the revised *T'ang History* replaced the old history. For more than 200 years, it was widely read. It is a good example of how 'loving the ancient' was sustained during the dark years when the old order collapsed and the search for a new order had to start afresh. Through the ancient parallels of another dark age of division and chaos in China, for which Confucius provided the framework for a new order, the scholars of the ninth and tenth centuries (late T'ang, the Five Dynasties and the early Sung) could find comfort and confidence and thus sustained their faith in the moral and political principles which could be used to construct a new order.

Let me not exaggerate the role of these scholars. The new order had to be built on military successes; the scholars studied and taught and offered their services to the victors. And until one group of victors stayed in power long enough, no new order could be sustained. The scholars' job was to assist the victors to restore the imperial institutions. Most of them did no more than reproduce the institutions of the T'ang dynasty. But some of them, those who loved the ancient, went further. They wanted to restore the ancient virtues in order that the new order be founded on the highest principles. The *Annals* was ideal in that it was neither abstract and philosophical nor obsessed with ceremonies and institutions, but emphasized concrete historical examples. Even more helpful was that the examples came from ancient times for which there were no great details and on which Confucius, himself a lover of the ancient, was thought to have passed wise moral and political judgements.[5]

Hence it is significant that the revival of Confucianism on a significant scale at the beginning of the eleventh century began with a book of divination, the *Book of Changes*, on the one hand, and a work of ancient history, the *Annals*, on the other. Of the two, the latter was more prominent for the early decades. All three precursors of the Neo-Confucian movement used the *Annals*, while two of them, Sun Fu (992–1057) and his disciple Shih Chieh (1005–63), became famous teachers of the *Annals* and have left comments which showed how the *Annals* was relevant to their times.[6] Both drew on the *Annals* to underline the ancient values of Chinese civilization and their place in a new order and argue why the 'barbarians' had to be kept out of China and a 'barbarian' religion like Buddhism should be rejected. Of course, Buddhism was not rejected, but the whole atmosphere of turning to the ancient to find specific lessons for the present had reached a high point.

Soon afterwards, Ou-yang Hsiu, a contemporary of Shih Chieh, was to draw upon the *Annals* for new ways of writing history and passing judgments on the rights and wrongs of the more recent past. His role in revising the *T'ang History* and his own re-writing of the *Wu-tai History* are examples of how he loved the ancient. Ou-yang Hsiu fondly believed that, by following Confucius in the Sage's laconic judgments on the Spring and Autumn period, he too was drawing profound lessons from the recent past, in his case from the T'ang and Wu-tai dynasties. The ancient was not merely useful in helping the present to give order to the recent past. It was fundamental and permeated civilization. It was essential if the highest standards of government were to be restored, China to become stable and the people contented again. To underline his non-utilitarian approach to antiquity, he founded the art of studying and collecting things ancient on a large scale. Although it did not give rise to the science of archaeology, it went a long way towards a systematic examination of ancient artefacts which culminated in his own great compendium, the *Collection of Ancient*

Inscriptions, the first of several major collections made during the Sung dynasty (Liu 1967: 101; Wang 1979b: 1084). It was the physical manifestation of his love of the ancient, but what impressed Ou-yang Hsiu much more was something no less tangible, the tradition that Confucius had revised the *Annals* of the state of Lu in order that historical judgments could establish political and moral standards for the future. He admired the way Confucius decided which rulers were right or wrong, who had been guilty of assassination or usurpation or of organising a coup against their predecessors. Similarly, also, which ministers, officials or subjects were loyal or disloyal, who had been wrongfully executed or deservedly punished. He followed Confucius in believing that it was vital to determine precisely how a man had died and to use the correct word to indicate the moral issues surrounding the circumstances of his death. Where the ruling houses were concerned, of particular importance was the question of betrayal within the family, fathers by their sons and brothers by their brothers. This may be seen in the commentaries to the first twelve chüan of *Hsin Wu-tai Shih*, attributed to Hsu/Wu-tang but probably by Ou-Yang Hsiu himself (Liu 1967: 110). No less vital were attitudes towards the proper rites and the use of punishments; the first determined the legitimacy of a reign or a dynasty, the second expressed arbitrariness and cruelty (see Commentaries, *Hsin Wu-tai shih* chuan 1–12; Yao Ying-t'ing 'Lun *Hsin Wu-tai shih* ti jen-wu p'ing-chia', *Chung-kuo ku-tai shih lun-ts'ung*, Fuzhou, I, 1981: 263–8).

Thus there are no better examples of Ou-Yang Hsiu's love of the ancient than in his historical judgments. He exercised these judgments with extreme care, revealing approval and disapproval often in no more than a word or two. But he also wrote longer comments. I have recently translated (yet to be published) the fifty eight such comments written by him in the *New History of the Five Dynasties*. One example would be enough to convey the flavour of these judgments:

Alas! the Liang dynasty has long been condemned by all under Heaven. Ever since the Later T'ang, it has been considered illegitimate. When I came to comment on the Five Dynasties, however, I did not single it out as illegitimate. Some people criticize me as having failed to conform to the principles of the *Annals*. They think Liang had done great wrongs and therefore should be left out of the legitimate succession. To legitimize it was to encourage usurpation. This surely was not in accordance with the purposes of the *Annals*.

My answer is that it is in accordance with the purposes of the *Annals*. In the *Annals*, Duke Huan of Lu took over the state by assassinating Duke Yin; Duke Hsuan (also of Lu) did the same by liquidating Tzu Ch'ih; Duke Li of Cheng drove away the legitimate Prince Hu in order to seize power; and Kung-sun Piao of Wei became ruler by driving away his former ruler K'an. In the *Annals*, the Sage did not prevent [all four] from being recognised as rulers. So my not treating Liang as illegitimate is an application of the principles of the *Annals*.

Is it true then that usurpation was encouraged by the *Annals*? No, the meaning of the *Annals* can only be seen in its not refusing these four rulers the legitimacy of their titles. The Sage intended the *Annals* to have a deep meaning so that wrongs were suitably warned against, and if what was said in it always proved true, then the distinction between good and evil would always be clear. (*Hsin Wu-tai shih* 2: 21–22)

There are indeed many other examples I can give of Ou-yang Hsiu's conscious embracing of an ancient duty: the moral and political role of the historian to draw upon the ancient to illuminate the principles of order and authority and especially the authority of the ruler. The contrast between his judgments and the conventional comments by historians a hundred years earlier brings out sharply the extent to which 'loving the ancient' had led his generation away from the pious and hollow clichés of the tenth century.

Of course, the ancient was loved not only by the historians. Both the philosophers and politicians had also accepted the vitality of the past for their thinking and actions. Ou-yang Hsiu, in fact, represented only one of the ancient threads that were woven into this remarkable 'renaissance' of the eleventh century. The philosophers soon went well beyond the ancient to construct new foundations for Confucianism. That is a rich and variegated story – the story of Neo-Confucianism – which is beyond the scope of this essay. The politicians, however, brought out one thread which would be of great interest to the second period I want to talk about, the last hundred years since the 1880s. This is the thread using the ancient to justify reform, radical reform, and it was clearly found in the eleventh century in one of the most dramatic ways the ancient was used.

Again, the story is well known. One of Ou-yang Hsiu's fellow provincials and one-time disciple was Wang An-shih (1021–86). He is best known for having been the greatest radical reformer in Chinese history before modern times. Less emphasized has been his scholarly background and the love of the ancient which he had absorbed from Ou-yang Hsiu. But he took a different tack from his mentor. Instead of looking to the *Annals* he turned to the *Chou Li* (The Rites of Chou), a work reflecting the idealism of the Warring States period after the death of Confucius and one that had been influential in stirring up utopian hopes for China (Liu 1959: 30–40). Let me simply say that 'loving the ancient' did not only lead to conservatism as one might expect. The return to ancient texts, examples and models led to the most thorough debate and re-statement of Confucian values on the one hand and, on the other, to the most radical attempt at reform for more than a thousand years and nothing as radical was to appear for another 800 years.

Let me now come to my second period, the past hundred years. In some ways, it can be said to have begun where Wang An-shih left off. I refer to the radical reforms proposed by K'ang Yu-wei (1858–1927) at the end of the nineteenth century. There were other superficial similarities. Ch'ing China was under severe foreign pressures just as the Northern Sung had been threatened by the northern Khitan and the northwestern Tangut empires. The need for reform following upon the disastrous Taiping rebellion was, of course, even greater. The defeats by France and then Japan in the decade after 1885 were as humiliating as having to send tribute to the northern barbarian Liao and Hsia Empires in the eleventh century. But the differences were probably more important, notably in two areas pertaining to attitudes towards the ancient past. For one thing, loving the ancient in China had long been revived and had long been the orthodoxy: especially notable was the excellent classical scholarship of the eighteenth century. K'ang Yu-wei therefore did not represent the climax of a movement to return to the ancient. On the contrary, his was the first generation to doubt whether long held interpretations about the ancient could save China. For another, foreign learning was of quite a different order from anything China had experienced in the past. The conventional rejection of the foreign which 'loving the ancient' (under Han Yü, Sun Fu and Shih Chieh) had brought about was not applicable. Again, on the contrary, K'ang Yu-wei's generation was the first to give some attention to the West and acknowledge that, since great religions and some enduring, political and moral philosophy had been produced in ancient times outside China, there was now more to the ancient than what had happened on Chinese soil.

The times demanded radical change. For such times, 'loving the ancient', as all Confucian scholars since the Sung had done, surely had nothing to offer. If anything, these scholars might have loved the ancient too much, so much so that, instead of owning the past, it could be said that the past owned them and had them bogged down in that past for centuries. K'ang Yu-wei had studied the ancient classics. He was ambitious and wanted to be a sage. He saw he had to be a radical sage who would turn to the ancient in a totally different way. He wrote prolifically about the classics, but his two most important works setting out his justification for radical reforms were his study of 'the forged classics' and his 1891 book on *Confucius as a Reformer* (1956, 1958; cf. Hsiac Kung-ch'uan 1975: 69–72 and 90). By showing how several of the standard classics had been forged at the beginning of the first century AD, he argued that many of Confucius' ideas had been misrepresented if not totally distorted. He offered to identify what Confucius really intended and attacked the idea that Confucius merely 'transmitted and did not create' and 'believed in and loved the ancient'. From this statement attributed to Confucius, the conservatives had interpreted the source of wisdom as the Duke of Chou, the brother of the founder of the Chou dynasty who lived several centuries earlier than Confucius, who created all the great institutions which Confucius believed in and loved. K'ang Yu-wei rejected this and demonstrated that Confucius and all the philosophers of his age and afterwards appealed to the ancient only to argue for institutional reforms. Confucius did create; he wrote all the six classics (K'ang *K'ung-tzu* 243–66 cf. 47ff for using the ancient to reform the present). 'Loving the ancient' did not mean blindly following the ancient, nor to stress the study of history, but was simply expressing respect for the past, readiness to use the past to enlighten the present.

K'ang Yu-wei's disciple, the martyred T'an Ssu-t'ung (1865–98), went further. Also a believer in innovation and progress, he took on those whom he said had boasted that they 'loved the ancient': 'If the ancient is to be loved, how can one be of the present?' Confucius was not like that, he said. 'When he was young, he followed the institutions of Chou. But later, when the Way was not accepted, he hid his tears on hearing of the appearance of the *ch'i-lin* (the mythical animal whose appearance meant that the time for a Sage had come) and knew that the laws simply had to be reformed. He was determined to compose the *Spring and Autumn Annals*, and by abandoning all the ancient learning, changed the present institutions. So how can there be references to his loving the ancient'. T'an Ssu-t'ung went on to quote another scholar (name now lost) saying that the whole statement about 'transmitting and not creating' or 'believing in and loving the ancient' was a forgery and he himself thought that the insertion of the phrase 'loving the ancient' when Confucius spoke about earnestly seeking knowledge was also a forgery. He concluded that Europe and America flourished because they loved the new and now the Japanese imitated them to the point of changing their own dress and food preferences (implying that the Japanese were successful because they had done this). In contrast, the three continents of Asia, Africa and Australia (he was referring to Aboriginal society here) perished because they 'loved the ancient'. He ended by condemning China for hanging on to the ancient even when on the point of death, resting in its decadent state of barbarism and blindness to the present (Tan Ssu-t'ung 1954: 35–36; cf Hsiac 1975: 83).

These were the first radical views rejecting the idea of 'loving the ancient'. K'ang Yu-wei and his disciples had set out consciously to *change* the ancient (*pien-Ku*) in order to save the future. They did so by opposing the dominant view of Confucius as a trans- mitter, scholar and historian and erecting a new image of him as a reformer, philosopher and politician. Their attack on the well- developed tradition was so fundamental that it aroused violent opposition from their peers. It also produced ironies and contradictions. For example, their reformist credentials depended on brilliant arguments about the *real* Confucius, about his role in his own times and about his success in changing the ages that fol- lowed. These led K'ang Yu-wei to turn to the ancient past to justify making Confucius the founder of *the* Chinese religion (K'ang *K'ung-tzu* 1897: 164–93). The more radical reforms were thereby tied to a new focus on the ancient, and although ancient, the uni- versalist nature of Confucian values and ideas.

On the other hand, in order to establish Confucius as a radical reformer, K'ang Yu-wei had to argue that the ancient sages Con- fucius had kept on quoting were not themselves sages (if they existed at all). All their sage sayings were put into their mouths by Confucius himself. This was a cynical view of the use of the ancient and one that undermined ultimately Confucius' own cre- dentials as a sage. Without intending to, K'ang Yu-wei implied that a sage could appropriate the past for his own use. He then suggested that, although one should not be a slave to the past, one should respect this sage, who had created the past in order to reform his age, just as K'ang Yu-wei himself was doing. In the end, he taught his disciples to be sceptical of the ancient, in particular, of the classics as sanctified knowledge. Instead, all the classics could be subjected to historical criticism like any document of history (Lev- enson 1968, III: 12–15, 27–32, 72–82). The greatest irony was that, even while he was persuading his followers to love the ancient sage as a religious founder, he had planted seeds of doubt about the whole of the Chinese past.

After K'ang Yu-wei, 'loving the ancient' could never be the same again. There could be no return to the idea that the ancient was always superior to the present, or to the time when those who loved the ancient were always superior to those who did not. But there were attempts to restore respect to the idea of continuity which allowed that Confucianism was for all time and therefore still vital and relevant for China. The view developed that a dangerous political and cultural vacuum had been created by people like

K'ang Yu-wei and the young activists of the May Fourth Movement. Some went so far as to say that the leaders of the Kuomintang had become bearers of the 'sage-succession (*tao-t'ung*) from Confucius down the centuries to Sun Yat-sen'. K'ang Yu-wei's own belief in evolution and progress, however utopian, made him sure that Confucius the Sage had foreseen a progressive history for China. In this, he had been influenced by modern ideas from the West, and soon afterwards a new generation of thinkers and activists were even more directly influenced. It openly used Western ideas of criticism and scientific criteria to re-examine all aspects of China's ancient past.

When the Ch'ing dynasty fell and the first republic was created in 1912, there were no holds barred to that re-examination. The ancient was no longer protected by the Confucian state; the classics were no longer sacred texts embodying all wisdom. The ancient philosophers described in these historical documents could, of course, arouse a different kind of love of the ancient, a love arising from curiosity, knowledge and understanding. As Chou Yü-t'ung, the historian of classicial learning, summed it up, Chinese attitudes towards the ancient this century had moved from being mired in or being addicted to the ancient (*ni-ku*) to doubting the ancient (*i-ku*) and then to studying the ancient (*k'ao-ku*) (which has now become the word for archaeology) and finally to explaining the ancient (*shih-ku*) (Chou Yü-t'ung 1941). He does not mention 'loving the ancient' because that has been too closely tied to Confucius' personal preference and, as has been suggested earlier, might have been forged by those who used Confucianism to support conservative ideas.

But Chou Yü-t'ung understood that studying and explaining the ancient could be a different kind of loving. And indeed the new forms of patriotism and nationalism that emerged in the 1920s called directly and sometimes rather passionately for new ways of caring for the ancient. There were many strands to this. The most notable were the following:

1. A new sceptical historiography that questioned every ancient classic with great care to test its historicity. Western methods of authentication were to be used at all times side by side with the best critical techniques developed within China (especially in the eighteenth century) in order to expose the false and verify the genuine. At the end of such an exercise, a totally credible ancient history would be re-written and that could be loved as a true heritage. The best examples of this were the work of Hu Shih on the ancient history of Chinese philosophy (1919) and that of Ku Chieh-kang, Ch'ien Hsuan-t'ung and their colleagues which were gathered together in the seven vol-

umes of *A Critique of Ancient History*, published between 1926 and 1941.[7]

2. The dramatic beginnings of scientific archaeology. This began with the spectacular oracle-bone finds at the turn of the century. The challenge that these inscriptions posed to classical philologists was successfully met and this greatly boosted the morale of all those who had begun to wonder at the antiquity of China's past. And when these finds were followed by others in Central Asia (ranging from ancient artefacts to more recent fragments of manuscripts), a new era dawned for the ancient in China. Systematic archaeology became possible in the 1920s and China has not looked back ever since (Cheng Te-s'un 1959, 1960 and 1963). Whether it was the Shang Yin capitals with even more oracle bones or the Peking Man at Choukoutien or neolithic pottery in Kansu or Shantung, the excitement was soon overcome by a resurgence of pride in China's antiquity. Again, 'loving the ancient' is not the most appropriate word to describe this feeling and no one used it at the time. Yet for the professionals involved, I wonder if they did not share the sentiments so simply expressed by Confucius when he said 'I transmit but do not create. I believe in and love the ancient'.

3. A new use for the ancient past that opened up a half-century of debate about the history of Chinese society. This began with Kuo Mo-jo's application of a Marxist historical analysis to the ancient classics – *The Book of Poetry*, even *The Book of Changes*. Even more than archaeology and the new historiography, Kuo Mo-jo's *The Study of Ancient Chinese Society* (1930) consciously sought to place China in the context of world history, with, of course, a particular theoretical framework in mind. He concluded that the ancient classics responded well to the new class analysis and that they yielded results which could be used to determine the existence of a slave society in ancient China and, what was more, the transition of that society to a feudal society, as Marx and Engels had found in Western Europe. The enquiries were not limited to Chinese scholars. Japanese, Germans, Russians also joined in with comparative studies, but the excitement the debate aroused within China was simply astonishing (Dirlik 1978: 46–53, 135–140). Scholars of different political persuasions were drawn into it and even non-Marxists tried to use the analysis. Certainly, no one claimed that they had rediscovered love for the ancient, but the number of scholars now engaged in the study and explication of ancient texts and inscriptions was unprecedented.

Even more significant was that the three strands above gradually ran together. The critical examination of all writings, the scientific excavation of more documents and artefacts and the use of Marxist analysis to re-write ancient history combined to make the ancient much more alive and significant than at any time in Chinese history.

That should have been the end of my story. This kind of love for the ancient is normal and examples abound for every country in the world. Chou Yü-t'ung's sequence of change from addiction to explication certainly describes a healthy condition. I am reminded of Fan Wen-lan's lectures at Yenan in 1940 (some of them in the presence of Mao Tse-tung) on the history of classical scholarship in China (Fan Wen-lan 1979: 265–99). While the war with Japan was still going on, when it was far from clear that Marxism would be victorious within the decade, Fan Wen-lan summed up the history of all the devotion that had gone into the study of the ancient classics. He showed how vigorous the debates had been. Despite many efforts by imperial regimes to demand conformity in attitudes towards the ancient and to control thought through prescribed texts and commentaries, there remained some fierce disputes about what the ancient meant for China. Did 'loving the ancient' mean treating antiquity as sacred and developing through such respect an orderly and conservative society? Or did it really require all Chinese to study the ancient carefully in order to learn how to reform and change the present? Indeed, who loved the ancient more – those who helped the state, as we might put it, own the past and thereby allowed the state to manipulate the people through owning their past? Or those who insisted that everyone had a right to that past, that all could learn lessons from it and could play their part in moulding the kind of state and society they wanted? Fan Wen-lan's answer at that time was that Mao Tse-tung's 'New Democracy' was a liberating force:

China's new politics and new economy had grown out of China's old politics and old economy. China's new culture had also grown out of China's old culture. Thus, we must respect our own history and never cut ourselves off from our history. But this kind of respect is to give history its rightful scientific place, is to respect the dialectics of change in history and not to praise the ancient in order to criticize the present and not to praise its feudal poisonous elements.[8]

Fan then went on to show how 'loving the ancient' in the feudal period had positive features. It encouraged high standards of scholarship which made it possible for us now to read and understand the difficult and authentic texts which illuminated ancient history. In this way also, it revealed the democratic and revolutionary elements in the ancient past which could be usefully translated for present use among the liberated proletariat.

Fan Wen-lan was too optimistic. The study and use of the ancient remained a stormy area for scholars and intellectuals even after the establishment of the People's Republic of China. By 1958, after the anti-Rightists movement had begun, Ch'en Po-ta, formerly Mao Tse-tung's secretary, devised the slogan 'Emphasize the present and play down the ancient' (*hou-chin po-ku*).[9] This was to attack those intellectuals who were still using the ancient to criticize the present, who criticized the Chinese Communist Party for 'looking down on the past and being irrationally hopeful about the future'. Kuo Mo-jo, the president of the Academy of Science, joined in (in his open letter to the history students of Peking University) and underlined the need for a balanced and scientific attitude. He singled out the two sayings 'study the ancient to serve the government' and 'love the ancient and earnestly seek knowledge from it' as no longer usable. He warned that, without the spirit of emphasizing the present and playing down the ancient, we would be the prisoners of ancient sages and ancient artefacts and become a cluster of antiquarians and bookworms with no real scholarship and of no use to the real world. He advocated a new critical spirit towards the past, so that 'we do not become the prisoners of the sources, but grasp them and possess them and become the owners and managers of these sources' (open letter, 16 May 1958; Kuo Mo-jo 1961).

A great deal of pressure was put on scholars and intellectuals to observe this critical spirit towards the ancient. But the battles continued. And the power struggles of the 'cultural revolution' from 1966 onwards highlighted the persistence of non-revolutionary attitudes towards the past. These attacks were far-ranging and almost no one was spared from accusations of disloyalty towards Mao Tse-tung's achievements and his vision of the future. By this time 'loving the ancient' was really not the central issue, although many of those attacked, like the historian Wu Han and many others, were accused of using the past to mock the present (Goldman 1981: 118–24; Pusey 1969: 23–29). Far more important interests were at stake. What was astonishing, however, was the revival of a traditional form of political discourse that specifically used the ancient to fight modern battles. It reached its highest form in the movement to criticize Lin Piao and Confucius.

The dimensions of this conflict need not detain us here. The remarkable thing is that for over three years, the ancient texts and interpretations were paraded before us as being vital to the outcome of the Cultural Revolution. It was not surprising that the campaign attacked Confucius and things conservative. What was unexpected was the continuous use of ancient history to establish that the Legalist opposition to Confucius also spanned some 2400 years. Thus, the point was made that among the contemporaries of Confucius and his later followers were progressive thinkers who were held down by the Confucians but nevertheless survived and appeared from time to time to contain the decadence and reactionary policies of the imperial Confucian state. And, instead of rejecting the ancient, which the early violent years of the Cultural Revolution might have led us to expect, an elaborate case was made to love the ancient selectively. That is, using the criteria that Legalists were good and Confucians were bad, the whole of Chinese history could be re-written. Every Legalist or everyone who could provide some evidence of having either used Legalist ideas or attacked Confucianism along Legalist lines, could be picked out and pointed to as worthy models for the present. These few would confirm that the dialectical process was at work even in ancient Chinese history and that even ancient Chinese history was permeated with evidence of the class struggle. In short, ancient history supported the Marxist interpretation of history. More than that, ancient history could be used to fight contemporary battles and guide the revolutionary cause. The extraordinary result of the campaigns was that the Chinese people were exhorted to study ancient history by both sets of protagonists in the power struggle, whether to prevent a reactionary restorationism or to confirm the historicity of Marxist analysis or to counter-attack by showing that Lin Piao and all those who opposed Premier Chou En-lai were obscurantist lovers of decadent Confucianist values. On the surface, the use of the ancient reminded one of earlier periods when 'loving the ancient' was the prevalent mode of discourse, especially the Northern Sung (eleventh century) which 'drew from the ancient to rectify the present' or to 'verify the present'; and the late nineteenth century when K'ang Yu-wei and his enemies both drew from the ancient to condemn each other, when K'ang claimed that he was, like Confucius, merely using the past to reform the present. But the use in the early 1970s was very crude, often simply the abuse of ancient history by using selective quotations out of context to make political points (Wang 1975: 1–2, 20–24 and 1979a, I: 4–10).

Indeed, this was not 'loving the ancient' at all, merely a parody of that sentiment that revealed a contempt for tradition reminiscent of, but surpassing in scale, earlier abuses of the ancient. The question is, was that episode of using the ancient to attack the present merely an aberration, or was it the inevitable farce that appears when an ancient people continually appeal to the past whether they care for it or not? Let me sum up the verdict of the intellectuals in China today by quoting one of them, T'ang Chih-chün, one of the senior and most prolific scholars writing today, in his essay 'The May Fourth Movement and the End of Classicism'.

After the establishment of the new China and the land reforms, the economic foundations of the feudal landlords are gone. But the poisons of feudalism left after several thousand years have not been totally removed. On the contrary, they have flourished under the surface out of sight and directly obstruct and undermine the development and strengthening of socialism. Lin Piao, 'the Gang of Four' and their ilk with their feudal fascism can be linked to the classicism attacked by the May Fourth Movement. They created idols for worship, religious rituals; they advocated feudal ethics, policies to keep the people ignorant; they waved a red flag to oppose the red flag; they pretended to criticize Confucius when they really respected Confucius; they caused modern superstititions like 'every sentence is the truth', '(we must) act according to every sentence' to poison the whole country, and used them as an important spiritual weapon to rebel against the party and seize power, as a means of locking up thought and suffocating democracy. This shows how important it is to liberate thought and complete the task begun during the May Fourth Movement of the revolution against feudal (modes of) thinking. (T'ang Chih-chün 1980: 296)

This was written in 1980. It might be the verdict against the poisons of the ancient, but it was not directed against the need to understand the ancient. Since 1976, numerous articles calling for critical reappraisals of Confucius, critical readings of the classics and a critical appreciation of ancient history have appeared. And, while they all call for rejection of the reactionary and conservative use of the ancient, some of them, especially those on archaeology, clearly capture the sense of 'loving the ancient', not of blindly following the past but of really respecting and caring for the ancient heritage.

What has all this to do with the question, 'Who owns the past?' Let me return to the four points made by Confucius in the two quotations I started with: loving the ancient; believing in it; transmitting and not creating; learning from the past. The combination of all four had led to the sanctification of the past to the point when it became suffocating. Together, the four points seemed to advocate uncritical acceptance of ancient ideas and values if the Chinese were to become wise; and that wisdom created a world in which the past owned the Chinese, as we may well feel was what happened in China for a thousand years. On the other hand, there can be no objection to learning from the past if believing and transmitting were done critically. I have no doubt that the approach of critical enquiry is necessary before the three points of belief, transmitting and learning are possible, and if that can be achieved, surely that is the essence of 'loving the ancient'. I cannot, of course, speak for Confucius. Indeed, he is elusive and has always been difficult to pin down. But I would venture to suggest that by 'loving the ancient', he asked that we cultivate an attitude of respect and caring for the past and with that we can hope to own the past and to deserve to own it.

Notes

1   For the first quotation the translation comes from Chan Wing-tsit. I have modified it by using 'the ancient' instead of 'the ancients'; I find support for this in D.C. Lau's 'devoted to antiquity'. Both James Legge and Arthur Waley use 'the Ancients' or 'the ancients'. (Chan 1963: 31; Lau 1979: 86; Legge 1960, I: 195; Waley 1938: 123). The second quotation is also Chan's translation which I have modified. He adds in parenthesis (teaching) after 'ancient' and this I have omitted. Lau and Legge both say 'fond of antiquity' while Waley says 'loves the past'. Chan 1963: 32; Lau 1979: 88; Legge 1960: 201; Waley 1938: 127.

2   Specially noticeable in the biographical chapters of *Hou Han Shu* but hinted at earlier in K'ung An-Kuo's Preface to the *Book of History*, in Yen K'o-Chün (1958, I: 196). A fine expression of this may be found at the end of the Western Han in an essay on the restoration of ancient music by P'ing Tang (Yen 1958, I: 390).

3   The details are carefully recorded and criticized in the 36 surviving essays (*nei-p'ien*) of Liu Chih-chi, *Shih T'ung* (T'ung Shih edition), Shanghai, 1978, vol. 1. For examples of mindless use of ancient models by historians, see his essay on the use of historical dialogue, I, 149, 153.

4   The civil officials in the Biographies sections of the Old and New *T'ang History* and the Old and New *Five Dynasties History* as well as those of the *Sung History* have numerous references to the importance of the Tso Commentary. The most accessible English text of the Tso Commentary is still James Legge, *The Chinese Classic*, V.

5   Preface and commentary by Tu Yü (222–84) and additional commentary by K'ung Ying-ta (574–648), both attributing much to Confucius. It was this edition of the early T'ang dynasty (618–917) which Liu Pen and all his contemporaries most probably used.

6   Huang Tsung-hsi, *Sung Yuan Hsueh-an*, Kuo-hsueh chi-pen ts'ung-shu edition, Shanghai, 1929: 2, 66–104; also Sung Shih 432, 12832–8. The third was Hu Yuan (993–1059).

7   *Ku Shih Pien*, volumes I–III, V, edited by Ku Chieh-kang, 1926–35; IV and VI, edited by Lo Ken-tse, 1933 and 1938; VII, edited by Lü Ssu-mien and T'ung Shu-yeh, 1941.

8   For a slightly different translation of this passage, *Selected Works of Mao Tse-tung*, London, 1954, III, 'On New Democracy' 155.

9   Lecture given on 10 March 1958; Ch'en Po-ta, 'P'i p'an ti chi-cheng ho hsin ti t'an-so', *Hung-ch'i* (*Red Flag*) 13 (July 1959), Appendix 46–49, translated in extracts from *China Mainland Magazines*, No. 183 (11 September 1959).

References

Chan, Wing-tsit (1963), *A Source Book in Chinese Philosophy*, Princeton University Press, Princeton.

Cheng Te-k'un (1959, 1960, 1963), *Archaeology in China*, 3 vols, Heffer & Sons, Cambridge.

Chou Yü-t'ung (1941), 'Wu-shih nien lai Chung-kuo chih hsin shih hsueh' *Hsueh-lin*, Shanghai 4, 1–36.

Dirlik, Arif (1978), *Revolution and History: The Origins of Marxist Historiography in China, 1919–1937*, University of California Press, Berkeley and Los Angeles.

Fan Wen-lan (1940), 'Chung kuo ching-hsueh ti yen-pien' in *Chung-kuo weh-hua* Yenan (reprinted in *Fan Wen-lan li-shih lun-wen hsuan-chi*, Peking, 1979).

Goldman, Merle (1981), *China's Intellectuals: Advice and Dissent*, Harvard University Press, Cambridge, Mass.

Hsia Kung-ch'uan (1975), *A Modern China and a New World: K'ang Yu-wei, Reformer and Utopian, 1858–1927*, University of Washington Press, Seattle.

Huan K'uan (1958), *Yen-t'ieh Lun*, Shanghai.

Hu Shih (1919), *Chung-kuo che-hsueh shih ta-kang*, Shanghai.

K'ang Yu-wei (1956), *Hsin-hsueh wei-ching k'ao*, (1891), Ku-chi edition, Peking.

—— (1958), *K'ung-tzu kai-chih k'ao*, (1897), Chung-hua editions, Peking.

Kuo Mo-jo (1930), *Chung-kuo ku-tai she hui yen-chiu*, Shanghai.

—— (1961), 'Kuan-yü hou-chin po-ku wen-t'i, *Wen-shi Lun-chi*, Peking, 11–16.

Kracke, Edwards, A. Jr (1953), *Civil Service in Early Sung China, 960–1067,* Harvard University Press, Cambridge, Mass.

Lau, D.C. (1963), *Tao te Ching*, Penguin Classics, Harmondsworth.

—— (1979), *Confucius, the Analects* Penguin Classics, Harmondsworth.

Legge, J. (1960), *The Chinese Classics*, 5 vols, Hong Kong University Press, Hong Kong.

Levenson, Joseph, R. (1968), *Confucian China and its Modern Fate: A Trilogy*, University of California Press, Los Angeles.

Liu, James, T.C. (1959), *Reform in Sung China: Wang An-shih (1021–86) and His New Policies*, Harvard University Press, Cambridge, Mass.

—— (1967), *Ou-yang Hsiu: An Eleventh Century Neo-Confucianist*, Stanford University Press, Stanford.

Lo Ken-tse (1937), 'Wan Chou chu-tzu fan-ku-k'ao, *Ku-shih Pien*, 1–49.

Pei-ching ta-hsueh (1979), *Hsun Tzu Hsin-chu*, Beijing.

Pulleyblank, E.G. (1960), 'Neo-Confucianism and neo-Legalism in T'ang intellectual life, 755–805' in Wright, A.F. (ed.) *The Confucian persuasion*, Stanford University Press, Stanford.

Pusey, J.R. (1969), *Wu Han: Attacking the Present Through the Past*, Harvard University Press, Cambridge, Mass.

T'an Ssu-t'ung (1954), *Jen-hsueh* in *T'an Ssu-t'ung ch'uan-chi*, San-lien edition, Peking.

T'ang Chih-chun (1980), 'Wu-ssu yun-dong he ching-hsueh ti chung-chieh', *Chung-kuo che-hsueh* 3, 287–297.

Waley, Arthur (1938), *The Analects of Confucius*, George Allen and Unwin, London.

Wang Gungwu (1975), 'Juxtaposing past and present in China today', *The China Quarterly*, 61, March, 1–24.

—— (1979a), 'Recent reinterpretations of history' in Lee Ngok and Leung, C.K. (eds.) *China: development and challenge*, Hong Kong University Centre of Asian Studies, Hong Kong, Vol I, 3–18.

—— (1979b), 'The Writing of Pre-modern History in Modern China' Proceedings of Seventh Conference International Association of Historians of Asia (August 1977), Bangkok.

Watson, Burton (1968), *The Complete Works of Chuang Tzu*, Columbia University Press, New York.

Yen K'o-chün (1958), *Ch'üan Shang-ku San-tai Ch'in-Han San-Kuo Liu-ch'ao wen*, vol. I Beijing.

Index